Teaching Reading and Writing in Spanish and English in Bilingual and Dual Language Classrooms

Teaching Reading and Writing in Spanish and English in Bilingual and Dual Language Classrooms

Second Edition

Yvonne S. Freeman
David E. Freeman

HEINEMANN
PORTSMOUTH, NH

Heinemann
361 Hanover Street
Portsmouth, NH 03801–3912
www.heinemann.com

Offices and agents throughout the world

© 2006 by Yvonne S. Freeman and David E. Freeman

Library of Congress Cataloging-in-Publication Data
Freeman, Yvonne S.
  Teaching reading and writing in Spanish and English in bilingual and dual language classrooms / Yvonne S. Freeman, David E. Freeman.—2nd ed.
      p. cm.
  Edition for 1997 has title: Teaching reading and writing in Spanish in the bilingual classroom.
  Includes bibliographical references and index.
  ISBN 0-325-00801-9 (alk. paper)
  1. Spanish language—Study and teaching—United States. 2. Language arts—United States. 3. Education, Bilingual—United States. 4. Literacy—United States.   I. Freeman, David E.   II. Title.

LB1577.S7F74 2006
372.6'044—dc22   2006002859

Editor: *Lois Bridges*
Production: *Vicki Kasabian*
Cover design: *Jenny Jensen Greenleaf*
Cover photographer: *Julie Farias*
Typesetter: *Publishers' Design and Production Services, Inc.*
Manufacturing: *Louise Richardson*

Printed in the United States of America on acid-free paper
10 09 08 RRD 3 4 5

We dedicate this book to teachers and administrators in schools that are implementing high-quality literacy instruction in two languages. We also extend this dedication to our daughter Mary, who is using two languages to help older newcomer students learn to read and write in a new language; to our son-in-law, Francisco, who is providing high-quality literacy instruction in Spanish to his bilingual students; and to our daughter Ann, who is conducting research and educating new teachers on the best ways to teach reading and writing to all students.

Contents

Acknowledgments

This second edition builds on the first. We want to thank again the teachers and teacher educators who helped shape our first edition with their insightful comments and classroom examples. It is those teacher stories and their students' writing that bring the research and theory in this book to life.

This second edition includes many new stories and new examples. We especially want to thank the teachers who provided detailed accounts of their classrooms and examples of their students' writing. These teachers include Francisco Soto, Delia Iris Ojeda, Rosa Chapa, Paula Garcia, Elda Valdez, Nancy Cavazos, Irma Magaly Carballo, Anna Barbosa, Patricia Cardoza, and Yudith González. We also wish to thank the children whose writing and photos are included within the pages of this book and provide us with a close look at what children know and can do. In particular, we would like to thank Juliana Arisleidy Chapa, Nallely Peña Cavazos, Flavio César Cardoza, Leslie Pesina, Alexis González, Alexis Chapa, and Citlaly Villareal.

In addition, we wish to thank the administrators and district and regional specialists who facilitated our visits to schools to observe classes in which wonderful teachers were providing high-quality education for their bilingual students. These administrators include Joe González, Ofelia Gaona, Emmy De la Garza, David Villarreal, Debbie González, Noemi Green, Gregorio Arrellano, all of Donna ISD, and Perla Roerig from Region One. We also need to thank the teachers in the Runn Elementary, Garza Elementary, and W. A. Todd schools who graciously allowed us to photograph their students and classrooms.

We also want to thank the people who actually turn manuscript pages into a finished product. Abby Heim and Vicki Kasabian, our production editors, have applied their considerable professional skills to create this book. In addition to the usual work they do, they traveled from New Hampshire to South Texas and spent two days with us visiting classrooms and advising Julie Farias, an energetic photographer, as she snapped picture after picture of bilingual teachers and students. As a result of their dedication, this book includes pictures of the students and teachers in the classrooms we write about. Among the pictures taken are those on the cover: one that shows Francisco Soto with his student, Daniel Volaños; and another of Mary Soto and two of her students, Yulissa Morales and Griselda Olivo.

Finally, we want to thank our editor, Lois Bridges. Lois is a remarkable editor who provides the feedback we need to revise and refine our writing. Her knowledge of literacy and best practices enables her to give us the advice we need. And she always does so with incredible speed. We respect Lois' professionalism and value her friendship. We look forward to writing more books working with the great team from Heinemann.

Introduction

Over the past seventeen years, we have been working with preservice and inservice teachers who want to help all their students succeed in school. These teachers know that reading and writing are key to school success. However, teaching students to read and write is a challenge, especially in bilingual and dual language classrooms.

Yvonne teaches a graduate course in biliteracy development. In their responses to the assigned readings, Yvonne's students have written about the complexities of teaching reading and writing in two languages. They have reflected on their own experiences of learning to read in a second language, on trying to implement new methods in schools in which administrators and other teachers are concerned only with test score results, and on the difficulty of putting into practice the approach and strategies they have been studying in Yvonne's class. The following quotes reflect the challenges that these teachers face.

> When I attended the elementary schools as a student who was Spanish dominant, I remember my teachers always teaching the lessons through direct instruction in English. It was difficult for me to understand some of the concepts that the teacher would explain because it was done in my second language. The teacher would do all the talking. I would just be listening and trying to comprehend as much as I could. On some occasions when we were reading aloud, the teacher would constantly be correcting all the errors I would make when reading in English. I felt really sad because I was not able to pronounce the words as I should.
>
> *Elda Valdez, bilingual second-grade teacher, two years' experience,*
> *teaching in an early transition bilingual program*

Como maestra, puedo ver día tras día las caras de desesperación de mis colegas por tener que enseñar un programa en el que no creen. Un programa hecho por manos inexpertas, por mentes que no tienen ni idea de lo que deben hacer para ayudar a un estudiante a aprender a leer y a sobresalir en la escuela. Los maestros de mi escuela están totalmente cansados de tener que administrar exámenes, ensayos tras ensayos y todo para estar siguiendo las leyes del gobierno federal. Lo más triste, es que los mismos estudiantes reflejan en sus rostros cansancio y fastidio por unos exámenes que para ellos no tienen ningún sentido.

Translation

As a teacher, day after day, I can see the desperate faces of my colleagues because they have to teach a curriculum they don't believe in, a curriculum created by hands of those without expertise, by those who have no idea of what to do to help a student learn how to read and to succeed in school. The teachers at my school are totally fed up with the tests they have to administer, practice test after practice test, and all to follow federal mandates. The saddest part is that the students' faces reflect their deep tiredness and boredom with tests that have no meaning for them.

Nancy Cavazos, bilingual pre-K–K teacher, seven years'
experience, teaching in a dual language program

Durante los últimos meses, en los cuales he estado leyendo los artículos, así como los capítulos de los diferentes libros de texto de mi clase, al tiempo que realizaba entrevistas y prácticas de lectura con mi hija y las observaciones a mis alumnos, he podido comprobar que la lectura es un área fascinante, sobre todo para el docente que realmente esté comprometido con su labor . . . Ha sido para mí muy gratificante poder aprender y conocer cuáles son las mejores opciones en el proceso enseñanza-aprendizaje de la lectura y reconocer que el niño no sólo lee letras aisladas en los textos, sino que utiliza múltiples recursos para interpretar y comprender su lectura.

Translation

In the last few months during which time I have been reading the articles as well as chapters from the textbooks for this class, doing interviews and trying out different reading activities with my daughter, and observing my students, I have realized that reading is a fascinating subject, especially for the teacher who is really dedicated to his or her profession . . . It has been very gratifying to be able to learn about and recognize which are the best options in the teaching/learning of the reading process and to realize that the child doesn't just read isolated letters but uses many resources to interpret and understand his or her reading.

Irma Carballo, kindergarten and first-grade bilingual teacher,
twenty years' experience, seventeen in Mexico, three in the United States,
teaching in a dual language program

The readings for this graduate course were eye-opening. I didn't go through the traditional route to become a teacher. I went through the alternative certification program. Common sense told me there were different approaches to teaching reading, but I had no idea the differences and their impact were so great. For many years I thought reading was reading and that if you were a good reader, the meaning would automatically come to you. Boy, I was way off. I will definitely consider the approaches I use and how they impact our students . . . Yes, there are many factors to consider like socioeconomic status, book availability, but it all leads to the fact that we must allow them free time to read and let them read what they want to read. I have spent so much of my own money to build up my classroom library and make sure it has culturally relevant books. I want to make sure my students read in both languages and that they have a good selection of books to choose from.

Anna Barbosa, third-grade bilingual teacher, six years' experience,
teaching in a transitional bilingual education program

"How do I teach reading and writing in Spanish and in English?" This question is one that both beginning and experienced bilingual teachers often ask themselves. As the previous quotes show, many factors influence the kinds of reading and writing programs teachers develop. These factors might include the teachers' own experiences in being taught to read and write, the teaching preparation they received in college, and their previous teaching experience. In addition, teachers must consider their students' access to books at home, their literacy backgrounds, and the materials available in the school and classroom libraries. In this era of accountability, teachers must also comply with federal, state, and district testing requirements. Because literacy is so critical for students' academic success, it is important for educators to take these factors into account so they can make informed decisions about their literacy programs.

The quotes from teachers help set the stage for the complexity of teaching students to read and write in two languages. Teachers in bilingual and dual language classrooms face an even more complex task than other teachers. They are trying to respond not only to reading mandates and the pressures of raising test scores but also to opposition from the public and even other educators because they are teaching in two languages. There is a great deal of misunderstanding about bilingual education, and bilingual teachers are caught in the middle.

Goals of the Second Edition

In this era of accountability, in which every student is expected to achieve grade-level literacy standards, teaching students to read and write in two languages is especially difficult. However, when teachers adopt effective practices, their students become good readers and writers. One goal for this book is to provide the information bilingual and dual language teachers need to implement effective reading and writing instruction in their classes. We offer teachers, program directors, administrators, and parents concrete ideas that can help students in bilingual and dual language classes reach high levels of biliteracy in both Spanish and English.

However, it is not enough for teachers to implement practices that lead their students to biliteracy. They should also develop an understanding of why certain practices lead to success. Then, when a new program or set of practices is implemented at their school, they can evaluate that program in light of their own understanding of how reading and writing best develop in bilingual settings. For that reason, a second goal for this book is to provide teachers with the theory that supports the practices we advocate.

In addition to employing sound practice supported by theory, we want teachers to understand some of the history of literacy instruction. This history provides the context for current practices. A review of how reading has been taught in the past helps teachers understand current methods. A third goal of this book, then, is to give teachers a summary of methods that have been used to teach reading and writing in Spanish and in English. Armed with a knowledge of history, theory, and effective practice, bilingual teachers can succeed in helping all their students become biliterate and achieve high levels of academic success.

Reasons for a Second Edition

There are several specific reasons that we have written this second edition of *Teaching Reading and Writing in Spanish in the Bilingual Classroom*. Since the first edition, published in 1996, the contexts for both literacy and bilingual education have changed dramatically, as we will show. Because of the opposition to bilingual education, the increased use of scripted reading programs that emphasize basic skills, and the move toward accountability with constant testing, it is more important than ever for bilingual and dual language teachers to develop the skills needed to promote biliteracy for all their students and the knowledge to defend the practices they choose to use.

There are other reasons we wanted to publish a second edition. We have now had many more experiences with talented teachers in bilingual and dual language schools. In addition, graduate students who are bilingual teachers have done research with both young bilingual emergent readers and writers and more advanced students. Our experiences in schools and the findings of the teachers' research support our beliefs about the teaching of literacy and need to be shared.

Finally, in this second edition we update both professional and literature references. We include new bibliographies of books in Spanish and in English, many of which are part of the descriptions of extended scenarios from classrooms in which teachers develop thematic units of study.

 ## Organization of This Book

In Chapter 1 we open with the story of one bilingual teacher and his journey since the publication of the first edition of this book. We use this story to show how conditions for teaching literacy in bilingual settings have changed in recent years. Next, we present the research and theory that support bilingual education. We explain a model that shows how English language learners who are instructed in two languages do better than those in English-only programs. In addition, we briefly review the history of bilingual education in the United States. To show the effects of current policy in both bilingual education and literacy, we present a scenario of reading lessons in a weather unit that follow a mandated reading curriculum in an English-only class. In this chapter, as in all chapters, we conclude with applications to help readers apply the ideas presented.

In Chapter 2 we look at the first of two views of reading. We begin with a scenario of reading lessons based on a weather unit in a bilingual classroom. The teacher teaches reading from a word recognition perspective. Next we explain the word recognition view. We show how this scenario and the scenario from Chapter 1 exemplify this perspective and present our concerns about using this approach.

In Chapter 3 we present a second view of reading. We describe reading lessons from a weather unit taught by a bilingual teacher who follows a sociopsycholinguistic approach to reading. We present evidence that supports this view, and we analyze the lesson to show how the methods and strategies this teacher uses reflect this second view of reading. We end this chapter with a checklist of effective reading practices that is consistent with a sociopsycholinguistic view, followed by descriptions of two additional units that show the checklist in action.

In Chapter 4 we give a historical overview of the methods that have been used to teach reading in Spanish and in English. This chapter provides the background for a description of each method. In Chapter 5 we describe the traditional methods that have been used to teach reading in Spanish. We include scenarios to bring each method to life. We also consider parallel methods that have been developed in English. In Chapter 6 we conclude our discussion of reading by presenting a principled approach. Principled teachers adopt methods and strategies consistent with their view of reading. We explain the methods and techniques that fit with a sociopsycholinguistic view.

We turn to writing in Chapter 7. We first show examples of writing from dual language classrooms, discussing what the goals for students should be. Just as we explained two views of reading, we present here two views of writing and the implications of each view for classroom practice. We contrast traditional approaches to teaching writing with a process approach. We introduce a checklist for effective writing instruction. Then we begin a description of how writing develops in both Spanish and English. We also look at the influence of English on Spanish writing and the influence of Spanish on English writing. We end the chapter with an example of a unit from a teacher who follows the checklist.

We begin Chapter 8 with three examples of writing that represent different stages in a developmental continuum. Then we continue our description of writing development. We show examples of more advanced stages as writers in both Spanish and English move toward conventional writing. We end this chapter with a unit from a fourth-grade teacher who is helping her students develop their writing skills.

Although we provide examples of classroom practice throughout the book, Chapter 9 brings the theory and methodologies discussed in the previous chapters together by describing how teachers using a principled approach plan and teach interesting thematic units. The examples we provide in this final chapter also include ideas for helping students move back and forth naturally between reading and writing in Spanish and in English as they become both bilingual and biliterate.

Teaching Reading and Writing in Spanish and English in Bilingual and Dual Language Classrooms

The Context for Developing Literacy
for Bilingual Students

Ser bilingüe es como vivir en dos mundos. Uno puede hablar con personas en español y entrar en su mundo. Lo mismo pasa cuando hablas, escribes y lees en inglés. Ahora que empecé el programa de educación bilingüe, puedo ver que tan valioso es ser bilingüe porque hay tantos niños que puedo ayudar en su primer idioma.

Translation
To be bilingual is like living in two worlds. One can speak to people in Spanish and enter into their world. The same thing happens when you speak, you write, and you read in English. Now that I have begun the bilingual education program, I can see how valuable it is to be bilingual because there are so many children that I can help in their first language.

Francisco's Teaching Journey

We open this book with a quote from Francisco, who wrote this a decade ago during his time in the teacher education preparation program at his university. Readers of our first edition of this book, *Teaching Reading and Writing in Spanish in the Bilingual Classroom*, might remember Francisco, a college student who was just entering the program to become a bilingual teacher. Yvonne was his university adviser and instructor. Much has changed in both bilingual and literacy education since Francisco wrote this quote. We include an extended description of what Francisco has experienced because we think it represents the reality of many bilingual teachers.

Francisco came to the United States from El Salvador when he was fourteen. His mother, a migrant worker, had lived and worked for several years in the United States before she could bring Francisco and her other children to join her. She wanted a better life for them than was possible in their native country. By the time Francisco arrived in Fresno, California, he was high school age. Like most students who come at the secondary level, Francisco received no first language support. He was submersed in classes given only in English. His English as a second language (ESL) classes focused on conversational language and did not prepare him for the academic demands of college.

Fortunately, Francisco was an outstanding soccer player. He attended a local Christian university on a soccer scholarship. He nearly dropped out of college because earning good grades was difficult. Nevertheless, he persisted with encouragement from his mother and his coach. Because he struggled with English, he remained quiet in his college classes. When, as a senior, he did some observations in a first-grade bilingual classroom, Francisco saw for the first time how English language learners in a bilingual setting were able to participate fully in classroom activities. He noted that the children felt good about themselves as learners because they could draw on their first language strengths as they studied school subjects. Francisco was inspired to use his bilingualism to help others so that they would not have to struggle as much as he had.

Because he had arrived in the United States at age fourteen with a high level of Spanish literacy that he further developed by taking college literature and Bible classes in Spanish, Francisco had a high level of academic Spanish. He was able to get an internship position in a rural school not far from Fresno because there was a need for teachers who could teach academic content in Spanish and in English. His first year he taught third grade. Then the district transferred him to another school.

Francisco's new school was growing so large that an additional class had to be formed. To accomplish this, the principal asked teachers to identify students who were significantly below grade level. The teachers identified twenty-six students, most of whom were boys, to form a second- and third-grade multiage bilingual classroom. This was the class Francisco faced at his new school.

Not surprisingly, Francisco found his second year of teaching with the struggling students challenging, but it was also rewarding. He organized his year around themes connected to the third-grade content standards, including the solar system, the tropical rain forest, the ocean, and the environment. He decided that since students could not really read or write very well in either language, he would first support them in developing literacy in Spanish.

During rug time, Francisco read and discussed a variety of books related to the themes his class was studying. He worked intensively with small groups doing guided reading and writing. While he instructed one group, the other students worked at centers. His centers included journal writing, math activity centers at which students wrote math problems related to the theme, silent reading, a listening center where students could listen to tapes of books, a center for individual story writing connected to the theme, and another center where pairs or small groups wrote plays and poems that they later presented to the whole class. Francisco always made a point of listening to his students and responding to individual writing. When his students shared their writing with him and others during an author share time, they got excited about writing and began to read and write more on their own.

Perhaps one of Francisco's greatest challenges was a student named Salvador, a third grader reading and writing at about a first-grade level. It was difficult for Francisco to convince Salvador to do any independent reading or writing. To avoid the embarrassment of trying to read and write, Salvador often engaged in disruptive behavior.

Francisco included Salvador and some other struggling third graders in one of the shared writing groups. Together with Francisco, the students created language experience stories. Francisco asked students what they wanted to write about and then helped them get their words down on paper, often going sound by sound. He also read many predictable, patterned books with the students, and they began to incorporate these patterns into their shared and guided writing.

Salvador particularly liked one story, *Los animales de Don Vicencio* (*The Animal Concert*) (Cowley 1987, 1983), which followed a predictable pattern and included the sounds of the farm animals who kept Don Vicencio awake at night. Salvador read the story over many times. One day, Salvador asked if he could take paper home to write a story. Francisco knew he had made great progress, because two days later Salvador brought his story back to read proudly to his teacher. The story closely followed the pattern of the story Salvador had read so many times in class, but Salvador had changed the characters to create his own version. He loved writing in the animal sounds. Under Francisco's guidance, Salvador continued to develop his reading and writing ability. At the end of the year, he was not at grade level, but he had improved greatly, and, more importantly, he had developed a love of reading and writing.

Francisco began by teaching the students to read and write in their first language, Spanish. The students in his class also improved in English as the year progressed. During English time each day, Francisco read them poems, and they sang or chanted together while he or one of the students tracked the words. Since the poems and charts were related to the theme they were studying, students were able to understand the English and build their English vocabulary. By midyear, groups of students were taking recess time to write and then read and edit their peers' writing pieces. The principal noticed the students' progress because students were constantly going to her with their writing in English as well as in Spanish and asking her if they could read it to her.

The following summer Francisco married a woman who had been teaching at the district's high school. They decided they wanted to relocate from the central valley of California to the coast. There they both found teaching jobs because they both had bilingual certification. Francisco was hired as a third-grade bilingual teacher. This time, however, Francisco found himself in a district that supported bilingual education only nominally. Several of the designated bilingual teachers had been hired because they promised to become proficient in Spanish within five years. However, since they were only at beginning levels, they were not able to teach in Spanish. The district offered bilingual classes only because the state required it. Francisco taught part of the day in English and part in Spanish.

That same year, Proposition 227, English for the Children, passed in California. This proposition made the teaching of children in a language other than English illegal unless the parents signed a waiver. The administration in Francisco's district quickly eliminated bilingual education. Administrators even warned teachers not to tell parents about the waiver option. By the second semester, all classes were taught in English. In his new school, Francisco used both Spanish and English the first four months, but after that, all his teaching had to be done in English. He commented, "I was hired as a bilingual teacher, but I only taught in English."

For the next four years, most of Francisco's teaching was done in English. Sometimes he was able to briefly preview or review a lesson in Spanish, but he was warned not to teach in Spanish or he would be in trouble with the district.

Francisco continued to emphasize the importance of reading and writing. He regularly read books connected to his themes to and with his students. By his fourth year of teaching in the district, Francisco began to notice that his English language learners, who had received all their instruction in English since kindergarten or first grade, were significantly behind the students he had taught the first year he came to the district. Before, the students had developed literacy in Spanish and then added English. Now, the students were being taught to read and write in English from the beginning. Even though all their instruction had been in English, they could not read third-grade material in English.

Another factor made the teaching of Francisco's English language learners more difficult. New reading mandates adopted at his school called for direct instruction in phonics and phonemic awareness. The required time for language arts was extended, but instead of being involved in meaningful reading and writing, Francisco's students were required to focus on basic skills. In addition, administrators carefully scrutinized scores on standardized tests. To prepare for these tests, teachers were required to give practice tests and benchmarks. Francisco's students did well enough on their tests, but he was finding it increasingly difficult to engage his students in interesting reading and writing and to organize around themes because there were more and more required tests and activities being assigned. Francisco could see that his students were losing interest in school. Toward the middle of the year, Francisco and his wife, Mary, decided to take a sabbatical. They applied to teach abroad for the experience and, perhaps, to avoid the test mania that seemed to be sweeping the country.

Francisco and Mary were hired in an American school in Guadalajara, Mexico. Francisco was hired as a third-grade teacher again. However, his students were the equivalent of fourth graders in the United States, as the Mexican school system provided students with two years of first grade so they could acquire enough English to study content area subjects in English.

This year of teaching proved to be educational for Francisco and Mary as well as for their students. The students in the Guadalajara American school were very different from the Mexican-origin students the couple had taught in California. In California their students were the children of immigrants who had come to the United States to seek a better life. In Guadalajara, the students were the children of wealthy Mexican and American businessmen. These students were assured of a comfortable life no matter the level of their academic achievement. While they were respectful and did their work dutifully, they were also used to a life that did not require too much of them. Francisco and Mary missed the sense of mission they had in teaching their students in the United States. The students in Guadalajara would succeed without their teachers' help.

The following year, the couple returned to their school districts in California. Francisco was moved to a new school where he did not know the administration or the other teachers. He was again assigned to the third grade. However, things had changed drastically from when he had left a year before. Now, a new reading program was being implemented, and facilitators at mandated training workshops emphasized how teachers would have to follow the script exactly for more than two hours a day. Teachers were told they would be evaluated on the test results their students achieved, and the trainers emphasized that if teachers followed the program exactly, all students would succeed, even English language learners. No special support was offered for the English learners, though the program trainers promised some materials were on the way.

For Francisco these workshops proved to be especially frustrating, since the trainers promoted what they called "scientific research," research he knew was flawed and not relevant to English language learners. Once school began, he quickly saw that he could not teach around themes, organize around centers, or engage his students in meaningful activities as he had done in the past.

To make matters worse, the economic crunch in California led to larger classes, so Francisco suddenly was teaching a class of thirty-five students. In the class, there were five students who were newcomers and spoke no English at all. Almost all his students were struggling with reading and could not read independently. Little time was allotted to writing other than filling out worksheets. One story was the basis of more than a week's lessons that emphasized the teaching of skills. On top of all this, Francisco and the students found the stories did not make much sense. He commented, "I hated what I was doing. I was not teaching. Someone taken off the street could follow the manual. I was not helping the kids at all."

Recently, Francisco, his wife, and their baby moved to Texas, a state known for teaching to the test. However, in Texas they both got jobs in a district committed to bilingual education and to helping the English language learners studying there. More than 50 percent of the students in the district are classified as limited English proficient (LEP). The superintendent has asked the bilingual director to implement dual language education in all elementary schools. Dual language, or two-way bilingual education, is a model that has proven to lead to academic success for bilingual students (Collier and Thomas 2004; Lindholm-Leary 2001). The move was a drastic step for the couple, but they both hope that despite the emphasis on testing in Texas, they can be given a chance to help the bilingual students in their classrooms.

Francisco's story may sound familiar to bilingual teachers in California and other states that have reduced the number of bilingual programs for English language learners. Despite a strong theoretical and research base that supports teaching students in their primary language while they are acquiring English, there has always been opposition to bilingual education. In the following sections, we first look at the research and theory that support bilingual education and then give a brief overview of the historical opposition to programs that include native language instruction.

 ## Research That Supports Bilingual Education

Research studies that provide support for bilingual education generally compare the academic achievement in English, as measured by standardized test scores, of similar students in different types of programs. The assumption is that if the students entered school with similar backgrounds, then differences in test scores could be attributed to the model of instruction they received. Since it takes from four to nine years to develop academic competence in a second language (Collier 1989; Cummins 1994; Skutnabb-Kangas 1979), test scores for English language learners must be measured over time. For that reason, studies should be longitudinal.

An important long-term study was conducted by Ramírez (1991), who compared groups of students in three kinds of programs: structured English immersion, early exit bilingual, and late exit bilingual. The structured English immersion programs provided ESL support for English language learners but generally no primary language support. The early exit programs included teaching in the primary language until about second grade. Then instruction shifted entirely into English. Students in the late exit programs continued to receive primary language instruction through at least fourth grade. Ramírez concluded that students in the late exit programs had higher academic achievement than students in either of the other two programs. In addition, he found little difference between students in structured English immersion and early exit programs.

Among his conclusions, Ramírez noted that teaching students in their native language did not interfere with their acquisition of English. Spanish-speaking students in late exit programs caught up with native English–speaking peers on standardized tests in English in about six years. On the other hand, native Spanish speakers in the structured English immersion programs did not catch up. Short-term studies do not reveal these positive effects of native language instruction.

A series of studies by Collier and Thomas have provided additional support for bilingual programs (Collier and Thomas 2004; Collier 1995; Thomas and Collier 1997, 2002). In these longitudinal studies of thousands of students, Collier and Thomas compared the academic achievement of English language learners in different kinds of programs, including traditional ESL programs, content-based ESL, early exit, late exit, and dual language. Like Ramírez, they have consistently found that English language learners in programs that teach academic content in the first language at least through sixth grade achieve at higher levels academically than students in other types of programs. In addition, both native English speakers and English language learners in dual language or two-way programs score above the national norms on tests of reading given in English.

Additional research support for bilingual education comes from the meta-analyses conducted by Willig (1985) and Greene (1998). In a meta-analysis, the researcher summarizes the results of a number of studies to draw general conclusions across the research. For example, Greene examined seventy-five studies of bilingual programs. He chose eleven studies that met the minimal standards for the quality of their research design. He combined the statistical results of these studies, which included test score results of 2,719 students. Of these, 1,562 were enrolled in bilingual programs in thirteen different states.

Based on the results, Greene concluded that limited English proficient students who are taught using at least some of their native language perform significantly better on standardized tests in English than similar children taught only in English. Thus, these meta-analyses led researchers to the same conclusions as the large-scale long-term studies conducted by Ramírez and Collier and Thomas, that instruction in the primary language improves the school achievement of English language learners.

Reviews of the research on bilingual education consistently show bilingual education is the best model for educating English language learners. A recent meta-analysis (Rolstad, Mahoney, et al. 2005) incorporated many studies not covered in the Willig or Greene reports and included more current research reports. Once again, the results favored bilingual education. The authors state:

> In the current study, we present a meta-analysis of studies comparing effects of instructional programs for ELL students in an effort to clarify "the big picture" in this debate. Our approach differs from previously conducted literature reviews in that it includes many studies not reviewed previously, and we did not exclude studies a priori based on design quality. Although our corpus and methodological approach differ from those of previous researchers, our conclusions are consistent with most of the major reviews conducted to date. We find an advantage for approaches that provide instruction in the students' first language and conclude that state and federal policies restricting or discouraging the use of the native language in programs for EL students cannot be justified by a reasonable consideration of the evidence. (574)

The researchers found that bilingual education was more beneficial for ELL students than all-English approaches. They also found that students in enrichment bilingual programs, such as dual language programs, outperformed those in transitional programs. In general, the longer students received primary language instruction, the better they did on academic measures of English.

The studies discussed here involved large numbers of students over long periods of time. The researchers concluded that the use of the native language for instruction resulted in increased academic achievement for English language learners. However, many factors influence test score results. Some students may be in programs that are labeled *bilingual*, but as was the case in Francisco's school in California, the teachers may not be bilingual or may be limited in their knowledge of academic Spanish. In addition, the teaching methods affect student learning. The teacher may be experienced and have a high level of proficiency in the second language but, like Francisco, be required to teach literacy using ineffective methods. Finally, especially at the upper grades, teachers may have difficulty finding adequate materials to teach in the second language. The best schooling for English language learners must include good teachers, good methods, and good materials as well as extended instruction in the primary language.

Theory That Supports Bilingual Education

What theory can explain the consistently positive results from research studies of bilingual education? The key concept is Cummins' (2000) interdependence principle:

> To the extent that instruction in L_x is effective in promoting proficiency in L_x transfer of this proficiency to L_y will occur provided there is adequate exposure to L_y (either in school or the environment) and adequate motivation to learn L_y. (29)

In other words, when students are taught in and develop proficiency in their first language, L_x, that proficiency will transfer to the second language, L_y, assuming they are given enough exposure to the second language and are motivated to learn it. Cummins cites extensive research showing that there is a common proficiency that underlies languages. His CUP (common underlying proficiency) model holds that what we know in one language is accessible in a second language once we acquire a sufficient level of the second language.

To take a simple example, David learned about linguistics by studying in English. He knows about phonemes and syntax. David has also acquired a strong intermediate level of Spanish. Even though he didn't study linguistics in Spanish, he can draw on his underlying knowledge of linguistics when speaking about it in Spanish. What he needs is knowledge of linguistics in English and enough of the grammar and vocabulary of Spanish to discuss linguistics in Spanish.

The concept of a common underlying proficiency helps explain why English language learners do better in school when some of their instruction is in their native language. If students enter school speaking a language other than English and if all their instruction is in English, they won't understand the teacher and will fall behind. In contrast, as Krashen (1996) notes, students in bilingual programs can learn academic content and develop the skills needed for problem solving and higher-order thinking in their first language while they become proficient in English.

Early exit bilingual programs are based on this idea. These programs include primary language teaching through about second grade. By that time, students can speak and understand enough English so that they can benefit from instruction in English. The first language is viewed as a bridge to English-only instruction.

However, the research cited earlier shows that for programs to be effective, students need at least six years of instruction that includes their primary language. Late exit or dual language programs provide this extra time of first language development. When students receive instruction in their first language for an extended period of time, they more fully develop that language.

Consider native English speakers who are taught all in English. They receive English language arts instruction throughout their schooling because two or three years would not be enough time for them to develop academic proficiency in English. Or think of a foreign language class you took in high school or college. Did the two or three years of French or German classes result in a high level of foreign language proficiency? Most people who study a foreign language for a short time do not develop high levels of the language, and they usually lose the language if they do not use it on a regular basis. Many who studied French or German in college certainly would struggle to carry on a conversation in that language with a native speaker.

Another reason that early exit programs are not successful is that although students can learn what Cummins' (1981) termed basic interpersonal communicative skills (BICS) in one or two years, they don't develop cognitive academic language proficiency (CALP). Research has shown that the development of academic language takes from four to nine years. As a result, students who are exited to an all-English program after two or three years have not yet developed the academic proficiency in their first language needed for school success in English. In contrast, students who receive primary language instruction for at least six years develop academic proficiency in two languages.

Thomas and Collier's Model of Language Acquisition for School

Thomas and Collier's prism models (1997) expand on and also help clarify the idea that the development of the first language promotes the development of academic achievement in a second language.

The prism model represents the four major components of language acquisition: language development, cognitive development, academic development, and social and cultural processes (42) (see Figure 1–1).

In schools, all students should continue their language development. For many students, this involves learning to read and write as well as increasing their vocabulary and refining their syntax. In addition, students continue their cognitive development. They become better problem solvers and learn to deal with more complex concepts. By studying the different content areas, students also develop academically. That is the goal of schooling. The foundation for successful language, cognitive, and academic development is a familiar social and cultural context.

As the prism model illustrates, in effective bilingual and dual language settings, students develop two languages as they increase their cognitive abilities and academic knowledge. By including first language instruction, schools recognize all students' social and cultural backgrounds. Instruction builds on what students bring to school and adds a second language.

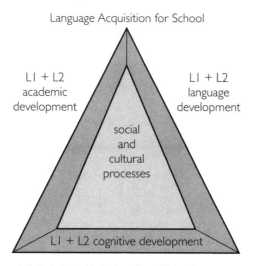

Language Acquisition for School

LI + L2 academic development

LI + L2 language development

social and cultural processes

LI + L2 cognitive development

FIGURE I–I. Thomas and Collier's Prism Model for Bilingual Education

The Context for Developing Literacy for Bilingual Students

The sociocultural component includes individual variables such as anxiety and self-esteem as well as larger social factors, like discrimination, overt or covert. For that reason, even if the school provides opportunities for positive language, cognitive, and academic development, social and cultural influences must also be examined because they have such strong positive or negative influences on students' language acquisition, cognitive development, and academic performance.

When all instruction is in English, English language learners are delayed in their language, cognitive, and academic development until they understand enough of the English instruction to receive any benefits. By that time, they are behind their native English–speaking peers, and, once behind, it is difficult for students to catch up. Further, when their native language is not used, the school fails to build on the social and cultural strengths English language learners bring to school. The only development that is promoted is the students' linguistic development in English. Figure 1–2 (Thomas and Collier 1997, 44) represents the prism model in an English-only setting.

A closer look at Francisco's educational experiences helps illustrates the effects of English-only programs as reflected in this second prism model. When Francisco came to the United States as a freshman in high school, he was suddenly thrust into a completely new sociocultural setting. He was not prepared for the large urban high school he attended, where neither teachers nor most other students had any understanding of his background. There were some students from El Salvador, but most Latinos in the high school were from Mexico, and many of his

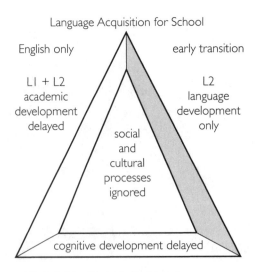

FIGURE 1–2. Thomas and Collier's Prism Model for English Only

TEACHING READING AND WRITING IN SPANISH AND ENGLISH

teachers assumed he was Mexican. Thus, his schooling did not build on Francisco's social and cultural backgrounds.

Although he came to school reading and writing at grade level in Spanish, no advanced Spanish classes were offered at the high school. It wasn't until he took Spanish literature and Bible classes in college that Francisco was able to continue his first language development. The high school did offer ESL classes, so he began to develop English proficiency. However, these classes focused on conversational English rather than the academic English he needed to succeed in school.

Francisco's academic development was also delayed. Since no academic content subjects were offered in Spanish, he could not continue his study of math or science while learning English. Instead, he was placed in ESL classes and other classes, such as P.E. and shop. Although Francisco was old enough to have completed much of his cognitive development when he started school in English, his classes generally required lower-order thinking skills. Most class periods were spent filling in worksheets.

Even though his high school experiences did not build on Francisco's social and cultural processes, delayed his academic and cognitive development, and failed to provide academic language development in English and Spanish, Francisco succeeded in college because of his early interest in schooling and reading, his own perseverance, and the strong support of his mother, his soccer coach, and his girlfriend, whom he later married. However, many English language learners who are placed in the school context represented by the second prism do not succeed academically.

Francisco now has developed high levels of bilingualism and biliteracy. And because he married his Anglo girlfriend and has spent time with her family, he has become bicultural too. Francisco hopes to enable his students to become bilingual, bilterate, and bicultural, but with less of a struggle than he endured. Francisco has moved to a school district that promotes dual language education. Dual language programs promote academic, linguistic, and cognitive development in two languages. The goal of dual language is to help students become not only bilingual but also biliterate and bicultural.

 ## Biliteracy

Francisco succeeded in school because he developed high levels of biliteracy. One of the goals of this book is to help teachers in bilingual classes understand how to promote biliteracy. Hornberger (2003) defines biliteracy as "any and all instances in which communication occurs in two (or more) languages in or around writing"

(xiii). We have observed that many bilingual students can carry on basic oral communication in two languages, but they cannot read and write at grade-appropriate levels in both languages. They are bilingual but not biliterate.

Hornberger examines the complexities of biliteracy. Different forms and levels of biliteracy develop in different social contexts. Even in the same contexts, individual differences result in varying levels of reading and writing proficiency in two or more languages. There may also be differences in an individual's ability to read a language and her ability to write it. Hornberger also takes into account other factors, such as whether an individual develops the two languages simultaneously or successively and the relatedness of the two languages in both their oral and their written forms. Her framework can help educators become aware of the many levels of biliteracy and the many factors that influence biliteracy development.

Language of Initial Literacy Instruction

Although not all programs have the goal of biliteracy for students, our view is that bilingual programs should strive to help students read, write, and learn with equal proficiency in two languages. A key question, then, that administrators and teachers must ask themselves is, "Should formal literacy instruction be introduced in the first language, in the second language, or in both languages simultaneously?" One approach is to have students learn to read first in their native language. A second approach is to have students learn to read in both languages simultaneously. In some 90/10 dual language programs, a third approach to initial literacy is to teach all students to read first in the minority language and then add reading in English later. In these later programs, all students, including English speakers, would first learn to read in Spanish and add English reading in second or third grade.

Students have succeeded in becoming biliterate in schools that introduce reading in two languages from the beginning as well as in schools that teach reading first in the native language. In addition, in dual language programs English speakers who are taught to read first in Spanish do well in reading in both languages by fifth grade (Lindholm-Leary 2001).

From our understanding of reading, there is no strong preference for teaching reading in one language or two from the beginning. If, in fact, written language can be acquired in the same way as oral language, then students could be expected to learn to read in two languages simultaneously in the same way that children brought up in bilingual households develop the ability to speak and understand two or more languages at the same time. As long as teachers make the written input comprehensible, students should be able to acquire the ability to read and write two or more languages at once. However, children could also acquire literacy in one language and then add a second language later.

Native English speakers who receive initial literacy instruction in Spanish in school often have been read to at home. Many of them come to school already at early stages of reading and writing development in English. As they learn to read in Spanish, they continue to receive support for English reading and writing at home. This pattern applies to many native English speakers and helps explain their success.

However, for Spanish speakers, in general, the same level of preschool support is not evident, and fewer of these students receive support for Spanish literacy at home. If these students are given initial literacy instruction in English, they may not learn to read in Spanish. An important study shows the value of having Spanish speakers begin to read and write in Spanish.

Edelsky (1986, 1989) conducted an extensive study of children's writing in Spanish. She analyzed the writing of twenty-six first-, second-, and third-grade bilingual children in a settled, semirural, migrant school. She described the purpose of the study:

> The study was an effort of qualitative research in which a team of researchers analyzed more than 500 written pieces from three different classrooms for code switching, invented spelling, nonspelling conventions (punctuation, segmentation), stylistic devices, structural features (e.g., beginnings, ending, links between clauses), and quality of content, in order to note changes over time as well as to make cross-sectional comparisons. (1989, 166)

Edelsky's research has helped dispel myths about biliteracy and bilingual education. Perhaps the most important myth that the study dispelled was the myth that "to begin literacy acquisition in Spanish and then to add English leads to interference with English literacy" (1986, 73). Instead, Edelsky concluded, first language literacy supported the acquisition of literacy in English. When the students Edelsky studied wrote in English, they used what they knew about literacy in their first language, and Spanish did not interfere with their acquisition of English. In fact, students who can read and write in their first language transfer those skills to second language literacy (Cummins 2000).

Edelsky's study also showed that students need extensive exposure to a wide variety of literature and other texts in Spanish. Students produced their best writing when they wrote for authentic reasons to respond to real audiences. Edelsky's study confirms many of the practices of effective bilingual teachers, and it provides important research support for teachers who are helping their bilingual students read and write in their first language.

In considering the language of initial instruction, it is important to consider the power of English. When schools introduce reading in both languages, English often gets more time and more emphasis. English language learners may conclude that their language, especially the written form, doesn't really count for much. On the other hand, the message a Spanish speaker gets when instruction is in Spanish is that Spanish is also an important language. English speakers do not ever get the message that their language is not valued. In the present political climate, it may be difficult for bilingual teachers to convince students that both Spanish and English are of equal value. Dual language programs try to develop true bilingualism and biliteracy. However, there is much resistance to any type of bilingual program in most of the country. A look at the politics of bilingual education provides important background to understand this resistance.

Political Influences on Bilingual Education

When the United States was being colonized and established in the 1600s and 1700s, bilingualism was accepted as natural. For example, Crawford (2004) explains that in 1664 at least eighteen tongues, not including Indian languages, were spoken on the island of Manhattan in the settlement in New York, and German-English schooling was common. In the first half of the eighteenth century, bilingualism was still in favor despite some efforts by President Thomas Jefferson and Congress to impose English-only policies on new colonies. Ohio established a law authorizing instruction in English, German, or both in 1839, and Louisiana followed suit with a law authorizing instruction in English, French, or both in 1847. In 1848 the Territory of New Mexico authorized Spanish-English bilingual education. In other parts of the country, local school boards allowed instruction in Swedish, Danish, Norwegian, Italian, Polish, Dutch, and Czech.

By the late nineteenth century, opposition to the use of languages other than English for instruction in public schools surfaced. The rise of nativist groups such as the secret society, the American Protective Association (APA), "marked the beginning of a gradual decline for bilingual education" (Crawford 2004, 86). Xenophobia was clearly evident as "Italians, Jews and Slavs began to outnumber Irish, Germans, and Scandinavians in the immigrant stream" and the "appearance, manners, living habits, and speech of these groups attracted more public notice and comment—usually negative" (87).

When the United States entered World War I in 1917, anti-German senti-ment led to language restrictionism, and laws were passed banning the use of German in schools, churches, public meetings, and even on the telephone. Ger-man teachers were reassigned to instructing children in Americanization and citi-zenship, and German textbooks were burned or sold as scrap paper. This fervor spilled over to other languages, and soon fifteen states legislated English as the basic language of instruction (Crawford 2004). By the mid-1930s bilingual in-struction was "virtually eradicated throughout the United States" (90).

In recent history several legislative acts have shaped policy for the education of English language learners. The National Defense Education Act of 1958, which strengthened mathematics, science, and foreign language education, was a re-sponse to the Soviet Union's launching of *Sputnik* and concern that the Soviets would win the space race. The Elementary and Secondary Education Act of 1965 (ESEA) addressed the needs of poor children and thus affected the education of many bilingual students. In the late 1960s several politicians from Arizona and Texas were brought together by the National Education Association (NEA) to make the plight of Spanish-speaking children in schools known. This meeting gave birth to the bilingual movement. The 1968 Bilingual Education Act, also known as Title VII of the Elementary and Secondary Education Act, eventually funded bilingual projects in schools and led to the mandating of bilingual educa-tion in some states, including Massachusetts, Texas, and California.

However, the civil rights and equal opportunity movements of the 1960s and the early 1970s came to an end as immigration waves and the growth of the His-panic population led to an anti-immigrant sentiment. Bilingual education was criticized as causing divisiveness. Opponents of bilingual education claimed that teaching students in their native language was detrimental to their learning En-glish and succeeding in school.

In 1983 immigration restriction activist John Tanton and retired politician S. I. Hayakawa founded U.S. English, an organization to promote English-only legis-lation in the country. Celebrities including Walter Cronkite and Arnold Schwar-zenegger endorsed the concept. William J. Bennett, the U.S. secretary of education, called bilingual education a failure. In 1998 Proposition 227, English for the Children, which called for English immersion programs for Limited English Proficient (LEP) students, was adopted by California voters, and stricter versions, Proposition 203 and Question 2, were approved in Arizona and Massachusetts in 2000 and 2002, respectively. When the No Child Left Behind Act was passed in 2002, Title VII came to an end. The needs of English language learners were now put under Title III. OBEMLA, the Office of Bilingual Education and Minority Lan-guages Affairs, in Washington, D.C., was eliminated and a new office, the Office of English Language Acquisition (OELA), was established to reflect the position of the government toward the education of English learners.

This brief overview of policy shifts in the United States reveals that much of the opposition to bilingual education comes from an attitude of isolationism and a fear of immigrants. Even though decisions about instructing students in their native languages should be determined by looking carefully at educational research, most of the decisions have had little to do with the realities of school. Ron Unz, the author and promoter of the English-only propositions, for example, has refused to visit bilingual classes. He has no background in teaching and learning. And yet he has managed to establish policies that affect thousands of English language learners.

An Extended Example of English-Only Mandated Reading Instruction

Policy related to both bilingual education and reading has affected all students and especially English language learners. To demonstrate the effects of English-only instruction coupled with reading mandates, we offer a scenario from a California classroom. The teacher is bilingual, and many of the students speak Spanish, but this teacher teaches language arts in English, carefully following the mandates set out at federal, state, and school levels.

Guillermo's Teaching Background

Guillermo is a first-year teacher in a first-grade classroom in a large elementary school in Los Angeles. Of his thirty students, twenty-one are classified as LEP. Some of these English language learners are at the beginning stages of English language development, while others are at the intermediate or the advanced level. Guillermo's students come from a lower-middle-class neighborhood. The class includes students with various cultural backgrounds—Hispanics, African Americans, Korean Americans, and Anglos. In addition to being at different levels of English proficiency, Guillermo's students are also at different levels of reading proficiency, ranging from students who are not yet reading to a few students who can read first-grade materials comfortably.

Guillermo completed his teacher preparation at a state university. State universities received instructions from the state board of education to follow the guidelines laid out by the government-promoted document *Put Reading First: The Research Building Blocks for Teaching Children to Read* (Armbruster and Osborn

2001). During his reading and language arts methods class, his professors explained the five components of a research-based reading program: phonemic awareness, phonics, fluency, vocabulary, and comprehension. Guillermo drew on the knowledge he gained in this class to pass the state-mandated test on how to teach reading. During his student teaching in a first-grade class, Guillermo's master teacher showed him how she taught reading. For the most part, she followed the lesson plans in the state-adopted textbook carefully. Each of her lessons included the five components Guillermo had studied. The master teacher made sure to give her English language learners extra work in the areas of phonemic awareness and phonics, fluency, and vocabulary, explaining that they were not yet ready to focus on comprehension.

Guillermo was hired to begin teaching the following year. In August, before classes started, Guillermo and the other teachers at his school were given a week-long inservice designed to help them implement the state-adopted textbook correctly. The facilitators assured the teachers that if they followed the scripted lessons carefully during the two and a half hours allocated for reading each day, all the students would learn to read. Guillermo felt confident as he began to teach. He had learned good classroom management skills during his student teaching. He had his plans for teaching reading laid out in the teacher's guide. All he needed to do was follow the plan and keep all the students actively engaged.

Guillermo's Weather Unit

Guillermo's reading textbook includes units that correlate with both the science and the social studies standards for grade one. A grade one standard for earth science is weather. Students are expected to know how to use tools such as a thermometer to measure weather conditions and record changes. The standards also call for students to understand that although the weather changes frequently, it is predictable during a season. In addition, students are expected to learn that the sun warms the land, the air, and water. These earth science standards include new academic vocabulary that Guillermo's students, especially his English language learners, need to learn.

Since much of the day is devoted to reading instruction, there is little time for either science or social studies. For that reason, Guillermo and the other teachers at his school try to cover science and social studies standards as they teach reading. The teachers are expected to concentrate on reading as the foundation of the content area studies. In addition, reading is what is directly tested.

The weather unit in the reading textbook includes several of the earth science standards related to weather. At the same time, this unit covers several of the

English language arts (ELA) standards (California Department of Education 1999) for grade one. The first reading standard states that by the end of first grade,

> Students understand the basic features of reading. They select letter patterns and know how to translate them into spoken language by using phonics, syllabication, and word parts. They apply this knowledge to achieve fluent oral and silent reading. (6)

This standard outlines specific skills and knowledge in the areas of concepts about print, phonemic awareness, decoding and word recognition, and vocabulary and concept development.

The English language learners in Guillermo's class are also expected to meet the state English Language Development (ELD) standards (*English-Language Development Standards for California Public Schools Kindergarten Through Grade Twelve* 1999), which specify the skills and knowledge students at different levels of English language proficiency are expected to meet. Each unit in the state-adopted textbook that Guillermo's school has chosen includes a section designed for English language learners. For the most part, these sections provide extra practice in phonemic awareness, phonics, decoding, and vocabulary. Although Guillermo feels somewhat overwhelmed by all the standards his students are expected to master, he is confident that the textbook includes stories and activities that will help him provide the instruction that all his students need.

Guillermo's Reading Lessons

Let's look closely at a lesson from the weather unit that Guillermo teaches in mid-September. We will point out both the ELA and the ELD standards that the different activities correspond to. Guillermo is bilingual, but his school does not provide bilingual education, so his reading instruction is given in English only.

On Monday, Guillermo introduces the big book that will serve as the basic text for the lessons during the unit. This is a fairly short decodable text of about twelve pages with a limited amount of text on each page. Decodable books include only words with phonics patterns or sight words that have been taught previously.

Guillermo asks the students to come and sit on the rug in front of an easel on which he has propped the big book. Following the teacher's guide, Guillermo reads the title of the book. He also reads the names of the author and the illustrator. He asks individual students to point to the title, the author, and the illustrator to be sure they understand these concepts. Knowing the title and the author is part of the concepts about print required for first graders. He points to the cover illustration, showing a boy walking his dog in a park, and asks students, "What do you see here?"

"A boy," calls out Ricardo.

"He's outdoors and he's walking his dog," Ana adds.

"Very good," Guillermo says. "This is a story about all the things this boy and his dog do together. Do any of you have a dog?"

"I do," chorus several students.

Guillermo continues by asking individual students about their pets and what they like to do with them. In this way, he is able to connect the story to his students' lives and build background knowledge for reading the story. He makes sure to introduce key words that might be difficult for students, such as *bark* and *jog*.

Next, he leafs through the book, asking students what they think is happening on each page. As he does this, he asks the questions from the teacher's guide for each page. In doing so, he introduces additional vocabulary from the story, including the weather words, *cloudy, rainy, windy,* and *sunny*.

The students return to their seats after this picture walk through the story. At their desks they complete two worksheets designed to reinforce the vocabulary that Guillermo has introduced. The first worksheet highlights four weather words from the story in a box. Students draw a line from each word to a corresponding picture. For example, for *rainy*, students draw a line to a picture of the boy and his dog in the rain. The second worksheet has five words like *boy, dog,* and *park*. Students use these words to complete five sentences, writing one word in each blank. Since this is a more difficult task, Guillermo pairs his English language learners with native English speakers, as the guide suggests.

When the students have finished their worksheets, Guillermo goes over the answers with the students, writing the correct answers on transparencies that all the students can see. He asks students to correct any mistakes on their papers. Then he has the students turn in their work. He is pleased that most of his students were able to complete the worksheets either individually or with the help of their partner.

Guillermo then calls the students back to the rug. Once they are settled, he reads the big book to them. It tells about a boy and his dog. It shows the different activities they like to do. They like to walk in the park when it is cloudy. They like to play inside when it is rainy. They like to fly a kite when it is windy. And they like to go to the beach when it is sunny. The pages follow a pattern. For example, if the first line reads, "Ted and his dog like to walk in the park," the second line continues, "They like to walk when it is cloudy." On the facing page, the text reads, "They like to walk, but not when it's snowy." For each page with "not when it's snowy," there is a picture of Ted and his dog sitting inside, looking out the window. The last page shows Ted and his dog, dressed in warm clothes, sliding down a snow-covered hill, with the line "Ted and his dog like to slide when it's snowy. They like it a lot."

The predictable pattern and the close text-to-picture match help all of Guillermo's students follow the story. As he reads, Guillermo tracks the words with a pointer. In this way, he helps students develop the skill to meet the standard that calls for them to match oral words to printed words. He reads the story through twice as the students follow along. Then he asks them to return to their seats for individual work. First they complete a comprehension worksheet. It shows five pictures from the story. Students are asked to color the pictures, cut them out, and assemble them in order. Guillermo circulates around the class to help any students who are having trouble deciding on the order of events in the story. Sequence is one of the comprehension skills first graders are required to master. When all the students are finished, Guillermo collects their papers.

He then calls them back to the rug for a final reading of the story for the day. This time, he encourages students to chime in on words or lines as he reads them. He is pleased that several of the students are able to do this. When he reaches the last page, he asks them to predict what will happen next. Some students say that Ted and his dog will catch a cold. Others say they will come inside and drink something hot. Guillermo praises them for their good predictions. Predicting is an important skill for first graders. For the last activity during the reading time, Guillermo writes the word *weather* on the board. Then he turns the pages in the book and asks students to pick out words related to weather. Students are able to identify words like *sunny* and *windy*. This activity meets the vocabulary and concept development standard for classifying categories of words. It also meets the concepts about print standard for identifying words.

Over the next week, Guillermo continues with the weather unit. Each day he rereads the story. Then he has students complete additional activities. For example, one of the comprehension worksheets shows two pictures from the story. Students are asked to put an X through things in picture 2 that are different from picture 1. Some of Guillermo's students are not familiar with this type of worksheet, so he has them work in pairs to complete it. A vocabulary worksheet has a sentence with a blank to fill in with the word *dog*. Students write *dog* and then look at a series of pictures on the worksheet. They are to circle the picture that does not have a dog. Then they color the dogs in the other pictures.

Although the students complete some vocabulary and comprehension activities, most of the worksheets and class exercises focus on phonemic awareness, phonics, and decoding. For example, Guillermo asks students to listen to the first sound in *dog* and tell him the sound they hear. This meets the English language development standard for beginners that requires that they recognize English phonemes that correspond to phonemes they already hear in their primary language. Guillermo knows that *d* is a phoneme in Spanish, although he isn't sure whether his Korean students would know that sound. He also checks to see if his intermediate ELD students can meet the standard to distinguish initial, medial, and final sounds in single-syllable words. Several of his students can do this with *dog* and *Ted*, but other students seem confused, and Guillermo decides to give them additional practice with identifying phonemes in words.

The advanced ELD students are expected to meet the standard to use morphemes to derive meaning by dividing words into syllables. They have some trouble with the weather words. Some students think that *rainy* should be divided into *rai* and *ny* while others believe it should be *rain* and *y*. Is *windy win* and *dy* or *wind* and *y*? Guillermo, following the teacher's guide, helps them see that each of these words has a base and a suffix, so students can understand a word like *rainy* or *windy* by finding the base word. Still some students find this difficult because they pronounce the words as *rai ny* and *win dy*. Guillermo has some advanced students find the words in their picture dictionary, so they can confirm the right answer.

All through the week Guillermo works on having his students match the sounds they hear in words like *dog* with the corresponding alphabet letters. His reading textbook presents all the English phonemes in a sequence, and each lesson emphasizes certain phonemes. Guillermo wants to be sure that all his students master the phonemes for the lesson. In addition to the big book, which he reads again each day, Guillermo reads both stories and content books related to weather.

Guillermo also provides his students with leveled books related to the theme that they can read independently or with a partner. To determine their reading level he had given his students an assessment at the beginning of the year. He makes sure to match his students with appropriate books. The books are leveled following strict guidelines. The first level, for example, contains only about twenty-five words with sentences of three to six words. The sentences at this level follow a pattern, and one word changes for each sentence. The first-level books also have a precise picture-to-text match with realistic pictures. For each level, the number of words, words per sentence, and variety of sentences increase while the picture support decreases.

Students practice reading their leveled readers each day. While most of the students read independently or in pairs, Guillermo works with small groups to provide additional instruction and to conduct further assessments. He also checks students' fluency. Each day, he asks five of his students to come to his desk one at a time. Each student reads a leveled book out loud. Guillermo times the reading and counts any errors the student makes. He charts their progress. Many of the students are proud of the progress shown on their fluency charts.

Guillermo and the students are very busy during reading time each day. They read together and separately and fill out worksheets. The students become accustomed to the routine and to the kinds of exercises the book requires. Although they are improving in their ability to complete the assignments, the students seem restless at times. Guillermo worries that they might not be enjoying their reading. They always like it when he introduces a new book, but by the end of the week, they seem somewhat bored when he reads it again and gives them another exercise to work on. He is a little concerned that the students who are less fluent in English seem completely lost when he gives them worksheets or tries to engage them in oral activities. Still, Guillermo is convinced that if he follows the teacher's guide carefully and steers all his students through each lesson, all of them will succeed.

 ## Conclusion

Both Guillermo and Francisco were required to teach reading in English, following the state guidelines. However, these two teachers are very different. Based on his teacher preparation and his previous experience, Francisco knew that he was not providing the best instruction for his English language learners. As a result, he chose not to continue working in his district. Guillermo, in contrast, had never taught in a bilingual class. In addition, the method he was asked to use to teach reading matched what he had learned at the university. As a result, he interpreted the students' response to instruction as normal. He had no experience to show that things could be different. Consequently, he did not offer his students the best possible instruction. His students were learning to decode, but they were not focused on comprehension. They were able to function in English, but they were not developing their first language.

It is important for teachers to have the knowledge that allows them to evaluate methods they are asked to use to teach reading. In the following chapters we examine two different views of reading. We offer scenarios from bilingual and dual language classes to show how these views are realized in classroom practice. We believe that once teachers understand the difference between these two approaches to reading instruction, they can make informed choices about methods and provide the best possible instruction for all their students.

Applications

1. This chapter began with an extended example of Francisco's teaching journey. Look over his story again. What events or experiences that he had over the years were positive? Which were negative? Make two lists. Which of these specifically influenced Francisco's teaching of reading and/or writing?

2. Consider the experiences of teaching reading and writing that you have had over the past eight to ten years, or interview an experienced teacher to find out what his or her experiences have been. How has reading instruction changed? If your experience in teaching literacy has only been within the last four or five years, how do you see reading as being taught?

3. What are the key findings of Ramírez (1991), Thomas and Collier (1997), and Greene (1998) in relation to bilingual education? List and be prepared to discuss.

4. Thomas and Collier (1997) present two different prisms. One shows what students get in bilingual programs and the other, what students get in English-only programs. We used Francisco as an example of the English-only prism. Find an example of someone whose schooling fits into one of the prisms. Be prepared to describe how.

5. This chapter includes a discussion about the language of initial literacy instruction. What is your view? Explain.

6. Proposition 207 in California, Proposition 203 in Arizona, and Question 2 in Massachusetts are antibilingual legislative mandates. If you live in one of these states, list some of the results of the legislation that you have seen. If you do not live in one of those states, what do you think the chances are of such a measure passing in your state? Interview at least five people to get their view of bilingual education.

7. We ended the chapter with an extended example of Guillermo's teaching. What is your opinion of his lessons? What are some strengths? What would you do differently?

A Word Recognition View
of Reading

How does reading happen? That is, what is the process that occurs as we look at marks on a page and try to make sense of what is written there? A teacher's view of that process strongly influences the methods and the materials he uses during reading instruction.

In this chapter and the next, we present two views of reading. A view of reading is a set of beliefs about how the reading process works. Although there are many variations in how reading is taught, the methods teachers use reflect one of the two views. The first view of reading is what we refer to as a *word recognition view*. This view holds that reading is primarily a process of learning to recognize words by converting written language to spoken language and then combining the meanings of individual words to construct the meaning of a text. The second view, the *sociopsycholinguistic view*, claims that reading is a process of constructing meaning from texts within a social context using background knowledge, psychological strategies, and linguistic cues.

We ended Chapter 1 with an example of a reading lesson in an English-only setting. We begin this chapter with a scenario of reading lessons from Elena's first-grade transitional bilingual class. Then we explain the word recognition view of reading. After explaining this set of beliefs, we analyze both Guillermo's lesson, described at the end of the last chapter, and Elena's teaching of reading to show how these teachers' methods reflect a word recognition view. In the following chapter we follow a similar format to illustrate and describe the sociopsycholinguistic view. The teachers whose lessons we describe may not be able to explain their view of reading, but the way they teach reveals their approach.

Elena's Teaching Background

Elena is a first-grade bilingual teacher in south Texas, in a small, rural town. In Texas, first language support is required by law. In fact, the importance of a student's first language is written into the standards. The TEKS (Texas Essential Knowledge and Skills) state the following in the introduction of the section on English Language Arts and Reading for grade one:

> For first grade students whose first language is not English, the students' native language serves as a foundation for English language acquisition. (TEA 1998c)

The first-grade TEKS call for students to develop listening and speaking skills and in reading to have print awareness, use letter-sound knowledge to decode, have word identification skills, and read for fluency. In addition, students should read from a variety of texts, develop vocabulary, and read for comprehension.

Elena teaches in a school that has transitional bilingual education, where students can be given instruction in Spanish through the third grade. Then students are transitioned into all English. Elena has noticed that her administration encourages teachers to move students into more English even as early as the end of first grade. Since Texas has high-stakes tests and third graders must pass a high-stakes reading test to get into fourth grade, there is pressure to move students into English before third grade despite the fact students can take the third-grade test in Spanish. Elena's principal prefers that teachers have students ready to take the test in English.

In the Valley, the area from Brownsville to Laredo along the Mexican and U.S. border, where Elena teaches, most of the students are Mexican or of Mexican origins. Many arrive in school with little to no English. Often new arrivals have had interrupted schooling or no previous schooling experiences. Many children live in *colonias*, unincorporated areas that often lack public services such as road maintenance, water, and even electricity.

Elena is a second-year teacher. She received her certificate in an alternative program during which she went to school evenings and taught under an emergency certificate until she finished her coursework. Her preparation for the teaching of reading was limited to one language arts class and one biliteracy course. In her coursework, she learned about the importance of being student centered, teaching through themes, and using literature, but she had little guidance as to how that would look in the classroom. Her program did not require a supervised student teaching experience. Because she feels somewhat insecure about teaching reading, Elena follows the lead of other teachers and tries to do the same kinds of things they do. Her principal has explained that she has to be sure to draw on the TEKS (TEA 1998c) as well as the content standards, and Elena feels the pressure to teach her students following those requirements.

If we could peek into Elena's bilingual second-grade classroom, this is what we'd see. Around Elena's room there is the alphabet in Spanish and in English; there is also a word wall with words in Spanish and in English under each letter of the alphabet, including the names of the children in the class. The words in Spanish are written in red and the words in English, in blue. On the bookshelves along the walls of her classroom, there are the books and workbooks in Spanish and in English from the basal series, some trade books, and many leveled books, mainly in Spanish with some in English, that are part of a reading program that the district requires. Students read books at their level, take a test on the computer, and get points that are part of their grade. Classrooms where students earn lots of points get prizes like pizza parties.

Elena's Weather Unit

Elena's theme, weather, designed to meet the first-grade science TEKS, is obvious from looking around the room. A teacher-made bulletin board with the titles What's the Weather Like? and ¿Qué tiempo hace? features pictures from magazines showing various types of weather under the titles *"Hace frío"* "It's Cold"; *"Está nublado"* "It's Cloudy"; *"Hace sol"* "It's Sunny"; and *"Está lloviendo"* "It's Raining." Another bulletin board contains student artwork: suns students made using paper plates. A poster with several clouds has weather words with common blends in English, including *snow, cloud,* and *spring,* and a poster in Spanish has some weather expressions with the verb *Hacer,* including *Hace frío* (It's cold), *Hace viento* (It's windy), *Hace calor* (It's hot), *Hace buen tiempo* (It's nice weather), and *Hace mal tiempo* (It's bad weather). Each of these is accompanied by a drawing to show the kind of weather. The calendar also has these expressions and drawings on each day as the children tell the weather during the daily opening.

The twenty children in the class have been divided into four groups, three for Spanish reading and one for English. Right now, three of the groups are busy at centers doing various activities. At the English center students are finishing pages in a take-home book that consists of pictures of weather conditions. Students find appropriate phrases from a list of sentence strips and cut and paste in "It's cold" under the picture of a boy shivering in the snow and "It's hot" under the picture of the boy lying in the sun on the beach. The children working in Spanish do the same thing using sentence strips that read, *"Hace frío"* (It's cold) and *"Hace calor"* (It's hot). The students then color the pictures and draw and color a cover for their book. Another group of children is working with the teacher's aide on a worksheet that asks them to start sentences with a capital letter and end them with a period. Meanwhile, Elena is sitting in a small circle with the five children who make up her middle Spanish reading group. First, Elena shows the children a list of words that she has printed on a paper: *viento* (wind), *lluvia* (rain), *frío* (cold), *cielo* (sky), *sopla* (blows), and *fresco* (cool). She begins by reading the words to the students and then asking them some questions about the words:

ELENA: ¿Qué notan ustedes en estas palabras?
FELICIANA: Todos tienen que ver con el tiempo.
ELENA: Sí, pero no estamos hablando del significado de las palabras. Estamos viendo las letras de las palabras. ¿Tienen algo en común las letras al final de cada palabra?
MARCO: Todos terminan con la letra *o* y la letra *a*.
ELENA: Muy bien, Marco. ¿Cómo llamamos letras como la *o* y la *a*?
TODOS: Vocales.
ELENA: Muy bien. Ahora, ¿Cuáles son las vocals en español?
TODOS: *A, e, i, o, u.*
ELENA: Muy bien. ¿Quién me puede decir el significado de las palabras? ¿Qué quiere decir *sopla*? ¿Quién puede enseñarme *sopla*?

ELENA: What do you notice about these words?
FELICIANA: They all have to do with the weather.
ELENA: Yes, but we are not talking about the meaning of the words. We are looking at the letters of the words. Do the letters at the end of the words have anything in common?
MARCO: They all end with the letter *o* or *a*.
ELENA: Very good, Marco. What do we call letters like *o* and *a*?
ALL: Vowels.
ELENA: Very good. Now, what are the vowels in Spanish?
ALL: *A, e, i, o, u.*
ELENA: Very good. Who can tell me what the words mean? What does *sopla* [blows] mean? Who can show me what *sopla* means?

After the children have identified the words, Elena takes the big book *El viento* (The Wind) (Flores 1986) and reads the book to the children, tracking the words with her hand. Then she reads the book again, page by page, having the students repeat the lines and then asking them questions about the book.

ELENA: Lean conmigo [La maestra y los niños leen juntos], "Cuando el viento sopla con fuerza, las nubes se mueven en el cielo con mucha rapidez."

ELENA: ¿Qué quiere decir, "el viento sopla con fuerza"? ¿Es que sopla mucho o poco?

ENRIQUE: Sopla mucho, maestra, mucho.

ELENA: ¿Qué pasa cuando el viento sopla con fuerza?

FRANCISCO: Hay mucho polvo como cuando estamos afruera en los *fields*.

ELENA: Sí, Francisco, tienes razón, pero ¿qué dice el libro?

MARIANNA: Dice, "Las nubes se mueven en el cielo con mucha rapidez."

ELENA: Muy bien, Marianna. Seguimos con la próxima página. Lean conmigo. [La clase sigue leyendo el libro y al final Elena les da direcciones.]

ELENA: El libro nos dice lo que la fuerza del viento hace. ¿Cuáles son algunas cosas que hace el viento?

JORGE: Empuja el barquito en el agua.

MARÍA: También empuja el papalote.

ELENA: Sí, y ¿qué palabra usan en el libro para *papalote*?

TODOS: *Cometa.*

ELENA: Quiero que ustedes trabajen en pares y que dibujen tres cosas que hace el viento. Al terminar, deben escoger un libro a su nivel, leerlo solo, y tomar el examen en la computadora. Recuerden que la clase necesita puntos para pizza y si ustedes no lean y tomen los exámenes no vamos a poder hacer una fiesta de pizza.

ELENA: Read with me [The teacher and the children read together], "When the wind blows strongly, the clouds move rapidly in the sky."

ELENA: What does it mean, "the wind blows strongly"? Does it blow a lot or a little?

ENRIQUE: It blows a lot, Teacher, a lot.

ELENA: What happens when the wind blows strongly?

FRANCISCO: There is a lot of dust like when we are outside in the fields.

ELENA: Yes, Francisco, you're right, but what does the book say?

MARIANNA: It says, "The clouds move rapidly in the sky."

ELENA: Very good, Marianna. Let's go on with the next page. Read with me. [The class continues reading the book and at the end Elena gives them directions.]

ELENA: The book tells us what the power of the wind does. What are some things the wind does?

JORGE: It pushes the little boat in the water.

MARÍA: It also pushes the kite. [Uses the word *papalote*]

ELENA: Yes, and what word does the book use for *kite*?

ALL: *Cometa.*

ELENA: I want you to work in pairs and draw three things the wind does. When you finish, you need to pick a book at your level, read it on your own, and take the computer test. Remember that the class needs points for pizza and if you don't read and take the tests, we won't be able to have a pizza party.

Since the students in this group are in the Spanish reading group, Elena also works with them on ESL (English as a second language). She knows she needs to get the children into reading in English and has been told the students need to work on their English sounds, so most of her ESL time is spent on going over the letters of the alphabet and having the students repeat each letter and the sound the letter makes. Then students repeat simple words that start with that letter. Some of the group can decode some simple words and read very limited-text books in English although they don't seem to understand the words they are decoding.

Elena has the students do phonemic awareness activities with words too: they change the first and last sounds of words she says to them. Although she notices that her students do not understand what they are repeating in English and that they get confused when asked to change the first and last sounds, she continues with these activities because she has been assured that students need to be able to manipulate sounds in words before they can read.

Elena has organized her curriculum around themes. She has good classroom management, and all her students are engaged in reading, writing, and talking about the weather. The children like their teacher, and it is obvious that she likes them. The students stay on task. While one group reads, children in the other groups exhibit excellent self-discipline, especially for first graders. The students read the leveled books in the school program and take the computer tests. Many of Elena's students will become successful readers and writers as a result of the experiences they have in this class.

A Word Recognition View

Both Guillermo, described in Chapter 1, and Elena hold a word recognition view of reading. They see the goal of reading as decoding words. Their lessons are organized to help students recognize that the black marks on a page correspond to words in oral language. Literacy is seen as the process of converting written language into spoken language. The idea is that once readers can translate written language into oral language they can recognize the words and combine the meanings of individual words to figure out the meaning of a text.

This approach is quite logical. Oral language development begins with the production of individual words, so written language learning must also begin with the identification of individual words. Instruction should focus on helping students develop the skills needed to recognize words. Guillermo and Elena taught these skills explicitly. The stories their students read were specifically designed so that follow-up exercises could focus on certain skills.

Both English and Spanish use an alphabetic writing system. In alphabetic writing, characters represent individual sounds rather than syllables or whole words.

While no language has a perfect match of one letter to one sound (Cañado 2005), most words in alphabetic languages can be analyzed to show the connection between the letters and the sounds. Spanish has a closer correspondence between letters and sounds than English does, but readers of either language can learn to sound out words by articulating the sounds of the individual letters.

The process of teaching reading in English usually begins with phonemic awareness. Next, students learn the letters of the alphabet and the sound or sounds each letter makes. Then students learn the phonics rules for combining the sounds of the individual letters to produce the sound of a word. Since some common words, such as *the*, *of*, and *one*, do not strictly follow phonics rules, students learn these as sight words, recognizing the whole word without analyzing it into its component parts.

Spanish follows a similar teaching pattern. However, Spanish words more easily divide into syllables than into individual letter sounds, so students learn the sounds of syllables and then combine the sounds to produce the whole word. For example, students usually find it easier to divide a word like *casa* (house) into *ca* and *sa* instead of attempting to sound out each letter. Students learning to read in Spanish can sound most words out, so they don't study sight words, although some words like *es* (is) are taught as wholes as sight words are in English.

The letters that represent vowels in Spanish generally have only one sound, so dividing the syllables does not affect the pronunciation of the vowels. The *a* represents the same sound wherever it appears in a Spanish word. This does not hold true for English, since a letter like *a* can have different sounds depending on the other letters in the word. For example, the *a* in *radio* has a different sound than the *a* in *rapid*. It would be difficult for a student to guess which sound the *a* represents by looking at an English word one syllable at a time.

 ## Research on the Word Recognition View

The word recognition view of reading is probably the most commonly held and most thoroughly researched view there is. The work of Thonis (1976, 1983), Braslavsky (1962), and Goldenberg and Gallimore (1991) in Spanish reading, and Adams (1990, 1994), Anderson, Hiebert, et al. (1985), and Chall (1967) in English reading are good examples of this research base. In general, this research supports the teaching of systematic, explicit phonics to increase students' word recognition skills.

Stanovich (1986, 1996, 1998) has argued for the important role of phonemic awareness in developing reading proficiency. In his article "Matthew Effects in

Reading" (1986), he pointed out that while good readers read more and get better at reading, poor readers read less and fall further behind. He reviewed research showing that one important difference between the good and the poor readers was their ability to recognize and manipulate the individual sounds in words, a skill known as *phonemic awareness*. A phoneme is the smallest unit of sound that makes a difference in meaning in a particular language. In English, for example, /p/ and /b/ are phonemes. In two words such as *pet* and *bet*, the only difference in sound is the difference between /p/ and /b/, so these two sounds are phonemes. Phonemic awareness is the ability to hear these differences in oral language. Tests of young children show that those with well-developed phonemic awareness at age four or five do much better at reading later in school than those who lack phonemic awareness.

Stanovich noted that the research did not clearly show whether increased phonemic awareness led to better reading or more reading led to increased phonemic awareness. Reading proficiency and phonemic awareness are correlated, but the research does not show clearly if one causes the other. For that reason, Stanovich termed the relationship reciprocal and argued that phonemic awareness increases reading ability *and* more reading increases phonemic awareness. He concluded that students who entered school lacking phonemic awareness should be given direct instruction in exercises that involved recognizing the sounds in words and manipulating those sounds.

For example, a student might be asked how many sounds they hear in a word like *cat*. Then they might be asked what word would result if the first sound were deleted or if the first sound were changed from /k/ to /r/. More advanced exercises would involve students in blending individual phonemes to produce a word. Although phonemic awareness is an oral skill, most exercises given to students also include work with the written language.

In an attempt to improve the reading ability of students in U.S. schools, the federal government convened the National Reading Panel (NRP) to review the research on reading and recommend effective methods for teaching students to read. The findings of this panel have strongly influenced reading instruction in this country because federal grants are available to schools that adopt materials and methods consistent with the research findings.

The NRP faced an overwhelming task since it would be nearly impossible to review all the research on reading. They narrowed the body of research by restricting their review to articles in peer-reviewed journals that reported experimental or quasiexperimental studies. These are studies that compare the results of some treatment on an experimental group with the results from a control group.

These were the only studies that were deemed *scientific* since they followed the scientific method quite strictly. This decision excluded qualitative studies. As a result, studies that examined the social context of reading instruction were not included.

Further, the NRP looked at studies in only five areas: phonemic awareness, phonics, fluency, vocabulary, and comprehension. These are considered the five essential components, or pillars, of reading. The choice of these five elements reflects a word recognition view of reading. Reading is seen as a process of developing phonemic awareness and then learning letter names and sounds and applying phonics rules to decode words. Once students can decode, their progress is determined by how fluently they read. Fluency is measured by a student's speed and accuracy in reading a passage. Students who can decode and read fluently work on increasing their vocabulary. Improved comprehension results from good decoding, adequate fluency, and a large vocabulary.

The findings of the NRP were widely disseminated in a summary document, *Put Reading First: The Research Building Blocks for Teaching Children to Read* (Armbruster and Osborn 2001). This short book outlines how to teach each of the five skill areas. Many schools received federal funds to implement Reading First grants. These grants fund programs that follow the NRP recommendations. In schools such as the one where Guillermo teaches, reading is taught at least ninety minutes each day, and each lesson includes the five research-based components of reading. Because of the federal funding, reading instruction based on the word recognition view has been widely institutionalized.

The National Institute of Child Health and Human Development (NICHD) has been the funding agency for most of the major research grants to study reading. This organization strongly supports the *scientific* view of research. This is not surprising, given that the medical research supported by the NICHD uses control and experimental groups. Until recently, Reid Lyon served as the chief of the Child Development and Behavior Branch of the NICHD. From his speeches and congressional testimony, it is clear that he takes a word recognition view of reading. For example, in speaking to a U.S. House of Representatives committee considering an educational bill, Lyon stated:

> What our NICHD research has taught us is that in order for a beginning reader to learn how to connect or translate printed symbols (letters and letter patterns) into sound, the would-be reader must understand that our speech can be represented by printed forms (phonics). This understanding that written spellings systematically represent the phonemes of spoken words (termed the alphabetic principle) is absolutely necessary for the development of accurate and rapid word reading skills. (*Testimony of G. Reid Lyon on Children's Literacy* 1997)

Lyon's comments clearly reflect a word recognition view of reading. He refers to a beginning reader having to translate printed symbols into sound. He states that to do this, the would-be reader must know phonics and understand the alphabetic principle. The goal is accurate, rapid reading of words.

Concerns with the Word Recognition View

Before turning to a second view of reading, we would like to point out certain concerns we have with the research base that the NRP used to support the word recognition view of reading and with the method of teaching reading they recommend. For one thing, the panel chose to examine research in only five areas. They assumed that these five areas constituted all of reading and that studies of each of these components taken separately would shed light on the complex act of reading. Scientists often try to break complex processes down into their component parts in order to be able to study each part. However, complex processes such as reading are often more than the simple sum of their parts. Looking at these five components separately obscures the interactions among them and ignores the psychological and social factors that influence readers.

The National Reading Panel (NRP) did not include elementary reading teachers. Instead, the members were researchers, many of them from fields outside reading or education. There were also problems with the way the panel selected research to review. They excluded many studies that did not meet their guidelines for scientific research. Reading is a social activity, and the context of instruction and the relationship between a teacher and students and among the students strongly influence students' reading development, but qualitative studies describing classroom interactions were not included. An additional concern is that the summary, *Put Reading First*, which was widely distributed and has helped shape classroom practice, does not accurately reflect the contents of the entire study.

Several books have been published critiquing the work of the NRP (Coles 2000; Garan 2002; Strauss 2005). Garan, for example, has looked carefully at the studies that were included and reanalyzed them to show that, in several cases, conclusions and recommendations did not reflect the research. For example, about the same number of studies showed the benefits of phonics and the benefits of sustained silent reading, but phonics is strongly advocated while the report does not support the use of sustained silent reading.

Coles' book *Misreading Reading* (2000) examines the research reviewed by the NRP to support certain claims. For example, one claim is that "phonemic awareness (hearing, distinguishing, and manipulating the sounds in words) is the chief causal factor in early reading achievement and the 'core deficit' in reading problems" (xx). His review of the studies supporting this claim reveals that the research shows only that " 'skilled readers' do better than 'less-skilled' readers on phonemic awareness and related skills tests, but the studies show only correlations, not causation" (xx). He concludes that phonemic awareness is a marker or indicator of reading ability, but it is not what causes that ability. This is like saying that a temperature of 101 degrees Fahrenheit is a marker of a fever, but the high temperature is not the cause of the fever.

In a typical study, children take a phonemic awareness test at the end of kindergarten. During first grade, the children who were "less skilled" get phonemic awareness training. They are tested again at the end of first grade, and then compared with other "less-skilled" readers who did not get the training. These studies show that the students who received the phonemic awareness training were better at identifying words or nonsense words than those who did not receive the training. However, Coles' concern is that there is no description in the different studies of what went on during the first-grade year and no attempt to determine why some children already did very well on phonemic awareness tests at the end of kindergarten while others did not.

"Difficulty understanding that words are made up of sounds and learning the 'alphabetic principle' (associating sounds with alphabet letters) are the primary causes of poor reading" (16) is another NRP claim that Coles examines. This claim echoes Lyon's Congressional testimony. However, a close examination of the research used to support the claim leads Coles to conclude that "beginning reading instruction that focused on the alphabetic principle and phonics failed to produce significant benefits in word reading" (16).

The study most often cited to support the NRP claim is one conducted by Barbara Foorman and her associates (Foorman, Fletcher, et al. 1998) and funded by the NICHD. Coles goes to some lengths to point out problems with this study. For example, the study does support Lyon's claim if all the results are lumped together, but an analysis of student scores on the posttest by school shows that one school that received phonics training had unusually high scores, while one school that did not have explicit phonics got low scores. Taking these two schools out of the data pool actually reveals a slight advantage for schools that did not receive the training. This is just one of the criticisms that Coles has of the Foorman study. Other researchers have also critiqued this widely reported study (see, e.g., Taylor 1998).

In his book *The Linguistics, Neurology, and Politics of Phonics: Silent "E" Speaks Out*, Strauss (2005) considers the claims of the NICHD researchers from his own scientific perspective. Strauss is well qualified to do this since he holds a doctorate in linguistics and a diplomate from the American Board of Psychiatry and Neurology. Strauss begins by questioning the claim that there is an alphabetic principle. He points out that no empirical studies have shown the existence of an alphabetic principle for English. His careful analysis of English sound-to-spelling correspondences confirms what most teachers already know: most phonics rules really don't work.

Earlier studies have also shown problems with applying the alphabetic principle to English. For example, Berdiansky and colleagues (Berdiansky, Cronnell, et al. 1969) analyzed about two thousand one- and two-syllable words taken from basal readers for six- to nine-year-olds. Each word was transcribed phonemically so that each letter could be associated with a phoneme. If a letter represented a certain sound (for example, the letter *b* represented the sound /b/) at least ten times in the sample, that was considered a phonics rule (*b* = /b/). If the correspondence occurred fewer than ten times, it was labeled an exception. The researchers found that to account for the words in the sample, one would need 166 rules, and there would still be forty-five exceptions.

Strauss points out that even if there were an alphabetic principle of the sort Lyon claims there is, no one could learn it. Certainly, the study by Berdinsky, Cronnell et al. confirms that claim. Another study that shows the problems with trying to teach or learn phonics rules was carried out by Clymer (1963). His examination of different reading textbooks revealed that different rules were presented in different orders. This led him to question these rules, so, like Berdiansky and colleagues, he analyzed a large number of words. In his analysis, Clymer tested the phonics rules he found in the reading textbooks to see how often they worked. What he found was that many commonly taught rules work less than half the time. For example, the rule that states that when there are two vowels side by side they receive the long sound of the first vowel (when two vowels go walking, the first one does the talking) works about 45 percent of the time, and the silent *e* rule works about 60 percent of the time.

Strauss (2005) also examines NICHD-sponsored research on the brain. This research has attempted to show that children with reading difficulties and those labeled dyslexic have a defective brain function. In other words, the research has tried to find a medical explanation for reading problems. This approach is consistent with the NICHD emphasis on scientific research.

However, as Strauss points out, brain studies of reading are quite limited. Despite claims that phonics is supported by brain research, "there is, in fact, no research at all that has ever demonstrated that the brain reads sound by sound. This is because no brain-research subject has ever read anything closer to authentic language than a word or short phrase" (73). Strauss goes on to show the difficulties scientists face when they try to isolate one aspect of reading from general brain activity. For example, for reading to occur, there must be arousal, perception, and visual processing going on in the brain, and trying to distinguish among these different aspects of brain activity is very difficult. Current methods of studying the brain, according to Strauss, are not sufficiently advanced to make the kinds of claims that are often published in the popular press. Neurologists such as Strauss recognize the limitations of their technology.

Additional Concerns for English Language Learners

We share the concerns about the research base and the resulting recommendations for teaching reading that Garan, Coles, and Strauss have articulated in their books. We discussed the linguistic concerns in detail in *Essential Linguistics: What You Need to Know to Teach Reading, ESL, Spelling, Phonics, and Grammar* (Freeman and Freeman 2004). Here we wish to briefly highlight additional problems with a word recognition view of reading that includes teaching phonemic awareness, phonics, and fluency to English language learners.

Phonemic Awareness

Phonemic awareness is usually defined as the ability to recognize and manipulate the sounds, or phonemes, that make up words. English-speaking four-year-olds have sufficiently developed phonology to distinguish between words like *cat* and *rat*. Otherwise, they could not communicate. As they communicate, children focus on the meanings conveyed by words, not on the sounds that make up the words. In school, however, they may be asked to tell how many sounds there are in a word, or they may complete an exercise in which they add, delete, or change sounds.

This sort of exercise is difficult for any young child because it is quite abstract and unlike anything people normally do with language. Speakers concentrate on what they are saying, not on the sounds in the words they are producing. Phonemic awareness tests and exercises are particularly difficult for English language learners. Each language has a different set of phonemes. English has about forty phonemes and Spanish has about twenty-two. Some sounds that are phonemes in English, such as *th* sounds, are not phonemes in Spanish. Native Spanish speakers learning English are still developing their English phonology. They may be confused when attempting to complete a phonemic awareness test or exercise in English for two reasons: their English phonology is still developing, and they have access to two phonological systems, so they may be applying their knowledge of Spanish as they attempt to answer questions about English.

Even though English words can be broken into individual phonemes, researchers have found that students more naturally divide them into onsets and rimes (Moustafa 1997). The onset is the consonant or consonant blend that precedes a vowel, and the rime (the part that rhymes) goes from the vowel to the end of the syllable. A word like *cloud* would be divided into the sounds represented by *cl* and *oud*. Often, word walls are based on rimes. For example, students may list other words that end with the same sound as *cloud*.

Spanish, on the other hand, breaks more naturally into syllables than into onsets and rimes. Students can easily divide a word like *masa* into *ma* and *sa*, but they would have trouble separating a word like *mar* into *m* (the onset) and *ar* (the rime). Denton and colleagues (Denton, Hasbrouck, et al. 2000) report that "some researchers think that the syllable may be a more important unit of phonological awareness in Spanish than it is in English, but there are mixed results in studies that have examined this issue" (339).

Even though words in Spanish divide more naturally into syllables than into phonemes, at many schools phonemic awareness in Spanish is tested in the same way as in English. Students are asked to tell how many sounds they hear in a word, to identify the first or the last sound, or to delete or add a sound. It is difficult for most Spanish speakers to tell the first or the last sound in a short word like *el*. It appears that they perceive the syllable as a whole, not the individual sounds. As a result, tests of phonemic awareness in Spanish that follow the same format as those in English ignore important differences between the languages. Students may score low on these tests, not because they lack awareness of sounds but because Spanish phonology is structured differently than English phonology.

Another problem is that tests of phonemic awareness often include nonsense words, such as *blem* and *flark*. Researchers use nonsense words to be sure students don't already know a word. Of course, since phonemes are sounds that make a difference in meaning, nonsense words pose a problem because they are not meaningful. But English language learners may just assume that any word on a test is a real word in their new language, a word they have not learned yet. When English language learners spend class time doing exercises with nonsense words, they are losing valuable time when they could be acquiring more English. The same holds true for native English speakers in a dual language program completing phonemic awareness exercises in Spanish that involve nonsense words.

Phonics

Phonics rules are a set of correspondences between the sounds in a language and the spellings. English language learners may have trouble understanding a rule because the students' pronunciation of the word does not match conventional pronunciation. If a Spanish speaker has trouble distinguishing English sounds such as /b/ and /v/, she is sure to have trouble applying rules that involve those sounds.

One aspect of English that causes problems for Spanish speakers is the difference between long vowels that occur in words like *seat* and the short vowels in words like *sit*. Spanish has a vowel sound that is shorter than the long English *i* and longer than the short English *i*. If Spanish speakers have difficulty hearing the difference between the English words, they will also have difficulty applying phonics rules for short and long vowel sounds. This is just one example of the kinds of problems second language students face in trying to learn phonics rules in a new language. The problem is further complicated if their teacher and classmates speak a variety of English that departs from conventional English pronunciation. English learners in rural Georgia hear a very different English than what those in Downeast Maine hear.

Fluency

Proficient readers can read a familiar passage aloud quite fluently. Their reading sounds smooth, and they emphasize the important words and pause at logical points in a text. Strecker, Roser, et al. (1998) conclude from their review of the research on fluency, "The issue of whether fluency is an outgrowth of or a contributor to comprehension is unresolved. There is empirical evidence to support both positions" (300). We would argue that fluency is a result of comprehension. That is, we can read fluently only when we understand what we are reading. It is true that proficient readers can read fairly fluently, but like phonemic awareness, fluency is a marker of proficiency, not a cause.

Flurkey (1997) has shown that proficient readers vary their speed to maintain a focus on meaning. They slow down when they are confused or puzzled, and they speed up when the text is making sense. Flurkey demonstrates that reading speed changes for words, sentences, and paragraphs. Good readers don't read at the same rate throughout a text, and they change speeds with different texts. Reading instruction should be aimed at helping students learn to vary their speed to fit the text they are reading.

Nevertheless, in many schools fluency is measured by how fast a student can read without making mistakes. A fluency score is usually generated by recording the time it takes to read a passage and subtracting for errors. This view of fluency fits with the word recognition view of reading because the goal of teaching phonemic awareness, phonics, and sight-word skills is to enable students to decode words quickly.

A better measure of fluency would include much more than speed and accuracy. Zutell and Rasinski (1991), for example, developed a multidimensional fluency scale that teachers can use to more accurately gauge students' oral reading. Teachers can use the scale to rate students' reading in three areas: phrasing, smoothness, and pace. This approach to fluency is more complex than simply measuring how fast and how accurately a student reads, but it provides much more useful information.

Since fluency is usually included on standardized tests, teachers may have students practice reading aloud rapidly each day. In many classes, teachers chart student progress. The problem with this approach to fluency for all readers is that they may come to consider good reading to be the rapid, accurate pronunciation of words, and they may not attend to meaning as they read. School practices that emphasize speed and accurate pronunciation pose additional problems for English language learners. These students may have trouble pronouncing English words, and this may result in a lower score on classroom or district tests, and a lower score can lead students to consider themselves poor readers.

 ## Summary

One view holds that reading is a process of word recognition. According to this view, reading involves translating written language into oral language. To convert the marks on a page into words they know in their oral communication, readers must first realize that spoken words are made up of individual sounds or phonemes. That is, they must develop phonemic awareness. In addition, they must be able to recognize letters and associate each letter with one or more sounds. Phonics rules help readers associate patterns of letters with patterns of sounds. Knowledge of sight words fills in the gap for words that do not follow regular phonics rules.

According to proponents of the word recognition view, students can read fluently once decoding of written language becomes rapid and accurate. Proficient readers do not need to think about the rules for converting letters into sounds. They can perform this task automatically, and this frees up mental space for attention to comprehension. Readers understand a text by combining the meanings of individual words. By reading a variety of texts and by direct study, readers can also increase their vocabulary. Teachers often directly teach unfamiliar words before students tackle a new story or content text. Good readers read more, and through extensive reading, they increase their proficiency. The key in a word recognition view of reading is for beginning readers to learn to decode words quickly and accurately.

Analyzing the Lessons

It is important that teachers understand how their view of reading is reflected by their classroom practices. If we look back at Guillermo's lesson from Chapter 1 and Elena's lesson in this chapter, we can deduce that both of them hold a word recognition view of reading. They may not be able to articulate this view, but the methods and materials they use reflect the beliefs about reading associated with a word recognition view. By reviewing and analyzing the lessons that both Guillermo and Elena taught, we can better understand how their teaching reflects their beliefs about reading.

Guillermo's Lesson

Guillermo's college courses and his experience as a student teacher taught him the importance of developing reading lessons that included the five components of research-based instruction: phonemic awareness, phonics, fluency, vocabulary, and comprehension. Before he began to teach, he attended a weeklong inservice that reinforced what he had learned. In addition, the materials he uses to teach his first graders to read are organized so that each lesson focuses on the five key components of reading.

The book Guillermo uses to introduce his weather unit is a short, decodable book. The words follow patterns of phonics rules the students have studied or sight words they have been taught. As he builds background for the story, he introduces and explains key vocabulary words. The students also complete and correct a worksheet on vocabulary from the story before reading it. Preteaching of vocabulary is normal practice in classes that follow a word recognition approach to teaching reading. Later, the students complete another worksheet to reinforce key vocabulary.

Guillermo's lessons also include comprehension. Students cut out and arrange pictures showing the sequence of events in the story. On another day, they look at two pictures showing events in the story and cross out things that are different in the second picture. However, the students don't discuss the story, so teaching is limited to literal comprehension.

Although Guillermo builds background for the story, has students connect the story to their lives, and has them predict what will happen next, most of his lessons focus on phonemic awareness and phonics. Students listen to words in the story and tell Guillermo the sounds that they hear. They divide words from the story into syllables. They match the sounds in the words they hear to letters of the alphabet as Guillermo reads the story. The students also read leveled books designed to help them practice the decoding skills they are learning. Guillermo has each student read aloud so he can check the student's fluency.

Guillermo rereads the big book many times so that students can match the sounds of his oral reading with the words on the page. The exercises and worksheets are all designed to reinforce the skills the students are learning. Guillermo wants all his students to develop rapid, accurate decoding skills. His unit on weather focuses on the skills rather than on weather concepts. Guillermo believes that his students must first learn to read. Then they can read to learn. In addition, all of Guillermo's instruction is in English. It is probable that much of what the students do as they practice decoding skills has little meaning for his beginning English language learners. The way Guillermo teaches reading is consistent with a word recognition view.

Elena's Lesson

Elena's preparation for teaching reading was not as extensive as Guillermo's. She had only two college classes to prepare her to teach reading. Both courses were taken while she was teaching on an emergency credential. Most of her teaching is based on what she sees others doing, what she perceives to be required, and the materials she has available. Elena is very aware of what her principal wants teachers to do.

Elena's teaching reflects a word recognition approach. Letters and words are highlighted around her classroom. In addition to the alphabet and word walls, Elena has posters with words that contain blends in English, such as the *sn* in *snowy*.

The exercises students complete at their centers also keep the focus on words. For example, students cut and paste a short sentence like "It's hot" or *"Hace frío"* under a picture. Other students fill out worksheets on punctuation. The students who sit with Elena answer questions about the letters at the beginning and the end of words and study the vowels in Spanish. When she rereads and discusses a story, she concentrates on specific words, like *cometa*. She does include comprehension, but as in Guillermo's class, the exercises are limited to literal comprehension. For example, after reading about the wind, students draw pictures of three things the wind does. When her English language learners study in English,

Elena involves them in phonemic awareness activities such as changing the first and last sounds in words.

Although the books Elena uses all connect to her weather theme, most of the activities are designed to teach students the skills needed to decode words. Little time is spent in investigating weather concepts. Elena follows the standards, takes the lead from fellow teachers, and works hard to keep all her students on task during their reading lessons. She does use her students' first language, which makes her instruction more comprehensible than if she were teaching only in English. An examination of Elena's methods shows that she is teaching reading as a process of recognizing words.

Elena's and Guillermo's students are kept busy completing the carefully controlled lessons. Although the reading texts have weather as a topic, the lessons are not focused so much on the concepts as on the development of the skills needed to decode the texts. The texts, for the most part, are designed to facilitate the teaching of a set of skills. The class activities and worksheets are meant to equip the students to decode words. Even though there are differences in the way that Guillermo and Elena teach, it is clear that their teaching reflects a word recognition view of reading.

Some teachers take a second view of reading. As Lilia, a bilingual teacher and one of Yvonne's students, explains: *"Lo importante es precisamente el encontrar el significado al leer. ¿De qué sirve leer sin entender lo que se está leyendo, entonces, en mera codificacion?"* (The most important thing is to make meaning while reading. What good does it do, then, if there is no comprehension while reading and only decoding?) In the next chapter we explain this second view of reading, the sociopsycholinguistic view.

 ## Applications

1. Write your own definition of the word recognition view of reading. Then explain what is meant when we say that this view is logical but not psychological.

2. Phonemic awareness is a hot topic in the teaching of reading. What is it? Interview two teachers who teach beginning reading. Ask them to define phonemic awareness and ask them if they think it is important to teach phonemic awareness and why. Be prepared to discuss their answers and your analysis of their answers in class.

3. What did the National Reading Panel do? Who was on the panel? How have the conclusions of this panel affected the teaching of reading at your school?

If you are not teaching in an elementary school, interview an elementary school teacher and ask what he or she knows about the NRP and if he or she has read *Put Reading First* (Armbruster and Osborn 2001). Be prepared to discuss.

4. Describe Berdiansky's analysis (1969). Why is this study important for teachers of reading?

5. Fluency is another hot topic in reading. What do teachers in your area understand about fluency? Interview three elementary school teachers about how they define fluency and how they teach and test it. Ask them why fluency is important. Be prepared to share your results.

A Sociopsycholinguistic
View of Reading

Many teachers, like Guillermo and Elena, teach reading in a way consistent with a word recognition view. However, some teachers adopt methods and materials consistent with a second view of reading, a sociopsycholinguistic view. We begin this chapter with an extended scenario from one such teacher, Cristina. The way she teaches reading clearly reflects the sociopsycholinguistic view she holds. Next we explain this second view of reading in detail. Following the explanation we analyze Cristina's teaching to show how it reflects a sociopsycholinguistic view. We introduce a checklist for effective reading that's consistent with the sociopsycholinguistic view and then describe two additional lessons from teachers who follow the checklist.

 ## Cristina's Weather Unit

In a dual language school in South Texas, on the other side of the town from where Elena teaches, Cristina's first-grade students are also reading and writing and learning about weather, one of the content standards specified in the TEKS for science. In addition, Cristina includes skills to meet the standards for language arts and reading listed in the TEKS. But if we could peer into her classroom, we would note some significant differences between her classroom and Elena's. On one bulletin board, labeled "What clothes do we wear?" "¿Qué ropa ponemos?," there are pictures of different kinds of weather, and next to the pictures, students have drawn and cut out the kinds of clothes people wear in each kind of weather. So, for example, next to the beach in the summer, there are bathing suits, sunglasses, and shorts, and next to the picture of fall with the wind blowing, there is a jacket, a sweater, and a hat.

In another corner of the room, Cristina has displayed a song chart with weather songs in English, including the traditional "Rain, Rain, Go Away," and poetry and songs in Spanish about the weather, including the song "Qué llueva" ("Let It Rain") (Longo 2004, 8) and weather poetry from *Días y días de poesía* (Days and Days of Poetry) (Ada 1991). Next to the poetry and song charts, Cristina has posted the most recent examples of the Daily News in English and *Noticias diarias* in Spanish. She uses the poetry, song, and daily news charts during the morning opening, which she does in English one day and in Spanish the next. These activities allow Cristina to work with her students on different skills, including spelling, capitalization, and sound-letter correspondence in a meaningful context. Cristina's students develop fluency as they read the charts, recite the poetry, and sing the songs.

Student science journals are displayed on a shelf. In the journals students have recorded the weather in English on their individual weather charts following the pattern of the limited-text book *Making a Weather Chart* (Dawson 1997). They draw and label weather pictures, writing words like *rainy, cloudy,* and *windy* under their drawings. In another area of the room, there is a thermometer and a large, student-made graph on which the temperature has been recorded by students daily. A map of the United States next to the graph has over it "¿Qué tiempo hace?" and "What's the weather?" On the map students have placed pictures of rain, clouds, and the sun in different parts of the country. One day a week the class watches the weather on TV and records the weather in two or three parts of the country just like the weather maps on TV show.

There are two word lists in the room: a weather alphabet chart and a cognate list. The chart contains words students have chosen related to the weather theme that they have been studying. Students place a word under the letter of the alphabet that matches the first letter in their word. The students know to write words in Spanish in red and words in English in blue. The second word list is made up of weather words that are cognates. On the list are words like *temperatura* and *temperature, termómetro* and *thermometer, clima* and *climate*, and *huracán* and *hurricane*.

In one corner of the room, there are student-made pinwheels and weather vanes and above these are drawings students have made to depict the traditional legend their teacher read in Spanish one day and in English the next, *El viento y el sol* (Pacheco 2000) and *Wind and Sun* (Parker 1997). In this fable Wind and Sun both claim to be the most powerful force. The bookshelves are stocked with books at different levels of difficulty that children can choose for SSR (sustained silent reading). On one side of the room, Cristina has grouped many books on weather. These books in Spanish and in English also range from very limited-text books to longer stories and content books Cristina has read to the students during read-aloud time.

A look at reading instruction over a couple of days provides a picture of Cristina's literacy program. Cristina bases her activities on her understanding of the reading process that she gained from the reading and language arts courses she took during her teacher-preparation courses and in her MA in Bilingual Education program. The morning opening is conducted while students are sitting on the rug in a corner of the room. Today is *Día de español* (Spanish Day). After the calendar activities, Cristina scribes as students dictate. Students and teacher share the pen in composing the *Noticias diarias* as one of the students records the daily temperature on the temperature chart. Then Cristina takes out three books, *El viento* (*The Wind*) (Flores 1986, 1997), *El señor Viento Norte* (Mr. North Wind) (Mañé 1997), and *¿Por qué soplan los vientos salvajes* (*Why the Wild Winds Blow*) (Ambert 1997a, 1997b). Showing the big book *El viento*, which Elena had also used, Cristina begins her lesson.

CRISTINA: El otro día leimos este libro. ¿Recuerdan? ¿Quién me puede leer el título de este libro?
VARIOS: "El viento."
CRISTINA: Sí, *El viento*. Y ¿de qué se trata este libro?
JUANITA: Habla del viento y nos dice que pasa cuando el viento sopla.

FELIPE: No podemos ver el viento.
CRISTINA: Sí, tienen razón los dos. [Hojeando las páginas] Aquí nos enseña como el viento mueve las banderas, y aquí como hace mover el rehilete, y aquí un pequeño barco de vela.

CRISTINA: The other day we read this book. Do you remember? Who can read me the title of this book?
SEVERAL: "The Wind."
CRISTINA: Yes, *The Wind*. And what is this book about?
JUANITA: It talks about the wind and tells us what happens when the wind blows.
FELIPE: We can't see the wind.
CRISTINA: Yes, you are both right. [Turning the pages] Here it shows how the wind moves the flags, and here how it moves a pinwheel, and here a little sailboat.

Hoy vamos a leer dos cuentos sobre el viento. Uno nos habla del señor Viento Norte que trae el viento frío del invierno, y el otro es un cuento de Puerto Rico que nos dice por qué hay huracanes. [Les enseña la portada del libro *El señor Viento Norte*] ¿Qué ven ustedes en la portada de este libro?

BERTA: Un señor entre los árboles y un niño. El señor debe de ser el señor Viento Norte.

CRISTINA: Sí tienes razón, Berta. Les voy a enseñar todas las páginas y las ilustraciones sin leer todavía. ¿Qué está pasando en el cuento?

MANUEL: Hay un conejo, un perro, y un ratoncito. Tienen puestos abrigos y parece que tienen frío. El niño habla con el conejo.

ESTÉBAN: El niño va caminando y se duerme en una casa.

[Los niños siguen comentando sobre todas las páginas.]

CRISTINA: Vamos a ver lo que pasa en este cuento. A ver si ustedes entienden más del cuento. [Lee todo el cuento.] Ahora, ¿qué recuerdan del cuento?

DIANA: Hacía mucho frío. El niño fue a hablar al señor Viento Norte porque querían que no soplara más.

PEPE: Tenía un regalo para el señor Viento Norte.

BERTA: Sí, fue un gorro blanco y azul.

FELICIANA: Cuando dormía, la niña tomó el regalo y le dio al señor Viento Norte.

FELIPE: Pero al señor Viento Norte no le gustó el regalo y le sopló bien lejos.

FELICIANA: El señor Viento Norte quería la bola blanca.

CRISTINA: ¿Qué era la bola blanca que mencionó Feliciana? El libro dice que era un vilano. ¿Diana?

Today we are going to read two stories about the wind. One tells us about Mr. North Wind who brings the cold, winter wind, and the other is a story from Puerto Rico that tells us why there are hurricanes. [She shows them the cover of *El señor Viento Norte (Mr. North Wind)*] What do you see on the cover of this book?

BERTA: A man in some trees and a boy. The man must be Mr. North Wind.

CRISTINA: Yes, you are right, Berta. I'm going to show you all the pages and the illustrations without reading yet. What is happening in the story?

MANUEL: There is a rabbit, a dog, and a mouse. They are wearing overcoats and it seems like they are cold. The boy is talking with the rabbit.

ESTÉBAN: The boy is walking and goes to sleep in a house.

[The children continue commenting on the pages.]

CRISTINA: Let's see what happens in this story. Let's see if you understand more of the story. [She reads the whole story.] Now, what do you remember about the story?

DIANA: It's very cold. The boy went to talk to Mr. North Wind because they didn't want him to blow anymore.

PEPE: He had a gift for Mr. North Wind.

BERTA: Yes, it was a white-and-blue cap.

FELICIANA: While he was sleeping, the girl took the gift and gave it to Mr. North Wind.

FELIPE: But Mr. North Wind didn't like the gift and blew her far away.

FELICIANA: Mr. North Wind wanted the white ball.

CRISTINA: And what was the white ball that Feliciana told us about? The book says it was a *vilano* [thistle]. Diana?

A Sociopsycholinguistic View of Reading   **49**

DIANA: No sé, pero tal vez es como estas bolas que vienen de la planta que al soplarlos, los pedacitos blancos se van volando.

CRISTINA: Sí, tienes razón. ¿Qué pasó al final?

MANUEL: El señor Viento Norte sopló suave para jugar con la bola blanca.

PEPE: Sí, y ya no hacía tanto frío.

CRISTINA: Ustedes han entendido muy bien. Tengo una pregunta. ¿Creen ustedes que este cuento es verdad? ¿Es que esto pasó en realidad?

TODOS: No.

CRISTINA: ¿No? ¿Por qué creen esto?

BERTA: El viento no habla. No es un hombre.

CRISTINA: Sí tienes razón. El cuento nos trató de explicar por qué el viento norte dejó que entrara la primavera. Dejó de soplar fuerte.

Ahora, les voy a leer otro cuento que nos explica por qué pasa algo en el clima. Es un cuento de Puerto Rico. ¿Dónde está Puerto Rico?

FELIPE: Cerca de Florida. Es una isla. La esposa de mi tío vivía en Puerto Rico antes de venir aquí.

CRISTINA: Sí, Felipe. ¿Nos puede enseñar en el mapa?

DIANA: I don't know, but maybe it is like those balls that come from plants that when you blow them the little white pieces fly away.

CRISTINA: Yes, you're right. What happened at the end?

MANUEL: Mr. North Wind blew softly so he could play with the white ball.

PEPE: Yes, and it wasn't as cold anymore.

CRISTINA: You have understood very well. I have a question. Do you think that this story is true? Is what happened real?

ALL: No.

CRISTINA: No? Why do you think that?

BERTA: The wind doesn't talk. It is not a man.

CRISTINA: Yes, you're right. The story tried to explain why the north wind let spring come. It stopped blowing strongly.

Now, I'm going to read you another story that explains why something happens with the weather. It's a story from Puerto Rico. Where is Puerto Rico?

FELIPE: Near Florida. It's an island. My uncle's wife lived in Puerto Rico before coming here.

CRISTINA: Yes, Felipe. Can you show us on the map?

Cristina reads the other story, *Por qué soplan los vientos salvajes* (*Why the Wild Winds Blow*) (Ambert 1997a), a legend that explains hurricanes. The students talk about what they remember and compare the two stories. Cristina writes down what they say about how the stories are alike and how they are different on a Venn diagram. The students take special interest in the second story because hurricanes often occur where they live. In fact, during the summer a hurricane passed through their valley. Though the hurricane veered to the south just before hitting the Texas coast, there was a great deal of concern about it among residents living in the area. Cristina promises that they will learn more about hurricanes.

The next day, Cristina does her opening in English. Students record the weather in their English science journals and then join Cristina on the rug for some ESL reading time. The teacher takes out the big book *What's the Weather Outside?* (Herzog 2003) and begins a discussion.

CRISTINA: What words do you recognize in the title?

FELICIANA: *Weather*! That's our theme!

CRISTINA: Excellent. Let's read the title together: *"What's the Weather Outside?"*

ENRIQUE: Teacher, the title is a question. It ends in a question mark.

CRISTINA: Very good, Enrique. You made a good observation. Looking at the title and the pictures on the cover, can you predict some words we will probably find as we read this book?

[Cristina writes the words the children predict on a large piece of paper. These include *cold, hot, wind, rain,* and *sun.*]

CRISTINA: Let's look at the first page. There are words and numbers after each word. Some are words you predicted, *hot, rain,* and *cold.* Does anyone know what the numbers after the words are for?

PEPE: I know, Teacher, that's the page that tells about the word.

CRISTINA: Yes, the numbers tell us where to find information about each of the words. This page is called a table of contents. It tells us where to find information. Let's go to each page and read the pages together.

[When the students get to the section on wind, they remember the stories they read the day before during Spanish reading time.]

ENRIQUE: Look, Teacher, that word is *wind, viento.* There is also a picture of a hurricane. We read about that yesterday. Last summer we had a hurricane come near here. I was scared.

CRISTINA: Yes, Enrique. I bet many of you heard about the hurricane.

ESTEBAN: My dad put boards on the windows so they won't break!

IRMA: Our family went to my *tía* [aunt] in San Antonio. We were afraid our trailer would blow over.

CRISTINA: Yes, many of you have stories. We're going to talk more about hurricanes today. One of the stories I read in Spanish yesterday I have in English today, *Why the Wild Winds Blow* [Ambert 1997b]. We talked about whether that story was true. You told me it was not. What about the wind and the hurricane in this big book, *What's the Weather Outside?* Is that true?

ALL: Yes.

CRISTINA: Good. Now, today I have another book that is about hurricanes, *Hurricane on Its Way* [Aparicio 1997b]. This book tells us how meteorologists—scientists who study the weather—can tell us when a hurricane is coming. Those people helped us know about the hurricane last summer. Let's look at the pictures, and I'll read the book to you.

[After Cristina reads the book to the students, she shows them that she has the book in Spanish too: *¡Huracán a la vista!* (Aparicio 1997a). She also shows the children several other books about the weather and tells them they can look at the books during SSR time and read them together in pairs. (See the weather bibliography in Figure 3–1.)]

CRISTINA: OK, class, we have read about the weather in Spanish and today in English, and we have put words up around the room and on our chart. In pairs I would like you to choose a book about the weather in English and read it together. Then, when you have finished, we will come back together and write about the weather. You will dictate to me, and I will write what you tell me.

[Later, the students return to the rug and Cristina has paper ready for the language experience activity about the weather.]

CRISTINA: OK. What should we write about the weather?

PEPE: "Weather can be scary."

CRISTINA: That's a good start. What is the first letter I am going to write?

ALL: *W*.

CRISTINA: Good. How do I write the letter?

BERTA: You write a capital *W* because it starts the sentence.

CRISTINA: OK. If I cannot spell the word, what can I do?

ENRIQUE: You can look for the word in a book or in the room.

CRISTINA: And sometimes we can sound out some of the letters. Do you see the word *weather* around the room? How do I spell *weather*?

SEVERAL: *W-e-a-t-h-e-r*.

CRISTINA: And what is the first sound you hear in *can*?

SEVERAL: *K*, Teacher, it sounds like *k*.

CRISTINA: You're right. Do you remember that we talked about the *k* sound before? It can be spelled with two letters. One is the letter *k* and the other is . . .

REBECCA: *C*! I know because my name has a *k* sound and I spell it with a *c*.

CRISTINA: Excellent! Rebecca, you helped us all.

After the students work with the teacher to write about the weather, they all read together what they wrote. Of course, they wrote a sentence about the hurricane from the summer before! Then they copy their paragraph in their notebook and take it home to read to their parents. Figure 3–1 lists the books Cristina used during her weather unit along with additional books on the weather.

Almada, Patricia. 1997. *Clouds*. Crystal Lake, IL: Rigby.

———. 1997. *Las nubes*. Crystal Lake, IL: Rigby.

Alonso, Fernando. 1989. *La vista de la primavera*. Northvale, NJ: Santillana.

Ambert, Alba. 1997a. *Por qué soplan los vientos salvajes*. Crystal Lake, IL: Rigby.

———. 1997b. *Why the Wild Winds Blow*. Crystal Lake, IL: Rigby.

Aparicio, Eduardo. 1997a. *¡Huracán a la vista!* Crystal Lake, IL: Rigby.

———. 1997b. *Hurricane on Its Way!* Crystal Lake, IL: Rigby.

Canizares, Susan. 1998. *Sun*. New York: Scholastic.

Chanko, Pamela, and Daniel Moreton. 1998. *Weather*. New York: Scholastic.

FIGURE 3–1. Weather Bibliography

Clark, Patricia N. 2000. *Goodbye, Goose*. Katonah, NY: Richard C. Owen.

Clevidence, Karen. 2004. *A Disaster Is Coming*. Barrington, IL: Rigby.

Costain, Meridith. 1966. *Clouds*. New York: Scholastic.

Crimi, Carolyn. 1995. *Outside, Inside*. New York: Scholastic.

Crum, Mary B. 2004. *The Power of the Wind*. Barrington, IL: Rigby.

Cusick, Pat. 1997. *How's the Weather?* Crystal Lake, IL: Rigby.

Dawson, Hamish. 1997. *Making a Weather Chart*. Crystal Lake, IL: Rigby.

Díaz, Katrina. 1997a. *Storm Trackers*. Crystal Lake, IL: Rigby.

———. 1997b. *Tras las tormentas*. Crystal Lake, IL: Rigby.

Ellis, Veronica F. 1997. *La isla de la nube lluviosa*. Boston: Houghton Mifflin.

Flores, Guillermo Solano. 1985. *La lluvia*. México, DF: Editorial Trillas.

———. 1986. *El viento*. México, DF: Editorial Trillas.

———. 1997. *El viento*. Big book. Boston: Houghton Mifflin.

Green, Josie. 2005. *Droughts*. Washington, DC: National Geographic Society.

Herzog, Brad. 2003. *What's the Weather Outside?* Barrington, IL: Rigby.

Hopping, Lorraine. 2000. *Today's Weather Is . . . : A Book of Experiments*. New York: Mondo.

Hughes, Monica. 1998. *Seasons*. Crystal Lake, IL: Rigby.

Jordan, Denise. 2004. *What Are the Seasons Like?* Barrington, IL: Rigby.

Kelly, Harold. 2002. *El sol*. New York: Rosen.

Lauber, Patricia. 1996. *Hurricanes*. New York: Scholastic.

Mañé, Carmen de Posadas. 1997. *El señor Viento Norte*. Boston: Houghton Mifflin.

Martel, Cruz. 1997. *Días de yagua*. Boston: Houghton Mifflin.

Nguyen, Rosemary, and Hieu Nguyen. 2004. *In the Rain*. Barrington, IL: Rigby.

Pacheco, Lourdes. 2000. *El viento y el sol*. Barrington, IL: Rigby.

Parker, John. 1997. *Wind and Sun*. Crystal Lake, IL: Rigby.

———. 1998. *I Feel Cold*. Crystal Lake, IL: Rigby.

Quinn, Pat, and Bill Gaynor. 1999. *El poder del viento*. Huntington Beach, CA: Learning Media.

Rius, María. 1985. *El aire*. Barcelona, Spain: Parramón Ediciones.

Sharp, Kathie. 1998. *Rain, Snow, and Hail*. Crystal Lake, IL: Rigby.

———. 2006. *Weather Words*. Austin, TX: Harcourt Achieve.

Shulman, Lisa. 2004. *The Wonderful Water Cycle*. Barrrington, IL: Rigby.

Stolz, Mary. 1997. *Una tormenta nocturna*. Boston: Houghton Mifflin.

Tsang, Nina. 2004. *The Weather*. Barrington, IL: Rigby.

Wachter, Joanne. 2004. *Around the Sun*. Barrington, IL: Rigby.

Waite, Judy. 2004. *Look Out the Window*. Barrington, IL: Rigby.

West, Loretta. 2006. *Maya's Storm*. Austin, TX: Harcourt Achieve.

Woolley, Marilyn. 2003. *Cuando llueve*. Washington, DC: National Geographic Society.

FIGURE 3–1. Weather Bibliography (*continued*)

The Sociopsycholinguistic View of Reading

Cristina's lessons reflect a sociopsycholinguistic view of reading. This view differs from a word recognition view in several ways, but the most important difference is that in this view, reading is seen as just one example of a general human ability to use language to make and get meaning. Reading is a process of constructing meaning, not just a set of skills for recognizing words. This process involves psychological, linguistic, and social factors. As Goodman (1993) puts it:

> Reading is a psycholinguistic process because readers rely on the same general psychological and linguistic processes to make sense of text that they use to make sense of speech. Reading is a social process because meaning can only be constructed within a particular social context. (89)

Much of the research that supports a word recognition view is quantitative. Researchers test one aspect of reading, such as phonemic awareness, by measuring the difference a specific kind of training makes on an experimental group that is compared with a control group. Usually, the treatment is evaluated by looking at the test results of a large number of readers. This is the kind of scientifically based research favored by the NICHD.

In contrast, the research that supports a sociopsycholinguistic view has been carried on in schools and other settings where teacher-researchers can sit down and listen as individual students read. In an early experiment, Goodman (1965) asked children at different grade levels to read a list of words and then read a story containing those words. He found that even first graders could read about two-thirds of the words within the story that they had missed on the list. Goodman's study has been replicated in both English and in Spanish. The results highlight the fact that reading does not concern itself primarily with recognizing words. Goodman says, "Eventually I believe we must abandon our concentration on words in teaching reading and develop a theory of reading and a methodology that puts the focus where it belongs: on language" (642).

If reading is not a precise process of identifying words, then what is it? Goodman (1967) calls it a "psycholinguistic guessing game." Rather than being exact, reading involves tentative information processing. Guessing is not completely random. We call something guessing only if we have some information but not all the information we need. Readers try to make sense of texts by using psychological strategies and linguistic cues as they read.

Psychological Strategies

Once readers recognize that something is for reading, they initiate the process. Even young children living in a literate environment soon realize that they can read a book but not the pattern in the wallpaper. Eventually, they discover that the part of the book they read is the black marks, not the pictures. This realization is a first step in reading.

Readers begin by sampling the text. Sampling is not the same as scanning. Eye movement research has shown that as people read, their eyes move in stops and starts (Paulson and Freeman 2003). The stops are called *fixations* and the starts are *saccades*. The only time that information is sent to the brain is when the eye stops for a few milliseconds. Even though the eye is really only taking snapshots of a page, the brain perceives the information as a smooth flow, not as a separate series of images. The process is similar to what happens as we view a movie. Although we are seeing a series of still frames, we perceive the movie as a continuous motion.

What eye movement studies have shown over the last one hundred years is that readers fixate only about two-thirds of the words in a text. This is true for both proficient and nonproficient readers. This is why we say that we sample text. The brain directs the eyes to fixate the key words. Research shows that the content words (nouns, verbs, adjectives, and adverbs) are fixated much more often than the function words (conjunctions, pronouns, helping verbs).

How can readers comprehend texts if they see only about two-thirds of the words? The answer is that they use the subconscious psychological strategy of predicting. We keep making predictions as we read. We predict at both the micro level and the macro level. That is, we are constantly predicting what letters we will see next in a word, what word will follow the one we are reading, where the sentence is headed, and what the whole text means.

Readers base their predictions on linguistic cues, on their background knowledge, and on the inferences they make. Writers never put every detail down on paper. They expect readers to be able to fill in what they have left out by using their knowledge of the world. That is, they expect readers to make inferences.

For example, suppose you are reading a novel, and the text reads, "The stranger walked into the seedy bar." Immediately, you begin to visualize this place. There is a bar, probably with a bartender and bottles on a shelf. The air might be thick with smoke. Perhaps a jukebox is blaring out an old favorite. Some of the patrons might be playing pool. Most of the people in the bar would be casually dressed, probably workers from a factory unwinding after a long day.

The writer might go on to provide some of these details, but your knowledge of seedy bars could allow you to picture the place and make some predictions. Inferences such as these depend on life experiences. Many texts for elementary students are written assuming the students bring background knowledge of certain kinds of places and activities to their reading. However, many English language learners lack the experiences that would build that background. These students need extra help in building background before reading.

The next psychological strategy a reader uses is confirmation or disconfirmation and correction of their predictions. As they continue to sample the text with a focus on meaning, readers check to see if their predictions were correct. If they were correct, they keep reading. If not, they might read on, or they might reread to see if they missed something. This is what proficient readers do. Struggling readers, especially if they think reading is primarily a process of recognizing words, may plow on, hoping to reach the end. The last psychological strategy readers use is what Goodman calls integration. This means that readers keep adding the new meaning to what they already understood. If the new information fits, they go on. If not, they go back to reread and start to build comprehension again. This is what proficient readers do. Struggling readers who are not focused on constructing meaning often continue even though the new information doesn't seem to fit the story or content text to that point.

Linguistic Cueing Systems

As readers sample text, make predictions and inferences, confirm or disconfirm their predictions, and integrate new information, they use cues from three linguistic systems: graphophonic, syntactic, and semantic. To test your knowledge of these cueing systems, try reading the following "story" out loud.

> Arn tib a phev was larzing two sleks. Ambily, ek plobbed one. "Blars!" ek gliffed. "O hwez to glif sleks. Ern are avily quinzy. O will larg aloftil slek. O grun to larg sleks."

Could you read the story? At the least, you were probably able to say the words (even though you didn't recognize some of them). To pronounce the words, you used your knowledge of graphophonics. This includes your knowledge of orthography (the writing system), phonology (the sound system), and phonics (the relationships between patterns of letters and patterns of sounds). For example, you might have stumbled on *phev* because you knew something was wrong. English spelling conventions don't permit words ending in *v*. Another word that could have caused trouble was *hwez*. The *hw* spelling pattern looks unfamiliar, even though we actually pronounce an *h* before the *w* in words like *when* or *where*.

Your knowledge of phonology allowed you to pronounce the *ed* of *plobbed* as a *d* sound and the *ed* of *gliffed* as a *t* sound. The *s* of *sleks* is pronounced as *s*, but the *s* of *Blars* has a *z* sound. This knowledge is subconscious. It's something you have developed by reading and talking. It isn't a set of rules you needed to learn before speaking or reading. It's an effect, not a cause. If you ask other people to read this passage, you will find that there will be much agreement on the pronunciation of these invented words. That's because all of you are operating on the same social conventions of orthography, phonology, and phonics.

In order to read this story out loud, you didn't have to rely solely on graphophonic cues. This text also offers syntactic cues. For example, you probably predicted that a noun would follow *a* in the first line and that a verb would follow *was*. You might even have decided that *ek* was a pronoun referring to *phev*. Whether you really thought about nouns, verbs, and pronouns is not so important as the pattern of nouns and verbs you predicted based on your intuitive knowledge of English syntax. You probably looked for a pattern that starts with a noun as the subject, then has a verb as the predicate, and ends with another noun that serves as direct object. If the story were in Spanish, you'd expect the same basic pattern although you wouldn't be surprised if a sentence started with a verb since Spanish can mark pronoun subjects on the verb and can delete the pronoun. Your knowledge of syntactic patterns is what helped you predict as you read the story. While some of the words are nonsense words, others, like *a* and *was*, are real words. These are the function words in the language that signal the syntactic patterns. So even though the story might not make sense, it does sound like English and follows a typical English syntactic pattern.

The third cueing system is semantics. Semantics refers to the meaning of words. But semantic knowledge also includes your knowledge of what words typically go together. In a sports story, if you see *baseball*, you can predict other words like *player*, *base*, and *run*. This knowledge helps you make predictions and helps you construct meaning as you read.

Since the content words in the story above—the nouns, verbs, adjectives, and adverbs—are all nonsense words, you couldn't very well access your semantic knowledge as you read. You could use only two of the three cueing systems. Meaning is at the heart of reading, and without the semantic system, all you could really do here is what Goodman (1996) calls recoding. When we decode we get at the meaning, but when we recode, we just change one code into another. In this case, you changed the written code into an oral code. But you did that without getting the meaning.

The students in many classes like Guillermo's and Elena's come to understand reading as recoding. They say the words, but they miss the meaning. This may seem hard to believe, but try the following exercise. Here are some comprehension questions based on the story above. See if you can answer them.

1. What was the phev larzing arn tib?

2. What did the phev do?

3. Are sleks avily quinzy?

4. What will the phev do?

5. What does the phev grun?

Many people can actually give complete-sentence answers to these questions. For example, by looking back at the story, they can say, "The phev was larzing a slek arn tib." You can answer even when the words don't make any sense. For someone who knew the words (who spoke this strange language), your answers would sound good. You might score 100 percent on the comprehension test. However, as you are aware, you didn't really understand anything here. The danger is that kids can sometimes fool us (and themselves) by following this same procedure. They can appear to show comprehension when no real comprehending ever took place. If reading is a process of constructing meaning, then kids who simply recode texts aren't really reading.

Miscue Analysis

Readers use various linguistic cues to make and confirm their predictions. Sometimes readers miss a cue or are misled by a cue, and then they produce responses that Goodman (1967) calls miscues instead of errors "in order to avoid value implications" (34). Insights into how readers use psychological strategies like predicting and linguistic cueing systems have been derived from studies of readers' miscues. These studies use a method called miscue analysis.

Miscue analysis was first developed by Kenneth Goodman in the early 1960s. Goodman noted that most measures of reading are indirect. Researchers often compare what students knew before reading with what they know after reading. For example, a test on a particular passage might first assess students' background knowledge on the topic and their knowledge of the key vocabulary. After reading, students could be tested on what they understand and remember. This is a measure of their comprehension. However, such comprehension tests are always indirect.

Goodman wanted to develop a more direct measure of reading that would reveal how children are comprehending as they read rather than just measure what they have comprehended after reading. He reasoned that if we want to develop lessons to help students become more proficient readers, then we must find a way to assess the actual processes they use as they read. Miscue analysis is the tool he developed.

In miscue analysis, readers are given a complete story or article to read, and this reading is recorded and analyzed. Afterward, the reader retells the story or article. Miscue analysis data constitutes the research base for a sociopsycholinguistic approach to reading. Miscues, or unexpected responses to text, help show us how the reader is attempting to make sense. It is only when readers leave a word out, insert a word, or substitute one word for another that we can start to understand the strategies and cues they are using during reading. As Goodman (1967) puts it, "expected responses mask the process of their attainment, but unexpected responses have been achieved through the same process, albeit less successfully applied. The ways that they deviate from the expected reveal this process" (127).

In other words, when readers produce the words we expect as we look at the story, we really can't say how they did it. But when readers produce unexpected responses, we get important insights into what they are doing as they read. For example, one young reader substituted "wants" and "set" for *went* and *suit* in the following sentence:

wants   set

Jack Jones always went around in overalls or a sun suit.

What insights do these miscues give us? For one thing, the reader used visual or auditory cues. Both *wants* and *set* look and sound like *went* and *suit*. In addition, the reader used syntactic information: He substituted a verb for a verb and a noun for a noun. He even added an *s* to *want* to make it agree with the subject. In addition, he used semantic information. He knew that *sun* and *set* go together in many contexts. Despite these strengths, this reader doesn't show a focus on meaning. He did not correct these miscues, and the result is a sentence that makes no sense. Of course, we can't evaluate this reading on just one sentence with two miscues. In miscue analysis, students read a complete text, and researchers look for general patterns in the miscue data.

Readers in every language make miscues. A number of researchers have carried out miscue investigations in Spanish (Barrera 1981; Hudelson 1981). In their research, they found Spanish readers making miscues such as the following:

tus

Gracias, Pedro, pero no quiero sus zapatos

your [informal]

Thanks, Pedro, but I don't want your [formal] shoes

Ⓒ la

Mientras comía y fregaba los . . .

Ⓒ the

While he was eating and washing the . . .

In the first sentence, the reader again used visual and/or sound cues. *Tus* looks and sounds like *sus*. The reader also used syntactic information, substituting one possessive for another. In fact, the reader showed good knowledge of the semantic system by substituting the familiar form of *your*, *tus*, for the formal form, *sus*. This substitution is logical in the sentence, and the reader doesn't correct it. It makes sense to use the familiar form of *your* when telling someone you know that you don't want to borrow his shoes.

The substitution of *la* (the) for *y* (and) in the second sentence shows that the reader was focusing on meaning more than on the visual or sound information. He used syntactic information to predict that a noun would follow *comía* (was eating), naming what was being eaten. When a verb instead of a noun occurred, the reader went back and corrected. This shows that the reader was focusing on meaning.

Crowell (1995), a bilingual teacher-researcher, explains how miscue analysis allowed her to discover what her students "knew about reading and texts and which reading strategies they needed to learn to use more effectively" (32). Two examples from one of her Spanish-speaking students reading *Los animales de Don Vicencio* (*The Animal Concert*) (Cowley 1987, 1983) are instructive:

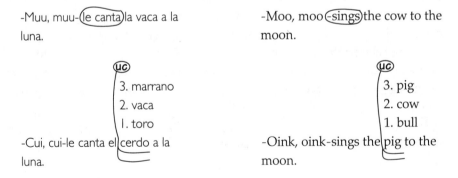

-Muu, muu- le canta la vaca a la luna.

-Moo, moo sings the cow to the moon.

UC
3. marrano
2. vaca
1. toro

-Cui, cui-le canta el cerdo a la luna.

UC
3. pig
2. cow
1. bull

-Oink, oink-sings the pig to the moon.

Crowell explains that in the first example the reader relied heavily on the picture cues in the book and the first words on the page, the sounds of the cow, to predict that the text that followed the *muu, muu* would be *la vaca*. Crowell points out that the reader "did not self-correct on this page, but did read *canta* correctly on the next page, and thereafter" (1995, 33). In the second example the reader does not self-correct but does finally substitute another word in Spanish for *pig*—*marrano* for *cerdo*—relying on picture cues and her own background knowledge. Because this reader relied too heavily on picture cues, Crowell engaged her in strategy lessons that focused on integrating all the cueing systems.

Universal Process

Goodman's theory of reading is based on a careful analysis of people reading complete texts. Over the last forty years, hundreds of miscue studies have been carried out in a variety of languages. In each case, a researcher sits and listens to an individual reader, records the results, and analyzes the reader's use of strategies and cueing systems. Based on this analysis, the researcher can suggest specific strategy lessons to help the reader become more proficient. Miscue analysis is not designed to test students. Instead, it is used to assess their reading in order to provide the best possible instruction.

Studies of both children and adults reading in a variety of languages—including nonalphabetic languages, like Japanese and Chinese, as well as languages that don't use a Roman script, like Arabic and Hebrew—have revealed that the reading process is universal. This is not surprising since all humans process language, both oral and written, in the same way. They do this by sampling the language (listeners don't hear every word and readers don't fixate every word) and using their background knowledge and linguistic cues (graphophonic, syntactic, and semantic). They make predictions and inferences, confirm or disconfirm and correct their predictions, and integrate the new knowledge into the meaning they are building. Throughout the process, they keep their focus on making meaning. Goodman (1984) states, "Though written language processes appear to vary greatly as they are used in the wide range of functions and contexts they serve, reading and writing are actually unitary, psycholinguistic processes" (81).

Although reading is a universal process, there are differences in the written forms of language readers encounter. For example, readers of traditional Chinese texts cannot use sound cues to get at meaning. Hebrew writing contains characters for consonants but none for vowels. Despite these differences, every written language offers graphic, syntactic, and semantic cues. English language learners have to figure out how English words are represented in texts, but if they know how to read in their first language, much of this ability transfers to reading in

English. Teachers should capitalize on similarities across languages as they teach reading rather than focus on areas of difference.

In addition, if reading is universal, then the same method should be used to teach reading in any language. In her article "How Will Bilingual/ESL Programs in Literacy Change in the Next Millennium?" Fitzgerald (2000) points out:

> there is little evidence to support the need for a special vision of second-language reading instruction. In general, with attention to minor modifications for certain second-language learner needs (such as increased emphasis on vocabulary meanings and developing background knowledge for specific reading material), reading methods considered sound for students reading in their native language can also be helpful with students reading in a new language . . . Collectively, current research and theory suggest a future in which reading processes and reading development across languages are viewed as more similar than different. (520–21)

From a sociopsycholinguistic perspective, reading is the same in any language because all readers use background knowledge, linguistic cues, and psychological strategies as they construct meaning from texts. Teachers like Cristina, who hold a sociopsycholinguistic view, use the same methods to teach reading in both Spanish and in English. In the next section, we briefly review aspects of Cristina's lessons to show that they are consistent with a sociopsycholinguistic view.

 ## Analysis of Cristina's Lesson

Cristina keeps the focus on helping her students build needed background by developing concepts and vocabulary related to weather as she teaches them to read and write. In this way she teaches written language through content studies that are meaningful to her students. This content emphasis is reflected in the bulletin boards around the room that contain weather pictures the students have drawn and labeled, charts with weather words the students have written, and the weather graph they add to each day. In addition, the daily news pages the students have composed with Cristina are prominently displayed. Many content and literature books, along with poems and charts, all related to the weather, fill the room. Cristina fulfills the knowledge and skills standards of the TEKS as she focuses on comprehension, has students read from a variety of texts, encourages writing in response to reading, and works on print and phonological awareness.

Cristina's students are involved in listening to, reading, and writing whole texts. They are learning how to communicate using written language. Instead of focusing on learning how to decode individual words, they begin by talking about the meaning of a story or content text. Cristina realizes that for students to use all three cueing systems together, they must have access to complete texts. When students are given exercises with individual words, they must rely primarily on the graphophonic cueing system since word lists do not provide syntactic cues or the context needed to determine which meaning of a word applies.

The students are also developing psychological strategies as they read. They are making and confirming predictions. They are filling in missing information by drawing on their growing background knowledge. And, because the focus is on constructing meaning, they constantly integrate the new knowledge about weather that they are gaining with what they already know.

Even though her students are focused on meaning, Cristina engages them in activities that build the skills they need to figure out individual words. For example, they write key weather words on the alphabet chart and find cognates. During daily news, they share the pen, and Cristina draws their attention to how words are spelled and punctuated. As they read poetry about the weather, they note how words at the ends of lines rhyme. As she reads big books each day, Cristina's students track the words and connect the letters to sounds. Cristina is deliberate about teaching all aspects of language as she plans her lessons, and she responds to standards on print and phonological awareness as well as word and letter-sound identification. However, even when she is teaching skills, she keeps the focus on meaningful reading and writing to build academic concepts and vocabulary.

The Checklist for Effective Reading Instruction

Cristina evaluates her teaching by using a checklist for effective reading instruction (see Figure 3–2). The first question on the checklist is Do students value themselves as readers, and do they value reading? Cristina's first concern is to help her students see the importance of reading. She knows that no matter how well a student can read, if the student does not see reading as worthwhile, that student will not become a lifelong reader. Some of Cristina's students still struggle as they attempt to read, so she makes every effort to find books that not only interest her students but are also within their current ability range. She wants all her students, reading in either Spanish or English, to experience success and thus build the self-confidence they need to value themselves as readers.

1. Do students value themselves as readers, and do they value reading?

2. Do teachers read frequently to students from a variety of genres?

3. Do students have a wide variety of reading materials to choose from and time to read?

4. Do students make good choices of books to read?

5. Do students regard reading as meaning making at all times?

6. Do students make a balanced use of all three cueing systems?

7. Are students provided with appropriate strategy lessons if they experience difficulties in their reading?

8. Do students have opportunities to talk and write about what they have read, making connections between the reading and their own experiences?

FIGURE 3–2. Checklist for Effective Reading Instruction

The second question on the checklist asks, Do teachers read frequently to students from a variety of genres? Cristina reads to her students several times each day. She chooses books that they would find difficult to read on their own. She knows that by reading aloud she is modeling fluent, proficient reading. To become readers, students need to see good readers in action. She includes both stories and content books when she reads because she wants students to realize that reading can provide information as well as pleasure.

The third question is Do students have a wide variety of reading materials to choose from and time to read? Since she wants all her students to have positive experiences with reading, Cristina has filled her room with colorful, interesting books. She makes sure that she has books at different levels of difficulty in each language so that every student can access books on the topic the class is studying. For example, some of the weather books have very limited text and close print-to-picture matches while others have more text and illustrations that extend the meaning. Cristina realizes that her students range widely in their reading ability, so she needs a variety of books for them to choose from. In addition, she plans time each day for independent reading. Since some of her students cannot yet read on their own, she pairs up students to read together during independent reading time. Other students go to the listening center, where they can listen to a story on headsets as they follow along in their own book.

Even when students have a good variety of books to choose from and time to read, some students make poor choices and become frustrated. The next question on the checklist is Do students make good choices of books to read? During the year, Cristina teaches her students how to choose appropriate books. She realizes that some students may simply choose a book because a friend is reading a similar book. For this reason, Cristina spends time teaching her students what makes a book easy, hard, or just right. During their independent reading time, she encourages her students to have an easy book, a challenging book, and a book on their level at their desk. She has to guide some students to find books they can read more easily and challenge other students to try more difficult books. She also encourages her students to read both informational texts and fiction.

The fifth question on the checklist is the one that guides each activity Cristina plans: Do students regard reading as meaning making at all times? In all the lessons she teaches, Cristina keeps the focus on reading for meaning. She organizes around interesting themes and engages students in investigating big questions, such as How does the weather influence our lives? Her students know that by reading they can investigate important questions. Although she teaches skills, she always keeps them in context so that every reading experience for her students is meaningful.

Question 6 asks, Do students make a balanced use of all three cueing systems? Cristina knows that some of her students rely on the pictures to get meaning from a story. If she has read the story to them, they may also use a few key words and the details they remember as they read. These students are relying primarily on semantics. A few of her students focus on the letters and the words, trying to sound out each word. Their strategy may reflect the way the kindergarten teacher introduced reading to them, or it may be the result of the instruction their parents give them at home. These students rely primarily on the graphophonic system. Cristina knows that proficient readers make a balanced use of all three linguistic cueing systems. They don't overrely on just one system. As she works with students in small groups, Cristina designs strategy lessons that build on the strengths of each reader and also build the skills they need to use all three cueing systems.

The next question asks, Are students provided with appropriate strategy lessons if they experience difficulties in their reading? Cristina knows that all her students need to improve their reading skills. She teaches some strategies, such as making predictions, to the whole class. For example, Cristina had students predict from the cover and did a picture walk through the book *El señor Viento Norte* (Mañé 1997) before reading and discussing the book. Other strategies, such as looking at the pictures to figure out the text, may be appropriate only for a few students. During shared and guided reading time, Cristina introduces different strategies that students can then practice during their independent reading.

The last question asks, Do students have opportunities to talk and write about what they have read, making connections between the reading and their own experiences? Cristina often introduces a book by showing the students the illustration on the cover and asking them questions to help them connect the book to their own experiences. She also chooses theme topics and specific books that she knows the students will be able to connect with their lives. For example, in the weather unit, she included books on hurricanes because the students live in an area where hurricanes are a threat. These connections promote lively classroom discussions during which students build greater understanding of the texts they read. Cristina's writing assignments also connect to what students have read and help them further develop and refine their ideas.

The checklist for effective reading instruction is a helpful tool for teachers as they work with students at different grade levels. It is a good way for teachers to see if they are following effective instructional practices that are consistent with a sociopsycholinguistic view of reading. We conclude this chapter by describing two additional units from classrooms of teachers who hold a sociopsycholinguistic view of reading. We evaluate each lesson by using the checklist for effective reading instruction.

Animal Unit with Reading Focus—Kindergarten

"Todas las cosas cambian al crecer" (All things change as they grow). This is the text for the first two pages of the big book *Cambios* (Change) (Allen and Rotner 1991), which Teresa reads to begin her unit on change with a focus on animals for the kindergarten students in her bilingual classroom. Teresa connects her instruction to the kindergarten science TEKS (TEA 1998a), which call for students to know about how things change and the difference between living and nonliving objects. The big question for her study with students is How do living things change? Teresa also follows the Texas language arts standards (1998b). She involves students in reading and discussing and students dictate to her as she does language experience writing with them.

After reading the first pages of *Cambios*, Teresa brainstorms with her students a list of all the things they know that change and grow. Once the children have listed many things including *las flores* (flowers), *mi perro* (my dog), and *mi hermanito* (my little brother), Teresa reads the rest of the big book to the children so that they can see how many of the things they thought of are included in the book. The book ends with several examples of baby animals and a human baby growing up. Teresa then moves to another big book and reads the first page:

> ¿Has visto alguna vez perritos chiquititos? Son preciosos, ¿no es verdad? Los animales nacen chiquitos. Pero todos crecen hasta llegar a ser igualitos a sus padres. (Kratky 1991)

Translation
Have you ever seen little puppies? They are precious, aren't they? Animals are born small. But they all grow up to be like their parents.

For Teresa this book, *Los animales y sus crías, "¡Qué maravilla!"* (Animals and Their Babies, How Marvelous!) is important because it introduces topics such as how mothers care for their young, which animals are hatched from eggs, and which are born alive. The topics in this book fascinate Teresa's young students, and the colorful pictures attract them. As they listen to their teacher read the first page, they watch her track the words by drawing her hand under them as she reads. Several of the children focus on the words. Others attend more to the pictures.

Many hands go up. Teresa's choice of topic has engaged her young learners. The kindergartners are eager to tell their teacher and their classmates about their experiences with puppies, kittens, and baby bunnies. She reads them another book about animal mothers and their babies, *Las mamás de los animales* (*Animal Mothers*) (Komori 1997, 1996), and students are fascinated that some mothers carry babies in their mouths, others in a pocket in their skin, and still others push their babies. To complement this content book, Teresa will later read the delightful story *Choco encuentra una mamá* (*A Mother for Choco*) (Kasza 1997, 1996), which tells how a little bird without a mother is cared for by other animals, *¿Tu mamá es una llama?* (*Is Your Mama a Llama?*) (Guarino 1993, 1989), about a baby llama looking for its mother, and *Oli, el pequeño elefante* (Oli, the Baby Elephant) (Bos and De Beer 1989), which reinforces the key concepts about baby animals her young learners will investigate during the unit.

Teresa has many small books in her classroom to read to the children, and she encourages her students to read these books alone or with a partner. The small books reinforce the concepts introduced by the big books and the storybook. There are four colorful, hardback books: *Un cariñito, mi bebé* (A Caress, My Baby) (Paqueforet 1993d), which explains how mothers care for their babies; *A pasear, mi bebé* (Let's Move About, My Baby) (Paqueforet 1993c), which tells how and where animals move; *A dormir, mi bebé* (Let's Sleep, My Baby) (Paqueforet 1993b), which describes where and how animals sleep; and *A comer, mi bebé* (Let's Eat, My Baby) (Paqueforet 1993a), which tells what animals eat and where they get their food.

Another book, *¿Cómo son los animales bebés?* (*Baby Animals*) (Kuchalla 1987, 1982), is particularly good for emergent readers. Working alone or in pairs, students can construct meaning as they read because the pictures support the text so well. Teresa's students love identifying different animal body parts, so the class reads together *¿De quién es este rabo?* (Whose Tail Is This?) (Barberis 1974). They also read another favorite predictable book, *Los seis deseos de la jirafa* (*Giraffe's Sad Tale*) (Ada 1989a, 1992d), in which a giraffe wants a different tail. Students love repeating the refrain, which changes with each new animal tail. Their favorite refrain reads, *"¡Pobre jirafa, con cola de chango!"* (Poor giraffe with the tail of a monkey!). For playful use of Spanish and work with rhyme and numbers, the teacher and students read *Me gustaría tener . . .* (I would like to have . . .) (Ada 1989b). The big book *Tres amigos* (*Three Friends*) (Brusca and Wilson 1995, 1997) gives students the opportunities to count and learn about desert animals. The children continue reading books about animals together in small groups with the teacher or the teacher's aide, including *Pistas de animales* (*Animal Clues*) (Drew 1993, 1990), *Veo, veo colas* (I See, I See Tails) (Kratky 1995d), *Orejas* (Ears) (Kratky 1995b), *Patas* (Feet) (Beck 1994), and *¿Quién está en la choza?* (*Who's in the Shed?*) (Parkes 1990, 1986). These limited-text picture books are very predictable. The patterns help students begin to build meaning as they make connections between the text and the illustrations.

During ESL time Teresa reinforces many of the concepts the students have been working on, sometimes reading big books in English that the students have read in Spanish, including *Animal Mothers* (Komori 1996) and *A Mother for Choco* (Kasza 1996). Teresa also works on shapes, numbers, and verbs in English within the context of the content. She reads *Color Zoo* (Ehlert 1990) and students make their own animals with shapes. She then reads *Count* (Fleming 1992) because the text counts animals in action. For example, the page about four kangaroos tells them, "Bounce, kangaroos!" (8), and the page about two zebras tells them, "Jump, zebras!" (4). Of course, the children can then do the actions the animals are told to do. Figure 3–3 lists some books in Spanish and in English that can be used in an animal unit for younger students.

Teresa includes both reading and writing in other activities she uses during her unit. For example, she brainstorms with the children what they know about different animals. For this activity, she puts pictures on the bulletin board, and the children tell her what they notice about the animals in the pictures. They use their background experiences and ideas they have picked up during reading. Teresa prints what the children say under the pictures so that they can later read what they have dictated and can also refer to these words during writing time. Teresa teaches language through content organized around a meaningful theme. As they investigate the big question, How do living things change?, Teresa's students develop both academic content knowledge and literacy skills in two languages.

Ada, Alma F. 1989a. *Los seis deseos de la jirafa*. Carmel, CA: Hampton-Brown.

———. 1989b. *Me gustaría tener*. Northvale, NJ: Santillana.

———. 1992. *The Giraffe's Sad Tale*. Carmel, CA: Hampton-Brown.

Allen, Marjorie, and Shelly Rotner. 1996. *Cambios*. Carmel, CA: Hampton-Brown.

Barberis. 1974. *¿De quién es este rabo?* Colección Duende. Valladolid, Spain: Miñon.

Beck, Jennifer. 1994. *Patas*. Literacy 2000, Nivel 3. Crystal Lake, IL: Rigby.

Bos, Burny, and Hans De Beer. 1989. *Oli, el pequeño elefante*. Barcelona, Spain: Editorial Lumen.

Drew, David. 1990. *Animal Clues*. Crystal Lake, IL: Rigby.

———. 1993. *Pistas de animales*. Crystal Lake, IL: Rigby.

Ediciones Litexsa Venezolana, ed. 1987. *Aprender a contar*. Caracas, Venezuela: Cromotip.

Ehlert, Lois. 1990. *Color Zoo*. New York: Trumpet.

Fleming, Denise. 1992. *Count*. New York: Henry Holt.

Guarino, Deborah. 1989. *Is Your Mama a Llama?* New York: Scholastic.

———. 1993. *¿Tu mamá es una llama?* New York: Scholastic.

Kasza, Keiko. 1996. *A Mother for Choco*. Boston: Houghton Mifflin.

———. 1997. *Choco encuentra una mamá*. Boston: Houghton Mifflin.

Komori, Atsushi. 1996. *Animal Mothers*. Boston: Houghton Mifflin.

———. 1997. *Las mamás de los animales*. Boston: Houghton Mifflin.

Kratky, Lada Josefa. 1991a. *Los animales y sus crías, "¡Qué maravilla!"* Carmel, CA: Hampton-Brown.

———. 1991b. *Animals and Their Young*. Carmel, CA: Hampton-Brown.

———. 1995. *Orejas*. Pan y Canela, Colección B. Carmel, CA: Hampton-Brown.

———. 1997. *Ears*. Carmel, CA: Hampton-Brown.

Kuchalla, Susan. 1982. *Baby Animals*. Mahwah, NJ: Troll.

———. 1987. *¿Cómo son los animales bebés?* ¿Cómo son? México, DF: SITESA.

Paqueforet, Marcus. 1993a. *A comer, mi bebé*. Libros del Rincón. México, DF: Hachette Latinoamérica/SEP.

———. 1993b. *A dormir, mi bebé*. Libros del Rincón. México, DF: Hachette Latinoamérica/SEP.

———. 1993c. *A pasear, mi bebé*. Libros del Rincón. México, DF: Hachette Latinoamérica/SEP.

———. 1993d. *Un cariñito, mi bebé*. Libros del Rincón. México, DF: Hachette Latinoamérica/SEP.

Parkes, Brenda. 1986. *Who's in the Shed?* Crystal Lake, IL: Rigby.

———. 1990. *¿Quién está en la choza?* Crystal Lake, IL: Rigby.

Sempere, Vicky. 1987. *ABC*. Caracas, Venezuela: Ediciones Ekaré-Banco del Libro.

FIGURE 3–3. Books for Kindergarten Animal Unit

Analysis of Teresa's Lesson Using the Reading Checklist

Teresa could answer yes to many of the questions on the checklist. She is helping her students understand the value of reading by engaging them with interesting texts. She also plans her lessons so that students can begin to read independently and thus start to value themselves as readers. Teresa reads to her students every day, and she helps students make good choices for their own reading as they become independent readers. She is sure to include a variety of genres when she reads so that her students will become familiar with both fiction and informational texts in their study of animals. Teresa keeps the focus on meaning by emphasizing the content of the texts. She teaches written language through academic content at her students' level, and she does not have them spend time on worksheets or abstract exercises in phonemic awareness.

Teresa observes how her students use the three cueing systems as they read. Since they are emergent readers, she is more concerned with keeping them engaged in reading than with giving them specific strategy lessons. She realizes that some of her students simply need more time engaged in texts, not more instruction. Teresa's students love to talk and write about what she reads and what they read. In Teresa's classroom this talk and writing is essential for building and developing the concepts introduced in the reading. Teresa's students are surrounded by interesting and imaginative texts written in language that is natural and engaging. All these elements are key to these children's early literacy development.

 ## Animal Unit with Reading Focus—Fourth Grade

At the beginning of the school year, Roberto, a fourth-grade dual language teacher, brainstorms with his students questions they have about their world. One main overarching concern his students have is how to care for the earth, so Roberto decides to develop a theme on conservation to answer the question How do we effect change in the environment? This theme also connects to the fourth-grade California science standards (Burton and Ong 2000, 9).

He begins the theme study in Spanish by reading the book *Conservación* (*Conservation*) (Ingpen and Dunkle 1991, 1987), a Spanish translation of a prize-winning book about how important it is for all people to conserve natural resources. The class discussion following this reading leads to one question in particular that interests Roberto's students: *¿Cómo se relacionan los animales y los humanos?* (What is the relationship between people and animals?). To begin the investigation of this question, Roberto reads *Zoológico* (*The Zoo*) (Browne 1993, 1992), another Spanish translation of an English book about a family's visit to the zoo. This colorful picture book raises questions about people's relationship to animals and the result of caging animals. After reading the book, which leaves the readers considering what might happen next, Roberto begins discussion by asking the two questions (see Figure 3–4), which help him check on students' literal comprehension and extend their understanding, *¿Qué recuerdan de lo que leí?* (What do you remember from what I read?) and *¿Qué más les gustaría conocer acerca de la historia?* (What else would you like to know?). The students share their memories of vivid scenes, the characters' responses to the animals, and the father's lack of respect for the animals. They also raise questions about what might happen next in the story. The discussion also leads to the question about whether zoo animals should be kept in cages.

Next Roberto reads another book by Browne, *Gorila* (*Gorilla*) (1991, 1983). Roberto then asks two additional questions (see Figure 3–4), *¿A qué les hace acordar esta historia?* (What does this story make you think of?) and *¿Qué otros libros has leído que puedes relacionar con esta historia?* (What other books have you read that you can connect to this story?). These two questions help students make text-to-self and text-to-text connections. During his lessons, Roberto often uses one or more of these questions (see Figure 3–4). Students remember their own visits to zoos and how unhappy the caged animals looked. In addition, they begin to make important intertextual ties, connecting ideas among the stories they have read.

Roberto extends this discussion by having the students compare two of the stories. He draws two large intersecting circles on the blackboard to form a Venn diagram. On the top of one circle he writes, "Diferencias *Zoológico*" (Differences in *The Zoo*); on the top of the second, he writes, "Diferencias *Gorila*" (Differences in *Gorilla*). Then Roberto writes *"Semejanzas"* (Similarities) over the area of the circles that intersect. Students use this diagram as a model and work in small groups to list how the books are different and how they are the same (see Figure 3–5).

---

1. What do you remember?

2. What else would you like to know?

3. What does it make you think of?

4. What other books have you read that you can connect to this story?

FIGURE 3–4. Comprehension Questions (based on Hansen 1989)

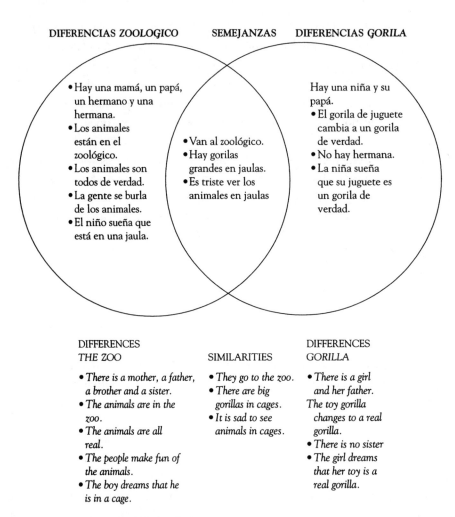

DIFERENCIAS ZOOLOGICO **SEMEJANZAS** **DIFERENCIAS GORILA**

- Hay una mamá, un papá, un hermano y una hermana.
- Los animales están en el zoológico.
- Los animales son todos de verdad.
- La gente se burla de los animales.
- El niño sueña que está en una jaula.

- Van al zoológico.
- Hay gorilas grandes en jaulas.
- Es triste ver los animales en jaulas

Hay una niña y su papá.
- El gorila de juguete cambia a un gorila de verdad.
- No hay hermana.
- La niña sueña que su juguete es un gorila de verdad.

DIFFERENCES THE ZOO **SIMILARITIES** **DIFFERENCES GORILLA**

- *There is a mother, a father, a brother and a sister.*
- *The animals are in the zoo.*
- *The animals are all real.*
- *The people make fun of the animals.*
- *The boy dreams that he is in a cage.*

- *They go to the zoo.*
- *There are big gorillas in cages.*
- *It is sad to see animals in cages.*

- *There is a girl and her father.*
The toy gorilla changes to a real gorilla.
- *There is no sister*
- *The girl dreams that her toy is a real gorilla.*

FIGURE 3–5. Venn Diagram for Two Stories

After the students fill in their Venn diagrams and compare them, Roberto writes another question on the board, "*¿Qué sabemos acerca de la relación entre el hombre y los animales?*" (What do we know about the relation between humans and animals?). After discussing this question in groups, the students make a list of their ideas. They include the fact that many animals are now extinct and many more are in danger of extinction. Roberto focuses on this point and asks, "*¿Qué queremos saber sobre los animales en extinción y las especies en peligro de extinción?*" (What do we want to know about extinct animals and the species in danger of extinction?). The students and their teacher decide to carry out further investigation into this question by reading additional books.

To help students with their research, Roberto fills the room with different resources in both Spanish and English. These include books rich with information and filled with illustrations of animals that are already extinct or must be protected: *¿Les echaremos de menos?* (*Will We Miss Them?*) (Wright 1993, 1992), *The Extinct Alphabet Book* (Pallotta 1993), *The Book of Animal Records* (Drew 1989), *La familia del chimpancé* (*The Chimpanzee Family*) (Goodall 1991, 1989), *La familia del león* (*The Lion Family*) (Hofer and Ziesler 1992, 1988), *Cocodrilos y caimanes* (*Crocodiles and Alligators*) (Barrett 1991a, 1989), *Monos y simios* (*Monkeys and Simians*) (Barrett 1991b, 1988), *Amazing Animals* (Drew 2000a), *Mountain Gorillas in Danger* (Ritchie 1999), and *Zoobooks* magazines about many animals, including one titled *"Los animales en extinctión"* (Extinct Animals) (Wexo 1981).

For his students who have less experience in reading in Spanish, Roberto provides stories and resource books with less text supplemented by photographs and illustrations that do not appear to be for very young children, including *Los animales del mundo* (The Animals of the World) (Granowsky 1986a), *¿Por qué nos preocupa?* (Why Do We Worry?) (Granowsky 1986b), *El bosque tropical* (The Tropical Forest) (Cowcher 1992), *Podría ser un mamífero* (*It Could Be a Mammal*) (Fowler 1991, 1989), *Animales con armardura* (*Animals with Armor*) (Smith 2002, 2001), *Animales de mar y tierra* (*Animals of the Land and Sea*) (Dawson 2003, 2001), *Animales y plantas viven aquí* (*Animals and Plants Live Here*) (Wong 2002, 2001), and *La culebra verde* (The Green Snake) (Urbina n.d.). Figure 3–6 lists animal books in Spanish and in English used in Roberto's lesson and others that can be used for older students.

Over the next two weeks students read and discuss these books and then write reports on different questions they choose to investigate. They also write an imaginative essay after reading *Si los dinosaurios regresaran* (*If the Dinosaurs Came Back*) (Most 1997, 1978) to tell what might happen if some extinct animals were still living. To culminate this unit of study, Roberto and his students work on a dramatic reading of *Fox, Beware!* (Waite 2000), which tells how the modern world encroaches on the habitats of wild animals. They also decide to make a class big book. Students work in groups, and each group creates a page that includes a picture of an endangered animal and information about the animal. They plan a day when they can present their dramatic reading and their findings to other classes in the school. They decorate the room with pictures of animals in their natural habitats. They also find recordings of wild animal cries. Each group creates a large-scale model of the animal it has studied. Then the students design centers

Atkinson, Kathie. 1998. *Hide to Survive*. Crystal Lake, IL: Rigby.

Barrett, Norman. 1988. *Monkeys and Simians*. New York: Franklin Watts.

———. 1989. *Crocodiles and Caimans*. New York: Franklin Watts.

———. 1991a. *Cocodrilos y caimans: Biblioteca Gráfica*. New York: Franklin Watts.

———.1991b. *Monos y simios: Biblioteca Gráfica*. New York: Franklin Watts.

Berger, Melvin, and Gilbert Berger. 1999. *Do Tarantulas Have Teeth?* New York: Scholastic.

Browne, Anthony. 1983. *Gorilla*. London: Julia MacRae Books.

———. 1991. *Gorila*. Trans. C. Esteva, A la orilla del viento. México, DF: Fondo de Cultura Económica.

———. 1992. *Zoo*. London: Julia MacRae Books.

———. 1993. *Zoológico*. Trans. C. Esteva, A la orilla del viento. Méxcio, DF: Fondo de Cultura Económica.

Cherry, Lynne. 1990. *The Great Kapok Tree*. New York: Harcourt.

———. 1996. *La ceiba majestuosa: Un cuento del bosque lluviosa*. Boston: Houghton Mifflin.

Comerlati, Mara. 1983. *Conoce nuestros mamíferos*. Caracas, Venezuela: Ediciones Ekaré Banco del Libro.

Cowcher, Helen. 1992. *El bosque tropical*. New York: Scholastic.

Dawson, Sarah. 2001. *Animals of the Land and Sea*. Washington, DC: National Geographic.

———. 2002. *Animales de mar y tierra*. Washington, DC: National Geographic.

Fowler, Allan. 1991. *Podría ser un mamífero*. Chicago: Children's Press.

Goodall, Jane. 1989. *The Chimpanzee Family Book*. Salzburgo: Neugebauer.

———. 1991. *La familia del chimpancé*. México, DF: SITESA.

Granados, Antonio. 1989. *Zoológico de palabras*. Hermosillo, Mexico: Editorial UniSon.

Granowsky, Alvin. 1986a. *Los animales del mundo*. Ed. C. Johnson, Especies del mundo en peligro de extinción. Lexington, MA: Schoolhouse.

———. 1986b. *¿Por que nos preocupa?* Lexington, MA: Schoolhouse.

Greenway, Shirley. 1997. *Two's Company*. Watertown, MA: Charlesbridge.

Hofer, Angelika, and Günter Ziesler. 1988. *The Lion Family Book*. Salzburgo: Neugebauer.

———. 1992. *La familia del león*. México, DF: SITESA.

Ingpen, Robert, and Margaret Dunkle. 1987. *Conservation*. Melbourne, Australia: Hill of Content.

———. 1991. *Conservación*. México, DF: Editorial Origen S.A.

Most, Bernard. 1978. *If the Dinosaurs Came Back*. New York: Harcourt Brace.

———. 1997. *Si los dinosaurios regresaran*. Boston: Houghton Mifflin.

FIGURE 3–6. Animal Bibliography for Older Students

Pratt, Kristin Joy. 1993. *Un paseo por el bosque lluvioso/A Walk in the Rainforest*. Nevada City, CA: Dawn.

Ritchie, Rita. 1999. *Mountain Gorillas in Danger*. Boston: Houghton Mifflin.

Sanchez, Isidro. 1989. *El elefante*. Barcelona, Spain: Multilibro.

Smith, Cathy. 2001. *Animals with Armor*. Washington, DC: National Geographic.

———. 2002. *Animales con armadura*. Washington, DC: National Geographic.

Urbina, Joaquín. n.d. *La culebra verde*. Caracas, Venezuela: Gráficas Armitano.

Waite, Judy. 2000. *Fox, Beware!* Barrington, IL: Rigby.

Wexo, John Bonnett. 1981. "Los animales en extinción." *Zoobooks*.

Willow, Diane, and Laura Jacques. 1993. *Dentro de la selva tropical*. Watertown, MA: Charlesbridge.

Wong, George. 2001. *Animals and Plants Live Here*. Washington, DC: National Geographic.

———. 2002. *Animales y plantas viven aquí*. Washington, DC: National Geographic.

Wright, Alexandra. 1992. *Will We Miss Them?* Watertown, MA: Charlesbridge.

———. 1993. *¿Les echaremos de menos?* Watertown, MA: Charlesbridge.

Zak, Monica. 1989. *Salvan mi selva*. México, DF: Sistemas Técnicos de Edición.

Zawisza, Tita. 1982. *Conoce a nuestros insectos*. Caracas, Venezuela: Ediciones Ekaré-Banco del Libro.

FIGURE 3–6. Animal Bibliography for Older Students (*continued*)

where they group the models of animals that live in similar environments. They pin up butcher-paper backgrounds to represent the habitats.

As other classes come in, the students are divided into small groups and directed to one of the centers. There they examine the models as they listen to the experts, the students from Roberto's class, tell about the different animals. The visitors rotate through the centers so they can learn about all the animals Roberto's class has studied. When all the small groups have presented to the visitors, the class does its reading of *Fox, Beware!* This culminating event provides a natural way for Roberto's students to present the knowledge they have developed. At the same time, students from other classes, particularly the third graders, get excited about what they will be doing when they are in Roberto's fourth-grade class.

Analysis of Roberto's Lesson

Like Teresa, Roberto could answer yes to the questions on the reading checklist. Roberto's students were involved in interesting and meaningful reading. This reading helped them answer important questions. During this process, Roberto reinforced for his students the value of reading. He also included books at different levels in each language so all his students could read successfully and value themselves as readers.

Even though his students are fourth graders, Roberto reads to them each day. He chose books to read aloud that were difficult for some of his students to read on their own. During the unit, Roberto brought in many books on the topic so that students had a wide variety of materials to choose from as they investigated different questions. As students read independently, Roberto counseled them to help them make good choices of books to read. Roberto encouraged students who were choosing books that were too easy or too hard to find more appropriate texts. Since students were reading to answer important questions, their focus was always on making sense of their books. Roberto taught important reading skills in context, but he never had his students waste valuable reading time filling out meaningless worksheets. He wanted them to regard reading as a source of pleasure and information.

While students were working in groups on their projects, Roberto called some of the students to read to him so that he could assess their use of the cueing systems. He also planned strategy lessons for both the whole class and individuals. The activity with the Venn diagram to determine similarities and differences was a whole-class lesson. For students who needed strategies for other aspects of reading, Roberto planned lessons suited to their needs. Roberto and his students frequently discussed what he read to them and what they read independently and in small groups. As they read and discussed books on a topic of interest, Roberto's students connected the ideas in the books to their own experiences. In addition, at the end of the animal unit, they had the opportunity to present all that they had learned to the other classes who came to see their display. The class' dramatic reading of *Fox, Beware!* gave all students the opportunity to practice fluency in a meaningful context and supported struggling readers in particular.

 ## Conclusion

We began this chapter by describing a unit on weather taught by Cristina, a teacher who takes a sociopsycholinguistic view of reading. Even though she taught the same content as Guillermo and Elena and used some of the same materials, her lessons were quite different from theirs. Cristina's lessons were designed to help her students use reading to learn about the weather. She taught reading through meaningful content studies.

We then explained the sociopsycholinguistic view of reading in some detail. The research base for this view is miscue analysis, a process that involves listening carefully to students as they read and then analyzing the way they substitute, insert, and omit words along with their corrections and retellings. This view of reading holds that reading is a process of constructing meaning by using background knowledge, psychological strategies, and linguistic cueing systems.

After analyzing Cristina's lessons to show how they were consistent with a sociopsycholinguistic view of reading, we introduced a checklist for effective reading instruction. Teachers like Cristina who have a sociopsycholinguistic view of reading can answer yes to each of the questions on the checklist. We concluded the chapter by describing two other units from teachers who take a sociopsycholinguistic view and then evaluating their teaching of reading by using the checklist. Current approaches to teaching reading have grown out of past theories and methods. In the next chapter, we provide readers with important background information by giving an overview of the history of reading methods in both Spanish and English.

 ## Applications

1. Cristina's lesson on the weather at the beginning of the chapter is different from Guillermo's and Elena's lessons. List eight to ten ways this lesson is different. Which of the three lessons did you like the best? Why?

2. As we began our discussion of a sociopsycholinguistic view of reading, we mentioned Ken Goodman's perspective on reading as a psycholinguistic guessing game. Why does he call reading a psycholinguistic guessing game? Be prepared to discuss.

3. Does eye movement research disprove a word recognition view of reading? How? Discuss this with a partner.

4. What is miscue analysis? What kind of information do miscues give us? How do the results of miscue studies support a sociopsycholinguistic view of reading?

5. We discussed psychological strategies readers use, including sampling, inferring, predicting, confirming or disconfirming, and integrating. Choose a favorite children's book. Go through the book with a group of children, having them predict and confirm or disconfirm their predictions. To check integration, have them write a short summary of the book.

6. We went through the reading of the "Arn tib, a phev was larzing two sleks" passage in order to help you understand graphophonics, syntax, and semantics. Have an adult read the passage and ask him or her some of the comprehension questions for each cueing system. Does this help you see more clearly how the three systems work?

7. Read over the checklist of effective reading practices. Evaluate a reading lesson you have recently taught or a reading lesson you observed using the checklist. Which elements in the checklist were present? Which were missing?

The History of Literacy Instruction in Spanish and in English

The more things change, the more they stay the same.

French saying

I n this chapter, we provide an overview of the history of reading methods in both Spanish and English. More detailed histories are available, but we hope our discussion will provide the background readers will need as they consider the methods currently being used to teach reading. What becomes evident from this look at history is that most ways of teaching reading have followed the logic that underlies the word recognition view of reading rather than the social, psychological, and linguistic research that supports the sociopsycholinguistic view of reading.

A Historical Overview of Early Spanish Reading Methods

Synthetic Methods

In his book *Los métodos de lectura* (Reading Methods), Bellenger (1979) provides a history of reading instruction. According to Bellenger, reading was taught using a synthetic, part-to-whole approach for more than two thousand years beginning with the ancient Greeks. In this synthetic approach, children were taught to read by first identifying letters, then syllables, then isolated words, then phrases, and finally whole texts. Recitation, memorization, and careful pronunciation were important parts of the pedagogy. The Romans followed the same practices, and this approach continued through the Middle Ages.

In Europe in these early times, literacy was restricted to the upper classes and members of the church. Then, in the 1660s, when the Spanish wanted to educate people in religion, priests at religious schools devised methods to educate the common people. Reading was approached synthetically, as it had been in the past, beginning with the parts and moving to the whole, because it was believed that the lower classes needed a very regimented, step-by-step progression in order to learn.

In the New World, reading instruction was also the province of the church. In the 1770s Spain's king, Carlos III, ordered that only Spanish be spoken in Nueva España. It was in this period that the famous *Silabario de San Miguel* (San Miguel's Reader) was developed in Mexico to teach both religion and Spanish to the masses, including the indigenous peoples. The front cover of the *Silabario* is known for its depiction of the archangel Saint Michael beating Satan (Barbosa Heldt 1971). López Guerra and Flores Chávez (2004) explain:

> El método de enseñanza del español se realizaba con un pequeño folleto de 8 hojas compuesto de 38 lecciones o ejercicios: el Silabario Método de San Miguel o Silabario de San Vicente. (5)

Translation
The method of teaching Spanish was realized with a small booklet of eight pages, composed of thirty-eight lessons or exercises, the Silabary Method of San Miguel or Silabary of San Vicente.

The first part of the *Silabario* presented the vowels, which students practiced reciting orally. In the second part the vowels were combined with consonants into syllables for oral practice. Then the students learned the alphabet, both the capital and the small letters. Finally, they read (or repeated) individual written words separated into syllables. The entire pamphlet had a religious theme and was used throughout the colonial period by priests to teach reading and religion (Barbosa Heldt 1973). The booklet was used broadly in parochial schools.

The *Silabario de San Miguel* is a classic part-to-whole reading document, termed by Barbosa Heldt as *un verdadero documento de la pedagogía tradicionalista y anticientífica, cuyo origen se remonta a siglos pasados* (a true document of the traditional and antiscientific pedagogy whose origin comes from past centuries) (29). Despite the rejection of this approach by Barbosa Heldt and other educators, *silabarios* were used broadly across Latin America and Europe and are still available. In fact, in 1990 a new *silabario* was produced in Spain, and in 1994 two *silabarios* were published in Venezuela.

Analytic Methods

Synthetic methods for teaching reading were widely used in Europe and the New World. However, criticism of synthetic methods arose because these methods were viewed as artificial and mechanical. In the early seventeenth century, Comenius presented a new method in his *Orbis Pictus*. He proposed starting with the whole rather than the parts. His goal was to educate universally, and not just the elite. He even proposed educating girls! He saw literacy as central to students' access to knowledge and understanding and encouraged students to use language and literacy to learn about science and other academic fields (Shannon 1991).

Others followed with critiques of the synthetic approach. In *De la maniere d'apprendre les langues* (The Way to Learn Languages), Radonvilliers rejected the idea that children should be spelling and sounding out syllables and words and proposed they could directly recognize whole words. Another Frenchman, Adam, agreed with this view, insisting that the synthetic method should be abandoned because (in Bellenger's translation),

> Se atormenta insistentemente a los niños para hacerles conocer y retener un elevado número de letras, de sílabas y de sonidos, de lo cual nada pueden comprender porque estos elementos no contienen en sí mismos ninguna idea que les atraiga ni les divierta. (1979, 72)

Translation
It constantly torments children to make them learn and remember a high number of letters, syllables, and sounds, which they do not understand at all because those elements do not have in them anything that is interesting or enjoyable [for children].

Even though this quote is well over one hundred years old, unfortunately, it still applies to many English language learners in schools in which reading is taught following a word recognition view.

In 1880, Block, building on the work of these French scholars as well as several German academics, introduced a daring new reading method that used whole words to illustrate the sounds and the letters students were to learn. Rather than starting with letters or syllables and building up to words, this method started with whole words that were later broken down into their parts.

In Mexico, Block's method was introduced by Rébsamen in 1899 when he published his *Guía metodológica de la enseñaza de la escritura y lectura* (Methodological Guide to Teaching Reading and Writing). Barbosa Heldt explains how this method works:

> A Rébsamen, pues, se debe la introducción a México del Método llamado de Palabras Normales . . . Es analítico-sintético, porque sigue un orden en que se presenta primero la palabra, pasando luego a su división en sílabas y por último a las letras, representadas por sus sonidos, para regresar a las sílabas y retornar a la palabra. (38)

> **Translation**
> Rébsamen introduced the method *Palabras Normales* to Mexico . . . It is an analytic-synthetic method because it follows the order of first [teaching] the word, going next to dividing it into syllables, and lastly into letter sounds, and [then] building back to syllables and returning to the word.

Rébsamen's method continues to influence the way reading is taught in Spanish. In Mexico, it was still referenced in the beginning reading text approved by the government in the 1980s (Alvarez 1979). However, it was criticized because of the nonsense children read and analyzed in order to learn sounds and letters. Block's method was rejected, then, because of *su negación de la lectura como medio de comunicación utilizable por el niño* (its negating of reading as a means of useful communication for the child) (Bellenger 1979, 70).

Analytic methods such as Block's were based on the idea of perceiving words and phrases globally. However, these early analytic methods were criticized for focusing on language and ignoring the reader. This concern led reading educators to place more emphasis on drawing on students' background knowledge and helping them comprehend texts. For example, the Belgian Decroly developed the ideovisual method in 1936. According to Bellenger, this method *se trataba de hacer que los niños comprendiesen lo que leían y de orientarles hacia la identificación del texto* (tried to help children comprehend what they read and relate to the texts) (1979, 76).

In 1947 the French educator Hendrix wrote a book describing the global method, which was an expansion of Decroly's ideovisual method. Hendrix's book was translated into Spanish as *Cómo enseñar a leer por el método global* (How to Teach Using the Global Method) (Hendrix 1952) and was widely read throughout Latin America. The book shows educators how to teach reading beginning with the sentence or the phrase and moving to the word, then the syllable, and finally, the letter.

This brief review of the history of reading methods in Spanish shows that even though there has been a concern for building on students' background knowledge and helping them comprehend text, the methods fail to do this. Both the synthetic methods and the analytic methods are designed to teach students to recognize words. The synthetic approaches start from the parts—the letters, sounds, or syllables—and build up to identifying the whole, but the whole is the word or at most a sentence.

In contrast, analytic approaches begin with the whole and break it down into parts. However, the whole is seldom even a complete sentence. Even when sentences and phrases are presented, individual words are analyzed. Students don't read connected text beyond the sentence. Little evidence exists that the construction of meaning was ever a serious consideration in most of the methods, although educators may have assumed that readers would comprehend a text once they could recognize the words. It is not surprising that currently the most commonly used method of teaching reading in Spanish begins by having students learn syllables.

 ## Early Methods for Teaching Reading in English in the United States

Early reading instruction in English in the United States, like the instruction in Europe and Latin America, was strongly influenced by the church. Children learned to read so that they could read the Bible or other religious books. During the 1800s the teachers who taught reading had often received little or no pedagogical preparation. Frequently these teachers had limited schooling themselves. They attended teacher institutes where presentations were motivational or gave them subject matter information. They were not well paid, and they faced large classes in the one-room schoolhouses of that period. Much like the *Silabario* method used in Latin America and Spain, approaches to teaching reading in the United States were "largely didactic, consisting of oral reading of texts with morals and lessons" (NCREL 2001, 1).

There were notable exceptions to this approach in a few pockets around the country. Parker, for example, drew on the work of Comenius, Rousseau, and Pestalozzi when he was superintendent of Quincy School in Quincy, Massachussetts, between 1875 and 1880. Under his leadership, lessons were connected to students' lives and interests. The Quincy School literacy lesson was based on real objects. Reading lessons dealt with topics that students studied in the different content areas. Teachers began by writing a word for an object related to their studies on the blackboard and repeating it. Students read the word after the teacher and then wrote the word on their slates. By using words for real objects connected to their other school subjects, teachers assumed that the lessons were meaningful and students would associate the symbols and the objects (Shannon 1991). However, it is clear that even this method was based on a word recognition view of reading because learning to read consisted of identifying individual words.

At the end of the nineteenth century and in the first half of the twentieth century, progressive education and ideas of child-centered approaches arose (Dewey 1929). Approaches to teaching reading changed, and there was a movement away from oral repetition of words and sounds and toward an emphasis on comprehension and silent reading. In the 1880s, Rice, a pediatrician who had studied psychology and pedagogy in Germany, observed more than twelve hundred teachers in thirty-six different cities in the eastern part of the United States. He found most teaching to be mechanical and lacking in any creativity.

Rice believed that literacy should be embedded in the study of academic content and that students should "read to learn something from books" and write "in order to record the thoughts of others and make clear their own thoughts" (Shannon 1991, 54). Up until the 1950s, others, including Dewey, Kilpatrick, Counts, Horton, and Mitchell, were involved in various schools or projects that approached literacy in meaningful ways as students wrote and read about the world around them, including social issues.

Scientific Management and Basal Readers

These movements did not dominate the entire literacy scene in the United States. Scientific management in industry became popular in the first decade of the 1900s, and this concept spread to education. Between 1915 and 1919, the Committee on the Economy of Time in Education was charged to "eliminate nonessentials from the elementary school curriculum, to improve teaching methods, and to set minimum standards for each school subject" (Shannon 1989). Two key results of this were the establishment of test scores to mimic industry's production figures and, in the teaching of reading, the rise of the basal reader with its accompanying teacher's guides, worksheets, and testing materials.

In the 1950s, with the launching of Sputnik, progressive education was attacked and there was a call for more direct teaching of academic content and a demand for results—efficient and scientific results like those called for by the Committee on the Economy of Time in Education. Reading during this period was dominated by the whole-word method, and most teachers used basal readers in which vocabulary was carefully controlled and the many exercises were designed to build decoding skills.

In her article on the four recent ages of reading philosophy and pedagogy, Turbill (2002) describes this period between 1950 and 1970 as "the age of reading as decoding." In her native Australia, as well as in the United States, she explains that "our focus in teaching reading . . . was on teaching skills including directionality, visual and aural discrimination, sound-symbol relationships (phonics), and word recognition" (2).

Word Focus in English and Spanish

During the 1960s in the United States, the federal government became involved in education with Lyndon Johnson's war on poverty. Head Start was initiated to give all children an equal chance at education, and the Elementary and Secondary Education Act provided funds to bring reading teachers to schools with children who needed extra support. As in the past, most methods were based on a word recognition view of reading. In both the United States and Latin America, reading research debates centered around the best way to teach children to recognize words. For English reading, Chall's famous *Learning to Read: The Great Debate* (1967), which is still often quoted by opponents of holistic approaches, was, in fact, a study of the difference between two word identification approaches to reading, phonics and sight words. It was never a comparison between a word identification approach and a sociopsycholinguistic approach.

For the Spanish-speaking world, Braslavsky (1962) published a widely read book about the teaching of reading in Argentina: *La querella de los métodos en la enseñanza de la lectura* (The Debate of the Methods for Teaching Reading). This book, like Chall's, is also basically about the identification of words. Braslavsky compares the synthetic methods with the global method, which she calls analytic. She uses Simon's 1924 definitions to distinguish the two methods to be debated:

A pesar de las apariencias, no existen verdaderamente más de dos métodos de lectura. Ambos tratan de hacer comprender al niño que existe cierta correspondencia entre los signos de la lengua escrita y los soniods de la lengua hablada; pero, para ello, uno de estos métodos comienza por el estudio por los signos o por el de los sonidos elementales, y el otro busca por el contrario obtener el mismo resultado colocando de repente al niño pequeño frente a nuestro lenguaje escrito. (Simon 1924, 24)

Translation
In spite of appearances, there do not exist more than two methods of reading. Both deal with helping children understand that there exists a certain correspondence between the signs of the written language and the sounds of the spoken language, but in order to arrive at this understanding, one of those methods begins with the study of the signs or the basic sounds and the other sets out by contrast to get the same results by suddenly giving the small child our written language.

Braslavsky's use of this quotation revealed her beliefs about reading in 1962. She believed that giving students whole words, phrases, and stories from the beginning was overwhelming ("suddenly giving the small child our written language") and that the phonetic approach, moving from part to whole, was much more effective. Both of the approaches she discussed took the word as the basic unit, broke words down, and analyzed them.

From Part-to-Whole to Sociopsycholinguistics

In the 1970s, reading instruction, influenced by B. F. Skinner's behaviorist principles, "gave birth to prepackaged programs of individualized instruction," during which children moved independently through a series of more and more difficult texts, working on specific skills (NCREL 2001, 2). Students worked independently to complete page after page. They were rewarded for correct answers and given additional practice if they gave wrong answers. These individualized instruction packets often supplemented the basal readers, which still dominated instruction.

By the late 1970s the pendulum began swinging away from a totally controlled approach to reaching literacy. Influenced by researchers such as Goodman (1967), Smith (1971, 1973), and Holdaway (1979) in psycholinguistics and reading, Graves (1983) in writing, and Halliday (1975) in functional linguistics, literacy educators in the United States, Canada, the United Kingdom, and Australia began to reject the fragmented, behaviorist approach to reading instruction that prevailed in most schools and adopt a more holistic and meaning-centered view of reading and writing.

Drawing on ideas developed during the progressive period of education, many literacy educators began to regard reading and writing as dynamic, interactive, and social. Students were encouraged to read good literature and write creatively. This sociopsycholinguistic view was popularly called *whole language*. The name reflected a belief that language should be kept whole, not broken up into meaningless parts.

These changes were especially apparent in many early literacy programs: Teachers were encouraged to surround young children with print and to encourage them to make their own meaning from this language. Young writers were told to *invent* spellings rather than copy words from a list. This era was the beginning of the "whole language versus phonics" wars, which persist to this day (NCREL 2001, 3).

Whole language began earlier in Australia. In fact, early whole language advocates in the United States frequently referred to Australia and neighboring New Zealand as models that should be followed. Turbill (2002) called the 1960s and the early 1970s "The Age of Reading as Meaning Making" (3). The message about reading was that "readers bring meaning to print in order to take meaning from print" (4). There was more reading of a variety of books to and with children. Teachers were no longer only implementing programs but were encouraged to learn new strategies and to understand the reading process itself. Instead of using the basals or other prepackaged programs, many teachers began to teach reading using children's literature.

In the 1970s and the early 1980s, both in Australia and in the United States, young learners were encouraged to read widely. Turbill describes the situation in Australia:

> Most classrooms seemed to be filled with lots of books—children's literature as well as new reading programs that looked and sounded far more interesting and relevant than the old department-supplied texts. Colorful "Big Books" were everywhere, all featuring the "3 Rs" of rhyme, rhythm, and repetition. (4)

During this time, there was also an emphasis on connecting reading with writing. Students read both literature and content books to learn about academic content subjects. Student projects involved students in reading the table of contents, graphs, diagrams, and the index, skills that were previously considered *library skills*. Teachers were involved in writing projects so that they could then help their students become writers in writing workshop. Standardized reading tests were criticized, and performance assessments such as miscue analysis, running records, cloze passages, informal reading inventories, and portfolios were widely used.

The early 1990s brought in an age referred to as the *postmodern period*, one of rapid change and diversity. This period brought turmoil to the field of reading. Turbill (2002) describes this period as "The Age of Reading for Social Purpose."

> While in many quarters there was a strong sense of human rights and equity for all in our "global village," there was also a strong backlash toward fundamentalism from the far conservative right. (7)

Critical literacy, literacy that helps readers understand their own history and culture and how they fit into and also shape the social structure, was popular in universities where diversity and reading as meaning making were valued. Advocates of critical literacy saw that literacy education could transform the social distribution of knowledge and give those who were not in power the cultural capital they needed to succeed (McCollum 1999).

The social in sociopsycholinguistics was emphasized at this time. Teachers taught students to read for personal pleasure, for academic enrichment, and to develop a greater awareness of their role in the social structure. As Freire (Freire and Macedo 1987) put it, students were learning to read the word *and* to read the world.

Sociopsycholinguistics in Latin America

In the 1980s publications about literacy in Spanish began to reflect an understanding of the sociopsycholinguistic view. As early as 1984, Dubois began questioning traditional, word-based approaches of teaching reading in favor of taking a psycholinguistic view. In 1989, Goodman's classic *What's Whole in Whole Language* (1986) was translated into Spanish in Venezuela and widely distributed throughout Latin America. The demand for the book was so great that it generated a newer translation into Spanish only six years later (1995).

In Latin America the whole language movement and the sociopsycholinguistic view of literacy coming out of the United States were closely connected to a movement called *constructivismo* (constructivism). While constructivism relates to learning in general, it has been applied to reading specifically. In 1992, Braslavsky, who thirty years earlier had written *La querella de los métodos en la enseñanza de la lectura* (1962), which advocated for a phonics approach to teaching reading, published *La escuela puede* (Schools Can), which promotes constructivism for teaching in general and for reading in particular. She now advises teachers to begin with the child and draw on the strengths and experiences of children to meet their varied needs. In this 1992 publication, Braslavsky described constructivism as a model for literacy that is *"didáctico, holístico, encuadrado en el contexto sociocultural y político"* (didactic, holistic, and framed by the sociocultural and political context) (13). She explained the basic philosophy of constructivism as an approach that builds on both the background of the student and the knowledge of the teacher:

> El alumno es el agente de la construcción del conocimiento, ya que sin su actividad mental no habría elaboración de significados. Pero es el profesor quien conoce en principio los significados que espera compartir y ese conocimiento le permite planificar la enseñaza. (26)

Translation
The student is the agent of the construction of knowledge since without his or her mental activity there would not be a construction of meaning. But it is the teacher who first knows the meanings he or she hopes to share and that knowledge permits him or her to plan his or her teaching.

Porlán (1993), in his study of constructivism and schools, expands on Braslavsky's definition and distinguishes constructivism from other approaches to learning, concluding that

> el proceso de enseñanza-aprendizaje no debe ser un reflejo mecánico de la planificación del profesor ni tampoco un reflejo simplista de la espontaneidad de los alumnos. Desde una nueva perspectiva curricular no simplificadora, debe ser el resultado de integrar de forma natural las intenciones educativas del profesor (expresados como hipótesis sobre el conocimiento escolar deseable) y los intereses reflexionados y organizados de los estudiantes (expresados como problemas a investigar en la clase). (164)

Translation
the process of teaching and learning should not be a mechanical reflection of the teacher's planning nor should it be a simplistic reflection of students' spontaneity. From a new, nonsimplifying curricular perspective, it should be the result of naturally integrating the educational objectives of the teacher (expressed as the hypothesis about the desired scholarly learning) and the reflective and organized interests of the students (expressed as problems to investigate in class).

During this constructivist period, education was looked at more broadly, and social, cultural, and political issues were seen as central to teaching and learning. In addition, educators from all fields began to call for making interdisciplinary connections. During this period, Ferreiro (1994) expanded this understanding by explaining how reading is influenced by and influences all the disciplines:

La alfabetización ha dejado de ser vista como la simple transmisión de una técnica instrumental, realizada en una institución específica (la escuela). La alfabetización ha pasado a ser estudiada por una multitud de disciplinas: la historia, la antropología, la psicolingüística, la lingüística. (5)

Translation
Literacy is no longer seen as the simple transmission of an instrumental technique realized in a specific institution, the school. Literacy is now being studied by a wide variety of disciplines including history, anthropology, psycholinguistics, linguistics.

Ferreiro moved from Argentina to Mexico and began working for the *Secretaría de la Educación Pública* (Secretary of Public Education). Her ideas and the ideas of other constructivist educators changed the kinds of materials used in schools. The first-grade primer, first published in 1993 and in its seventh edition in 2000, was titled *Libro integrado* (Integrated Book) (Chapela Mendoza 2000) and was organized around themes that connect to students' lives, including *"Los niños," "La familia y la casa," "El campo y la ciudad,"* and *"Medimos el tiempo"* ("Children," "Family and the Home," "The Country and the City," and "Let's Measure Time"). The introduction of the book showed the drastic difference this text represented from the former government-approved text, *Mi libro mágico* (My Magic Book), with its practice sheets that required students to repeat syllables and practice penmanship.

La renovación de los libros de texto gratuitos es parte del proyecto general de mejoramiento de la calidad de la enseñanza primaria que desarrolla el gobierno de la República. Para cumplir tal propósito, es necesario contar con materiales de enseñanza actualizados, que correspondan a las necesidades de aprendizaje de los niños y que incorporen las avances del conocimiento educativo. (Chapela Mendoza 2000, iii)

Translation
The renovation of free textbooks is part of the country's government project for the general improvement of the quality of elementary teaching. In order to fulfill this goal, it is necessary to provide up-to-date materials that correspond to the learning needs of children and that incorporate the latest educational knowledge.

Literacy, Society, and Politics

Although whole language was popular in the United States in 1980s, there were many who never understood the sociopsycholinguistic underpinnings of the movement. There were frequent attacks by those who misunderstood the theory or the classroom-based research that supported whole language. They also mistrusted critical theorists who warned that there would be social upheaval. In the United States, the United Kingdom, and Australia, the pendulum was swinging again.

> Toward the end of the 1980's, controversies were rampant. There were cries that students were not being taught spelling, that acceptance of invented spelling was creating a nation of illiterates, that our students were not being taught phonics, that student writing was too personal, and that there was a need for students to be taught the skills of reading and writing (including spelling and grammar) explicitly. (Turbill 2002, 6)

In the United States, the federal government began to take a much more active role in controlling educational methods. The government funded research by the Commission on Reading. Their report, *Becoming a Nation of Readers* (Anderson, Hiebert, et al. 1985), was widely distributed and strongly influenced reading instruction.

The commission included a number of prominent reading researchers, and, according to the foreword, the group reviewed studies in the area of human cognition, environmental influences on reading, and classroom practice. Despite this broad research base, the commission's description of the reading process begins by stating:

> Research on the reading process has provided fuller understanding of how children can learn the letter patterns and associated sounds in an alphabetic language such as English, the importance of fluent word recognition, and how a text's structure influences the meaning drawn from it. (v)

In light of this description of reading, which is consistent with a word recognition view, it is not surprising that one of the commission's recommendations is "That teachers of beginning reading should present well-designed phonics instruction" (118). The report explains, "Phonics is more likely to be useful when children hear the sounds associated with most letters both in isolation and in words, and when they are taught to blend together the sounds of letters to identify words" (118). Even though other recommendations call for devoting more time to comprehension and more time for independent reading, the recommendation that most influenced instruction was the strong call for well-designed phonics instruction. It is no wonder that Ken Goodman described this report as "a dangerous document" (personal communication).

Goodman's words proved prophetic. The end of 1980s brought a swing back toward the 1950s views on education. Madeline Hunter's (1994) curriculum model was especially influential. Her model, based on behaviorist psychology, involves a series of steps that include direct teaching, extensive student practice, testing, and reteaching.

At the end of the 1980s, an education summit in the United States resulted in a second government document that has influenced literacy education strongly, *Goals 2000* (U.S. Congress 1994). This document sets out a series of goals: all children should start school ready to learn, students should demonstrate grade-level competence at specific grades, and every adult should be literate. Even though *Goals 2000* didn't specifically advocate a method for teaching reading, phonics advocates became more vocal and political, claiming that reading scores were declining and students would not demonstrate grade-level competence in reading unless instruction emphasized phonics.

Another document supported by a government agency, the Office of Educational Research and Improvement, made very specific claims for the importance of phonics in beginning reading. The extensive research study was summarized and widely distributed by the Center for Reading, the same government-funded agency that had produced *Becoming a Nation of Readers*. This publication, *Beginning to Read: Thinking and Learning About Print* (Adams 1990) included statements such as "Good readers decode rapidly and automatically. Younger and poor readers rely on context, partly because they do not have efficient knowledge of spelling patterns to rely on instead" (92). Statements such as these provided fuel for the phonics advocates' demands for more phonics.

However, both the full report and the summary contain statements that could be used to support either a word recognition or a sociopsycholinguistic approach to teaching reading. For example, one of the first recommendations is that "approaches in which systematic code instruction is included along with the reading of meaningful connected text result in superior reading achievement overall, for both low-readiness and better prepared students" (125). For some, this means explicit teaching of phonics and reading of stories; for others, it means teaching decoding skills in the context of meaningful reading. The research could be interpreted either way.

Increasingly, political forces have come to determine how reading should be taught. Mandates from the federal and state legislatures in the United States, Australia, and the United Kingdom have shaped reading instruction. In Australia a strong group lobbies for extensive, explicit, and systematic instruction in phonemic awareness and phonics. The group claims that this approach is supported by scientific research (Turbill 2002). In the United States, the National Reading Panel reviewed "scientifically based" research to determine the best methods for teaching reading. In its review, the panel excluded qualitative classroom studies along with miscue studies and recent studies on eye movements, all of which support a sociopsycholinguistic view of reading. In fact, it looked only at studies of the effects of instruction in phonemic awareness, phonics, fluency, vocabulary, and comprehension. The report was strongly criticized (Garan 2002).

The National Reading Panel's report, like the previous reports, was summarized. This document, titled *Put Reading First: The Research Building Blocks for Teaching Children to Read* (Armbruster and Osborn 2001), was distributed to every elementary school in the country and led to government-supported Reading First grants. These grants provide monies for teacher training that emphasizes the direct teaching of phonics, phonemic awareness, and fluency with a minimum of emphasis on vocabulary and reading comprehension. Knowledgeable reading educators are concerned about this narrow view of reading, and they're especially concerned for English language learners who may learn to word call without understanding anything they are reading.

A Recent Latin American Perspective

A similar emphasis on learning to decode words is a source of concern for reading educators in Latin America. In 2004 at the age of ninety, Braslavsky published a new book, *¿Primeras letras o primeras lecturas?* (First Letters or First Readings?), that has received the attention of educators in Argentina and has been advertised by the press as a publication that *"ofrece aquí un nuevo estado del arte de la enseñanza de la lectura y la escritura"* (offers here a new state-of-the-art [publication] on the teaching of reading and writing) (Duer 2004, 1). This book reflects both Braslasky's views on reading and her concerns with the state of teaching reading and writing in Argentina and Latin America. For example, in an interview about her work, she comments:

> Aún se enseña-sobre todo en el interior-a reproducir letras. No se pone el acento en la comprensión. Hay que preparar a los chicos para que entiendan lo que leen, y no para que descifren letras . . . Algunos creen que el problema de la escritura es motriz, y promueven ejercicios con palotes para manejar el lápiz. (2004, 1)

Translation
Even today [reading] is taught, especially in the interior [of the country] by having students repeat letters. There is no emphasis on comprehension. It is important to prepare children to understand what they read and not to decode letters . . . Some believe that the problem with writing is fluency and encourage exercises [where children] practice strokes with the pencil.

Conclusion

This brief historical overview demonstrates that for hundreds of years, reading has been taught as a process of recognizing words. However, in recent years, in both Latin America and the United States, many educators adopted a method of teaching reading based on sociopsycholinguistic principles. Nevertheless, in response to government mandates, in most schools the kind of reading instruction embodied in whole language and constructivism has given way once more to traditional approaches. From a historical perspective, the widespread acceptance of a meaning- and child-centered approach to literacy instruction was short-lived.

Even though the pendulum seems to have swung back toward a part-to-whole approach in which reading is taught as a series of skills for decoding words, knowledgeable teachers and teacher educators are not willing to go back to simplistic views of reading. Turbill (2002) expresses this sentiment well.

> There is so much we know now, there are so many resources that we have access to, that it is often difficult to know where to start with our young emergent readers, writers, and spellers. We certainly know a lot more than the politicians and media . . . Teachers need to be reassured that they are no longer simply doers; we are thinkers and researchers in our classrooms and schools. We are professionals—better trained than ever before. (8)

Part of being a professional is knowing the history of our subject. This chapter has provided a brief overview of that history. In the next chapter we turn to a specific description of methods that have been used to teach reading in Spanish. Many of these methods parallel those used to teach reading in English.

Applications

1. Draw two parallel time lines. On one of the time lines list key events and/or approaches and methods of teaching reading in Spanish. On the other time line, do the same for reading in English. Compare the two time lines. Where are there similarities? Where are there differences?

2. *Becoming a Nation of Readers, Goals 2000,* and the National Reading Panel have had an impact on the teaching of reading in the United States. To evaluate the influence of the three locally, look at reading instruction at your school or interview a local elementary school teacher. What practices reflect the influence of *Becoming a Nation of Readers, Goals 2000,* and the NRP?

3. In Spanish-speaking countries in Central and Latin America, the constructivist approach has had a strong influence on reading practices. What evidence for this is given in the chapter? If you have access to an educator who lives in one of these countries or has recently come to this country, interview him or her about reading instruction in his or her home country. Alternatively, do a search on the Internet about *constructivismo* and be prepared to share what you find.

4. What materials and programs are used to teach reading in English at your school? In Spanish? What view of reading do these materials reflect? Be prepared to defend your conclusion.

5. The chapter opens with the French saying, "The more things change, the more they stay the same." How does the history of reading instruction in Spanish and in English reflect this saying?

Methods of Teaching Reading in Spanish

Muchos de quienes aprendimos a leer y a escribir con métodos mecánicos y rígidos, recordamos ahora el deletreo difícil, "la tonada" que aprendimos paralelamente al conocimiento del signo gráfico y rememoramos los castigos que se nos imponían para dar validez al refrán de que la letra con sangre entra.

Antonio Barbosa Heldt, *Como han aprendido a leer y a escribir los mexicanos*

Translation
Many of us who learned to read and write with mechanical and controlled methods, remember the difficult spelling, the "sing-song tune" that we learned at the same time as we learned the graphic symbols. And we remember the punishment that teachers imposed upon us to give validity to the saying that learning to read enters only with blood[shed].

The above quote seems an appropriate one for opening a chapter on methods of teaching reading in Spanish and in English. Certainly, we do not want our students to suffer through reading instruction based on the philosophy of *"la letra con sangre entra."* Some teachers have moved away from methods that are *"mecánicos y rígidos."* Nevertheless, in many schools teachers follow scripted lessons from prescriptive teacher's guides that require students to complete many different exercises and worksheets to build decoding skills.

To help teachers evaluate their teaching, we discuss the traditional methods that have been used and, in many cases, are still being used to teach Spanish reading. First we describe each method. Then we present a scenario of an actual lesson using the method and analyze it with the checklist of effective reading instruction. We also draw parallels between methods used to teach reading in Spanish and those used for English.

 ## Methods of Teaching Reading in Spanish

The methods used to teach reading in Spanish can be divided into two general categories: synthetic and analytic. Synthetic methods go from the parts, usually sounds, letters, or syllables, to wholes. In most cases, the whole is a word, though it could be a sentence. Students first learn the parts and then synthesize or combine them into wholes. Pacheco (1992) summarizes this approach:

> Sintéticos, los que parten de unidades menores o fonemas, letras, sílabas, y palabras, para llegar a la frase. También incluye la categoría de los métodos alfabéticos, silábicos y psiconfonéticos, lo que define técnicas variadas para la enseñanza de la lecto-escritura. (19)

Translation
Synthetic [methods are] those that start from the smallest units or phonemes, letters, syllables, and words, in order to get to the sentence. Included in this category are the alphabetic, syllabic, and phonetic methods, which lay out different techniques for the teaching of literacy.

A second group of methods, those that are analytic, go in the opposite direction, from whole to part. However, the wholes that these analytic methods begin with are usually no bigger than words or, at most, sentences. Students might start with a whole word and then analyze or break it down into component parts. Pacheco (1992) summarizes the analytic methods in the following way:

Analíticos o los que parten de la palabra, para llegar por descomposición o segmentación hasta las unidades menores llamadas fonemas. Dentro de ellos se ubica el método global y el léxico. (19)

Translation
Analytic [methods] or those that start from the word to get to the smallest units, called phonemes, by breaking the word down or segmenting. Among these one finds the global and lexical methods.

Even though these two groups of methods seem to be opposite, they really are more alike than they are different because both methods come from a word recognition view of reading. Synthetic methods often build up to recognizing words, and analytic methods begin with words and break them into parts (Dubois 1995; Freeman, Goodman, et al. 1995; Rodríguez 1995; Sequeida and Seymour 1995; Solé i Gallart 1995).

 ## *Métodos sintéticos* (Synthetic Methods)

Synthetic methods begin with different elements—letters, syllables, or words—and then combine the elements to form short texts, usually single sentences. Although the synthetic methods use different starting points, they all have in common the belief that reading is learned by starting with the parts and then moving toward the sentence, which is considered the whole.

El método alfabético *(The Alphabetic Method)*

This method begins with the teaching of the names of the letters. In its purest form, students begin by learning the names of the letters that represent vowel sounds. Then they learn the names of letters that represent consonant sounds. Next, they learn to combine the consonants with vowels to create syllables and then words. Students are asked to repeat the spelling of the syllables or words and then pronounce them. This procedure is repeated for the many different words students are given to learn to read. The *Silabario de San Miguel* is the classic version of this method. The following scenario shows part of a reading lesson in which the teacher follows the alphabetic method. In this lesson, the teacher has moved to the level of having students work with whole words rather than single letters or syllables.

Scenario for *el método alfabético* (Scenario for the Alphabetic Method)

La maestra escribe tres palabras en el pizarrón, *mamá*, *mano*, y *ama*. Después empieza la lección.

MAESTRA: Buenos días, niños.
NIÑOS: Buenos días, maestra.
MAESTRA: Hoy vamos a aprender a leer las palabras escritas en el pizarrón. Las voy a leer: "mamá," "mano," "ama."
    Repitan mientras yo señalo las letras con mi dedo:
    "Eme" "a" "eme" "a"—"mamá."
NIÑOS: "Eme" "a" "eme" "a"—"mamá."
MAESTRA: Muy bien. Ahora, seguimos con la segunda palabra:
    "Eme" "a" "ene" "o"—"mano." Repitan.
NIÑOS: "Eme" "a" "ene" "o"—"mano."
MAESTRA: Muy bien. Ahora, seguimos con la tercera palabra:
    "A" "eme" "a"—"ama." Repitan, por favor.
NIÑOS: "A" "eme" "a"—"ama."

Los niños siguen repitiendo las letras y pronunciando las palabras después de la maestro.

The teacher writes three words on the blackboard, *mamá* (mother), *mano* (hand), and *ama* (loves). Then she begins the lesson.

TEACHER: Good morning, children.
CHILDREN: Good morning, Teacher.
TEACHER: Today we are going to learn to read the words written on the chalkboard. I am going to read them: "mamá," "mano," "ama."
    Repeat while I point to the letters with my finger:
    "M" "a" "m" "a"—"mamá."
CHILDREN: "M" "a" "m" "a"—"mamá."
TEACHER: Very good. Now, let's continue to the second word:
    "M" "a" "n" "o"—"mano." Repeat.
CHILDREN: "M" "a" "n" "o"—"mano."
TEACHER: Very good. Now, let's go on to the third word:
    "A" "m" "a"—"ama." Repeat, please.
CHILDREN: "A" "m" "a"—"ama."

The students continue repeating the letters and pronouncing the words after the teacher.

Analysis of *el método alfabético* ◆ Using the checklist for effective reading instruction (repeated here as Figure 5–1), it appears that the answer to all the questions on the checklist is no. There is no attempt to help the children value themselves as readers or to value reading. The teacher reads only words to the students, not complete stories. The only reading materials available to the students are the words the teacher has written on the blackboard, and students are given no choice of what they read. The students are not making meaning as they repeat letters and words after the teacher because there is no connected text.

This method uses only the graphophonic system. Students can't access the syntactic or semantic systems since they read only isolated words. While it might be argued that each child has a *mamá* and a *mano* and that the child does love, *ama*, the teacher chose the words based on their letters and makes no real attempt

1. Do students value themselves as readers, and do they value reading?

2. Do teachers read frequently to students from a variety of genres?

3. Do students have a wide variety of reading materials to choose from and time to read?

4. Do students make good choices of books to read?

5. Do students regard reading as meaning making at all times?

6. Do students make a balanced use of all three cueing systems?

7. Are students provided with appropriate strategy lessons if they experience difficulties in their reading?

8. Do students have opportunities to talk and write about what they have read, making connections between the reading and their own experiences?

FIGURE 5–1. Checklist for Effective Reading Instruction

to relate the words to the students' lives. All students do is repeat the words, and this is not likely to spark their imagination nor help them make any connections to other topics or areas of study. After this kind of reading lesson, children have no reason to talk or write about what they have read.

Even other traditional reading educators saw how this method was senseless. Heldt (1971) pointed out that spelling a word like *hijo*, for example, caused serious problems:

> El niño lee y pronuncia por ejemplo: "hache," "i," "jota," "o," y se le pide el milagro, que al reunir todo eso pronuncia *hijo*, y pobre de él si sale o resulta con un *hacheijotao*. (22)

Translation
The child reads and pronounces, for example, "h," "i," "j," "o," and one asks of him the miracle of uniting all that to pronounce *hijo*, and poor child if out comes *aitch-eye-jay-o (h-i-j-o)*.

Although English doesn't have a method that parallels the complete alphabetic method, elements of this method are present in many classrooms today. Teachers begin with the names of alphabet letters. However, there are several differences. Usually, instruction in English begins with consonants instead of vowels. Further, consonants and vowels are not combined into syllables. Another difference is that in English letters can represent more different sounds than letters in Spanish, so more time is spent in English instruction on teaching the children the sounds associated with the letters.

El método onomatopéyico *(The Onomatopoeic Method)*

Onomatopoeia refers to words whose sounds mimic sounds in nature. In English, examples would include *hiss* and *buzz* and in Spanish, words like *zas* and *cataplán*. In the onomatopoeic method, reading instruction begins with words like these. For example, the Spanish vowel sound for *i* might be taught in connection with the squeal of an animal like a pig, a monkey, or a mouse, and the sound for *a* might be taught in connection with people laughing. Onomatopoeic words are used to teach students the sounds different letters make.

Scenario for *el método onomatopéyico*

La maestra enseña a los estudiantes un dibujo de unos monos dentro de una jaula. Los monos están jugando y haciendo los sonidos *hi, hi, hi*. También en el dibujo hay unos niños parados alrededor de la jaula. Ellos están riéndose y diciendo, *ja, ja, ja*.

MAESTRA: ¿Qué ven en este dibujo?

NIÑO: Una jaula con monos.
MAESTRA: ¿Qué más?
NIÑA: Hay gente mirando a los monos jugar.
MAESTRA: ¿Qué está haciendo la gente?
NIÑO: Todos están riéndose.
MAESTRA: ¿Qué sonido hacen las personas allí?
NIÑO: ¡Ja! ¡Ja! ¡Ja!
MAESTRA: ¿Y qué sonido hacen los monos?
NIÑA: Hi, hi, hi.
MAESTRA: Muy bien. El sonido que hacen los monos es el sonido de la letra *i*: hi, hi, hi. ¿Qué sonido hace la gente?

NIÑOS: ¡Ja! ¡Ja! ¡Ja!
MAESTRA: Sí. Este es el sonido de la letra *a*: ¡ja! ¡ja! ¡ja!

The teacher shows the students a picture of some monkeys in a cage. The monkeys are playing and making sounds *he, he, he*. Also in the picture there are some children standing around the cage. They are laughing and saying, *ha, ha, ha*.

TEACHER: What do you see in this picture?
BOY: A cage with monkeys.
TEACHER: What else?
GIRL: There are people watching the monkeys playing.
TEACHER: What are the people doing?
BOY: Everyone's laughing.
TEACHER: What sound are the people there making?
BOY: Ha! Ha! Ha!
TEACHER: And what sound are the monkeys making?
GIRL: He, he, he.
TEACHER: Very good. The sound the monkeys are making is the sound of the letter *i* [in Spanish]: e, e, e. What sound do the people make?
CHILDREN: Ha! Ha! Ha!
TEACHER: Yes. This is the sound of the letter *a*: ha, ha, ha!

Analysis of *el método onomatopéyico* ◆ This is an interesting lesson to analyze with the checklist because the only text the students see appears in cartoon bubbles and represents the sounds made by monkeys and people. The students are using only the graphophonic cueing system because there is no linguistic context to provide syntactic or semantic cues. Students are asked to make connections and predictions using their background knowledge of the sounds people and monkeys make as they identify the words in the picture. Students might be interested in the picture. However, since the students really have no text to read and are only identifying sounds that might later be found in other words, one could not say they are reading for meaning.

Children love to play with the sounds of language. As they learn to read, they make connections between patterns of sounds and patterns of spelling. The onomatopoeic method capitalizes on children's interest in language play. However, the method takes natural sounds out of context and uses them as building blocks to help students learn the sounds letters make so that they can eventually identify words. The method is quite limited. It is hard to find words to represent some sounds. Teachers can draw on children's interest in sounds by finding rhymes and songs that contain onomatopoeia. Children's interest in sounds is part of a love of reading but not the key for learning to read. It is possible to find examples of lessons in Spanish reading textbooks, such as the lesson shown here, but no parallel method is evident in the teaching of reading in English. However, as we will describe in the following chapter, books in Spanish and in English draw on sounds in nature, including animal sounds, and those books can be used effectively to support children's early reading.

El método fónico o fonético (The Phonics or Phonetic Method)

Like the onomatopoeic method, the phonics method focuses on the sounds that letters make. In this method, the students first learn the names of the letters of the alphabet. Then they identify the sounds of letters and put those sounds together to make syllables and then words. Generally, in Spanish this method has been used to teach the vowels only. Then, once the vowels are learned, the syllabic method is used to teach syllables and words.

Generally, students begin to learn the sounds of the letters by identifying objects that have those sounds, usually beginning with the initial sounds. A common worksheet for the phonics method would provide a series of pictures and ask students to circle the pictures that begin with the sound of the letter being studied. The following short scenario is an example.

Scenario for *el método fónico o fonético*

MAESTRA: Niños, recuerdan que estamos estudiando los sonidos de las vocals. ¿Cuáles son las cinco vocals?

NIÑOS: A, e, i, o, u.

MAESTRA: Sí. Voy a enseñarles unos dibujos. Algunos de estos dibujos comienzan con el sonido de la *a*. Algunos no. Ustedes me van a decir cuales comienzan con la *a*.

[La maestra coloca dibujos de un astronauta, un avión, pintura azul, y un pájaro en la pared.]

MAESTRA: ¿Quién me puede decir cuáles comenzan con el sonido de la *a*?

MAYA: Veo un avión. *Avión* empieza con el sonido *a*.

MAESTRA: Sí, Maya. Tienes razón. *Avión* empieza con el sonido *a*. ¿Hay otras palabras que comienzan con este sonido?

FELIPE: Veo el dibujo del astronauta y pintura azul. Estos empiezan con el sonido *a* también.

MAESTRA: Bien. Y ¿el otro dibujo? ¿Comienza con el sonido de la *a*?

NIÑOS: No, maestra.

MAESTRA: ¿Qué es?

NIÑOS: Es un pájaro.

MAESTRA: Muy bien. *Pájaro* no comienza con el sonido *a*. Ahora, tengo una página de práctica para todos ustedes. En la página hay varios dibujos. Ustedes van a encerrar con círculo cada dibujo que comienza con el sonido *a*.

TEACHER: Children, remember that we are studying the sounds of the vowels. Which are the five vowels?

CHILDREN: *A, e, i, o, u.*

TEACHER: Yes. I'm going to show you some pictures. Some of the pictures begin with the sound of *a*. Some don't. You are going to tell me which begin with an *a*.

[The teacher then puts pictures of an astronaut (*astronauta*), an airplane (*avión*), a blotch of blue paint (*azul*), and a bird (*pájaro*) on the wall.]

TEACHER: Who can tell me which ones begin with the letter *a*.

MAYA: I see an airplane. *Airplane* begins with an *a*?

TEACHER: Yes, Maya. You're right. *Airplane* begins with the sound of *a*. Are there are other words that begin with this sound?

FELIPE: I see the picture of the astronaut and blue paint. Those begin with the sound of *a* too.

TEACHER: Good. And the other picture? Does it begin with the letter *a*?

CHILDREN: No, Teacher.

TEACHER: What is it?

CHILDREN: It's a bird [*pájaro*].

TEACHER: Very good. *Bird* doesn't begin with the sound of *a*. Now, I have a practice sheet for all of you. On the sheet there are several drawings. You are going to circle the pictures that begin with the sound of *a*.

Analysis of *el método fónico o fonético* ◆ Again, in this lesson, the text consists only of isolated words that begin with *a*. Consequently, students cannot construct meaning through the use of the three cueing systems. Students are focused on the graphophonic system because they are asked to identify pictures and match the beginning sounds of the pictures with a letter. At this stage, they have not even reached the level of word recognition. No attempt is made to connect the lesson with the students' background experiences. While the pictures used may be attractive and colorful, the method does not involve students in reading a text.

The goal of the phonics method is to help beginning readers use initial sounds to identify words. Sounds provide important cues for readers, but like the onomatopoeic method, this method is limited. In Spanish the phonetic method has been used only as a bridge to the syllabic method. In English, on the other hand, the phonics method is commonly used. Students learn "*a* is for apple" and "*b* is for banana." Once students learn the sounds that letters make, they blend the sounds to pronounce whole words.

El método silábico *(The Syllabic Method)*

The syllabic method is by far the most widely used method to teach beginning Spanish reading. This method moves beyond the individual letter sounds and uses the syllable as the basic unit. As syllables are introduced and learned, they are combined to form words and sentences. Many teachers of Spanish reading prefer this method to the phonics method because consonants can be pronounced only in combination with vowels. Also, Spanish speakers point out that Spanish is a naturally syllabic language. Most words can easily be broken up into syllables of a consonant and a vowel.

In the syllabic method, the sounds of the five vowels are usually taught first. Then vowels are combined with consonants to form syllables. Words are learned by putting the syllables together. Many texts for beginning readers start by combining *m* with all five vowels. Students repeat *ma, me, mi, mo, mu*. These syllables are then used to form words, such as *mamá* (mother), *mimo* (pamper), *Memo* (Memo, a nickname), and *mami* (Mommy). Next, these words are used to form sentences: *Mi mamá me mima. Mi mamá me ama. Amo a mi mamá.* (My mother pampers me. My mother loves me. I love my mother.) During the course of the lesson the students repeat syllables, words, and basic sentences.

The syllabic method is taught sequentially. Each lesson builds on the one before by adding a new consonant. For example, in the second lesson there would be words with both *m* and *s*, so students would read sentences like *Mamá ama a Susú* (Mother loves Susu).

Scenario for *el método silábico* ◆ In earlier lessons, the students have already been taught the syllables *ma, me, mi, mo, mu*, and *sa, se, si, so, su*. For this lesson the students are learning the syllables with the letter *p*. The children have their books open to the page that is introducing *p*. There is a picture of a father with his son. The word *papá* is written next to the drawing. Under it on the page are written the syllables *pa, po, pu, pe, pi,* and words and sentences. On the opposite page is a picture of a map, a father, a cat, a dish of soapsuds (foam), and a box of raisins. Under each picture are lines so students can write the words that go with the drawing.

La maestra empieza la lección:	The teacher begins the lesson:
MAESTRA: Lean conmigo. *Papá.*	TEACHER: Read with me. *Father.*
NIÑOS: *Papá.*	CHILDREN: *Father.*
MAESTRA: Repitan: *pa, po, pu, pe, pi.*	TEACHER: Repeat: *pa, po, pu, pe, pi.*
NIÑOS: *Pa, po, pu, pe, pi.*	CHILDREN: *Pa, po, pu, pe, pi.*
MAESTRA: *Papá.*	TEACHER: *Father.*
NIÑOS: *Papá.*	CHILDREN: *Father.*
MAESTRA: *Pesa.*	TEACHER: *Weighs.*
NIÑOS: *Pesa.*	CHILDREN: *Weighs.*
MAESTRA: *Mapa.*	TEACHER: *Map.*
NIÑOS: *Mapa.*	CHILDREN: *Map.*
MAESTRA: *Pipa.*	TEACHER: *Pipe.*
NIÑOS: *Pipa.*	CHILDREN: *Pipe.*
MAESTRA: *Pasas.*	TEACHER: *Raisins.*
NIÑOS: *Pasas.*	CHILDREN: *Raisins.*
MAESTRA: *Espuma.*	TEACHER: *Foam.*
NIÑOS: *Espuma.*	CHILDREN: *Foam.*
MAESTRA: *Pepe.*	CHILDREN: *Pepe.*
NIÑOS: *Pepe.*	CHILDREN: *Pepe.*
MAESTRA: *Pisa.*	TEACHER: *Steps* [on].
NIÑOS: *Pisa.*	CHILDREN: *Steps* [on].
MAESTRA: Pepe es mi papá.	TEACHER: Pepe is my father.
NIÑOS: Pepe es mi papá.	CHILDREN: Pepe is my father.
MAESTRA: Papá ama a mi mamá.	TEACHER: Father loves my mother.
NIÑOS: Papá ama a mi mamá.	CHILDREN: Father loves my mother.
MAESTRA: Memo usa ese mapa.	TEACHER: Memo uses that map.
NIÑOS: Memo usa ese mapa.	CHILDREN: Memo uses that map.
MAESTRA: Ema pesa esas pasas.	TEACHER: Ema weighs those raisins.
NIÑOS: Ema pesa esas pasas.	CHILDREN: Ema weighs those raisins.
MAESTRA: Susú pisa esa espuma.	TEACHER: Susú steps on that foam.
NIÑOS: Susú pisa esa espuma.	CHILDREN: Susú steps on that foam.
MAESTRA: Ahora, en la otra página van a escribir debajo de cada dibujo el nombre que le corresponde. [Señalando los dibujos] ¿Qué van a escribir debajo de los dibujos?	TEACHER: Now, on the next page, under each picture, you are going to write the name of the picture. [Pointing to the pictures] What are you going to write under the pictures?
NIÑOS: *Mapa, papá, gato, espuma, pasas.*	CHILDREN: *Map, father, cat, foam, raisins.*

MAESTRA: Está bien, pero uds todavía no han visto las sílabas para la palabra *gato*. ¿Recuerdan el nombre del gato en la última lección?
NIÑO: ¿Susú?
MAESTRA: Sí, Juan, Susú. Entonces, deben escribir la palabra *Susú* debajo del gato y no la palabra *gato*.

TEACHER: OK, but you haven't studied the syllables for the word *cat* yet. Do you remember the name of the cat in the last lesson?
CHILD: Susú?
TEACHER: Yes, Juan, Susú. Then, you should write the word *Susú* under the cat and not the word *cat*.

Analysis of *el método silábico* ◆ When analyzing the syllabic method with the checklist for effective reading instruction, it does not appear that there is an attempt to help students value reading since what they read is limited to individual sentences. Teachers do not read complete stories to students and students do not choose what they read. In fact, after practicing pronouncing the sounds, they do exercises with isolated words. The sentences are meaningful, but they are not connected, and the focus is on individual words. The lessons are designed to help develop the graphophonic cueing system but do not tap into syntax or semantics. For the most part, the sentences consist of words that reflect everyday experiences a child might have. However, the words and sentences are presented in isolation with no real connection to one another, making prediction difficult. The exercise following the presentation of the vocabulary and basic sentences is merely a labeling exercise and could hardly be called either authentic writing or a true strategy lesson that supports reading. Students do not discuss what they read.

The lesson was not really interesting or imaginative. Sometimes Spanish basal reading programs have attempted to make lessons more imaginative and visually attractive to students despite the extreme limitations of the controlled vocabulary. For example, for the syllables with *m*, one series presents a short story about Manolo watching a *mono* (monkey) do funny tricks on television. Still, these stories are hardly predictable and the language is far from natural.

Pellicer (1969) discusses the pros and cons of the syllabic method, pointing out that it is good because it presents the language in a logical order; it requires very little in the way of materials; and teachers report they are satisfied with the method for both children and adults. However, he explains that the method depends too much on the student's memory in the first stages; the student can lose interest if meaningful words are not introduced early; there is the danger of a sort of mechanical learning, especially if the material is difficult or taught too quickly; and the method is not consistent with child psychology.

An additional problem with the syllabic method is that it often results in students' being able to pronounce words or sentences without attending to meaning. As a result, students often become word callers. They may appear to be good oral readers, but they are not developing comprehension. English has no method similar to the Spanish syllabic method because in English words don't easily divide into syllables with consonant/vowel, and each English vowel has more than one sound.

The methods described so far are all considered synthetic because readers are presented with letters, syllables, or words and asked to combine them to create larger units. These traditional methods of teaching reading in Spanish have as their goal the recognition of words. In most cases, students are working with parts of words, words, or individual sentences rather than with connected text. The textbooks present reading exercises rather than engage students in authentic reading experiences. None of the synthetic methods we have described meets the criteria for effective reading practices as outlined in the checklist. Next, we turn to analytic methods.

Métodos analíticos (Analytic Methods)

The methods in this section are considered analytic because they begin with some whole and then move to parts within the whole. Analytic methods may at first appear to be more consistent with a sociopsycholinguistic approach to reading than synthetic methods. As we explain, however, analytic methods do not represent effective practice because the goal is still word recognition. In analytic methods students seldom engage with connected text longer than a sentence, and our claim is that students need to engage with complete texts to develop the strategies they need to become proficient readers. As we did with the synthetic methods, we start with a short description of each analytic method, present a sample lesson scenario, and analyze the lesson using the checklist. We also consider parallels with English teaching methods.

El método global o ideovisual *(The Global or Visual Concept Method)*

In the early 1900s Decroly and Degand suggested the global method of teaching, explaining that reading *"no tiene relación alguna con el sentido del oído que, por el contrario, es una función puramente visual"* (does not have anything to do with the sense of hearing, and, on the contrary is a purely visual act) (Braslavsky 1962, 71). In addition, Decroly believed that people read ideas and not graphic symbols and that those ideas were related to something beyond the symbols themselves. Thus, the global method was also called at times the ideovisual method. Decroly believed that children need sensorimotor, intellectual, and affective preparation before they begin to read. He stressed the idea that children are at different stages of maturity at age six, when most reading instruction is begun, and for that reason, reading should be individualized. His entire ideovisual approach stresses readiness to read.

Hendrix (1952) wrote enthusiastically about the global method, explaining how the students he taught found this method so much more interesting than the synthetic methods that were normally used:

> En el transcurso de mi enseñanza de la lectura mediante el método global, siempre me llamó la atención el interés que suscitaba en mis alumnos y, me atrevo decirlo, en todos mis alumnus. (2)

> **Translation**
> In the course of my teaching of reading using the global method, I was always impressed by the interest that it provoked in my students, and I dare to say it, in all my students.

Hendrix explains that the global method does not ignore analysis of the parts, and he describes the stages of learning following this method as moving from the sentence to the word to the syllable. However, those who believed strongly in a synthetic approach to reading critiqued this system because students fail to acquire "a system for unlocking unfamiliar words beyond visual clues and visual patterns" (Thonis 1976, 31).

Moreno (1982), drawing on Braslavksy (1962), summarized four basic principles of the global or visual concept method:

1. Conceptualization is global. Thought is constructed not from part to whole, but beginning with chunks. Children get concepts *"en bloque sin análisis previo"* (in a block without previous analysis) (74).

2. Reading is a purely visual process. Reading has nothing to do with sounds, but instead is purely visual. The visual images are understood by the brain as wholes.

3. Reading is ideovisual, which implies a reading of ideas, not of symbols.

4. The global method is a natural method. The acquisition of reading is natural, just like the acquisition of spoken language is natural in a child.

With the global method, students are taught to read and write either whole words or complete sentences. Some Spanish literacy experts have been concerned that global lessons never have students analyze the parts (Thonis 1976). However, students often do get many readiness-for-reading activities before they are ever given texts to read. Eventually, students are involved in an activity in which they talk about a picture. The teacher writes down what the children say, and then they read it together. We describe both the readiness activities and the lesson for this version of the global method.

Scenario for *el método global o ideovisual*

Los estudiantes están viendo sus cuadernos de ejercicios (Figura 5–2) mientras la maestra les da direcciones para hacer los ejercicios que son para desarrollar habilidades para la lectura.

MAESTRA: Abran sus libros en la página veinte. Miren la página. Noten que hay varios dibujos que son iguales o casi iguales. En cada fila hay un dibujo que es un poco diferente a los demás. Encierren con un círculo alrededor del dibujo que ustedes crean que es diferente. Vamos a hacer el número uno juntos. ¿Qué ven ustedes en el número uno?

NIÑO: Veo cuatro ositos.
MAESTRA: Bien. ¿Son todos iguales?
NIÑA: No, uno es diferente.
MAESTRA: Muy bien. Encierren con un círculo el osito que es diferente. Ahora ustedes pueden continuar con las casas en el segundo ejemplo haciendo el resto del ejercicio.

The students are looking at their exercise books (Figure 5–2) while the teacher gives them directions about how to do the exercises, which are meant to develop skills for reading.

TEACHER: Open your books to page 20. Look at the page. Notice that there are several pictures that are the same or almost the same. In each row there is one picture that is a little different from the others. Draw a circle around the picture that you think is different. We are going to do number one together. What do you see in number one?
BOY: I see four teddy bears.
TEACHER: OK. Are they all the same?
GIRL: No, one is different.
TEACHER: Very good. Draw a circle around the bear that is different. Now you can continue with the houses in the second example and do the rest of the exercise.

FIGURE 5–2. Reading-Readiness Activity (Four Bears and Four Houses)

Después de terminar este ejercicio, la maestra les da a los niños las direcciones para la próxima página. En esta página hay dibujos de dos regalos de diferentes formas, dos niños con cajas de diferentes formas y dos palabras escritas *papá y lima* (ver Figura 5–3).

MAESTRA: Ahora vean la página veintiuno. ¿Qué están haciendo los niños en el número dos de esta página?
JUAN: Están cargando unas cajas.
MAESTRA: ¿Qué ven en el dibujo del número tres?
FRANCISCA: Veo una niña cargando una caja.
MAESTRA: ¿Hay algo dentro de la caja?

MAGDALENA: Sí, hay una palabra dentro de la caja.
MAESTRA: Muy bien. ¿Cabe bien la palabra dentro de la caja?
NIÑOS: Sí.
MAESTRA: Ahora, en el último dibujo, hay unas cajas vacías y unas palabras. Dibujen una línea desde la palabra hasta la caja donde ustedes piensan que cabe la palabra.

After finishing this exercise, the teacher gives the students directions for the next page. On this page there are drawings of two gifts of different shapes, two children with boxes of different shapes, and two written words, *papá* (father) and *lima* (lemon) (see Figure 5–3).

TEACHER: Now look at page 21. What are the children doing in number two on this page?
JUAN: They are holding some boxes.
TEACHER: What do you see in the drawing of number three?
FRANCISCA: I see a little girl holding a box.
TEACHER: Is there something inside the box?
MAGDALENA: Yes, there is a word inside the box.
TEACHER: Very good. Does the word fit inside the box?
CHILDREN: Yes.
TEACHER: Now, in the last picture, there are some empty boxes and some words. Draw a line from the word to the box where you think the word fits.

FIGURE 5–3. Reading-Readiness Activity (Boxes)

Ahora la maestra les enseña a los niños un dibujo de un niño en un salón de clase pintando un dibujo.

MAESTRA: Ahora vamos a escribir un cuento juntos sobre este dibujo. Ustedes me van a decir el cuento y yo voy a escribir lo que ustedes me dicen. ¿Quién quiere empezar?

ROBERTO: Yo, maestra. Yo sé lo que debemos escribir.

MAESTRA: Está bien, Roberto. ¿Qué debo escribir?

ROBERTO: El niño está pintando en la escuela.

MAESTRA [Al escribir]: "El niño está pintando en la escuela." Bien. Ahora, ¿Qué más?

ANA: El niño está pintando un árbol y un sol.

MAESTRA: OK, Ana. [Al escribir] ¿Algo más para nuestro cuento?

ALBERTO: Su camisa está sucia. Tiene pintura.

MAESTRA: Bien, Alberto. [Ella escribe y lee en voz alta.] "Su camisa está sucia. Tiene pintura." Ahora tenemos un cuento. Lean conmigo mientras yo señalo las palabras con mi dedo.

NIÑOS Y MAESTRA: "El niño está pintando en la escuela.

   "El niño está pintando un árbol y un sol.

   "Su camisa está sucia. Tiene pintura."

MAESTRA: Muy bien. ¿Quién quiere señalar las palabras mientras leemos otra vez?

FAUSTO: Yo, maestra, yo.

MAESTRA: Está bien, Fausto, ven acá. Ahora vamos a leer mientras Fausto nos señala las palabras.

NIÑOS: "El niño está pintando en la escuela.

   "El niño está pintando un árbol y un sol.

Now the teacher shows the students a picture of a boy in a classroom painting a picture.

TEACHER: Now we are going to write a story together about this picture. You are going to tell me the story and I am going to write what you tell me. Who wants to start?

ROBERTO: I do, Teacher. I know what we should write.

TEACHER: OK, Roberto. What should I write?

ROBERTO: The boy is painting at school.

Teacher [While writing]: "The boy is painting at school." Good. Now, what else?

ANA: The boy is painting a tree and a sun.

TEACHER: OK, Ana. [While writing] Something else for our story?

ALBERTO: His shirt is dirty. It has paint on it.

TEACHER: Good, Alberto. [She writes and then reads aloud.] "His shirt is dirty. It has paint on it." Now we have a story. Read with me while I point to the words with my finger.

CHILDREN AND TEACHER: "The boy is painting at school.

   "The boy is painting a tree and a sun.

   "His shirt is dirty. It has paint on it."

TEACHER: Very good. Who wants to point to the words while we read again?

FAUSTO: I do, Teacher, I do.

TEACHER: OK, Fausto, come here. Now, we are going to read while Fausto shows us the words.

CHILDREN: "The boy is painting at school.

   "The boy is painting a tree and a sun.

"Su camisa está sucia. Tiene pintura."
MAESTRA: Muy bien. ¿Quién quiere leer solo?
JORGE: Yo, maestra.
MAESTRA: OK, Jorge. Tú puedes leer mientras Fausto señala las palabras con su dedo.

"His shirt is dirty. It has paint on it."
TEACHER: Very good. Who wants to read alone?
JORGE: I do, Teacher.
TEACHER: OK, Jorge. You can read while Fausto points to the words with his finger.

Analysis of *el método global o ideovisual* ◆ This lesson really has two distinct parts. In the first part, students are focused on reading-readiness activities that are intended to check how children visualize wholes. Some early reading experts believed that students beginning to read were at different stages of maturity and that reading-readiness materials could help teachers determine if their students were indeed ready for reading. First, the students are asked to pick out the picture that is different from a series of pictures. Then they are asked to match words to boxes that represent the shapes of those words. Many approaches to teaching reading in English include similar readiness activities. The assumption is that students need to be trained to notice small differences so that they can apply that skill to noticing differences between letters or words.

Both of the readiness activities tie into the first two principles Moreno listed for the global or visual concept method. The two exercises reflect both that conceptualization is global and that reading is a purely visual process, unrelated to the sounds of language. Although readiness activities fit the principles of this method, they do not fit with a sociopsycholinguistic view of reading, and they do not appear on the checklist for effective reading instruction. Teachers who take a sociopsycholinguistic view of reading do not believe that preparation for reading should include exercises in visual discrimination. From a sociopsycholinguistic perspective, reading readiness involves exposure to meaningful print, not practice in picking out the picture that is different.

The second part of the lesson, the language experience activity, reflects the second two principles of the method: reading is ideovisual, that is, it is the reading of ideas, and it is a natural method. The teacher has the students discuss the drawing of the child painting a picture. Then the picture is used as the basis for a story the children dictate to the teacher and then read with the teacher's help.

Language experience is certainly a valid way for emergent readers to begin to construct meaning from text. When children dictate the text, it has meaning for them. The text of a language experience story is usually interesting, predictable, and reflective of students' background interests and experiences. The language experience approach fits several items on the checklist for effective reading instruction. Students do value themselves as readers when they read stories they have helped construct. Reading is always presented as meaning making. As students suggest letters and words for the teacher to write, the teacher can help students develop the three cueing systems. Students also talk about what they are writing and reading, especially if the story draws directly on their personal experiences. The lesson presented here did not do that, since the teacher simply showed students a picture and asked them to describe it instead of having them paint their own picture and then discuss what they did and write about the activity.

However, language experience was not conceptualized as the entire reading curriculum. Students also need to be exposed to a rich variety of children's books with colorful illustrations if they are to develop an interest in reading. Evaluation of the global method with the checklist would show that teachers do not read to students from a variety of materials, and students do not choose materials and read on their own. They are not given strategy lessons. Even though the language experience aspect of the global method comes closer to reflecting a sociopsycholinguistic view of reading than the other methods we have described, the complete method has limitations.

Methods of teaching reading in English often include language experience, a technique that Allen (1976) wrote about extensively. He described how teachers could use many different activities, such as art, cooking, and games, as a basis for a language experience activity. Most preschool and kindergarten teachers include language experience. In bilingual and dual language classes, the morning message and daily news routines that often start the day are good examples of language experience. An excellent resource on this topic for teachers is *Getting the Most Out of Morning Message and Other Shared Writing* (daCruz-Payne and Browning-Schulman 1998).

El método léxico *(The Lexical Method)*

According to Moreno (1982), the lexical method was developed over two hundred years ago in Germany. It included a series of steps:

1. Present the object or a picture of the word that is to be taught.

2. Say the name of the word.

3. Write and read the word.

4. Divide the word into syllables and letters.

5. Form new words with the now-known elements of the original word. (83)

The idea behind this method is that every word has its own form and is remembered individually by the reader. The goal of this method is to make the reading of individual words automatic. More recently, teachers have used just the first three steps and omitted the last two. In the whole-word method, flash cards are often used to introduce the words. The words are then put into sentences to provide some context and are repeated by the emergent reader. Once the words are learned, they can be used to construct new sentences.

Scenario for *el método léxico*

La maestra y los niños van a leer tres oraciones escritas en el pizarrón que tratan de una niña en la escuela que está pintando. Les va a enseñar a leer tres palabras: *¿quién?, sol,* y *amarillo.* Estas tres palabras están escritas en tres tarjetas que va a usar la maestra al enseñar.

The teacher and the children are going to read three sentences written on the blackboard that talk about a girl in a school who is painting. She is going to teach them three words: *¿quién?* (who?), *sol* (sun), and *amarillo* (yellow). The three words are written on three cards that the teacher is going to use.

MAESTRA [Enseñándoles a los niños una tarjeta con la palabra *quién* escrita sobre ella]: Repitan la palabra después de mí: "quién."
NIÑOS: "Quién."
Maestra: Ahora miren la primera oración en el pizarrón y léanla en silencio.
Maestra: Lean la oración después de mí: "¿Quién pinta?"
NIÑOS: "¿Quién pinta?"
Maestra [Enseñándoles a los niños una tarjeta con la palabra *sol* escrita sobre ella]: Repitan la palabra después de mí: "sol."
NIÑOS: "Sol."
MAESTRA: Ahora miren la segunda oración en el pizarrón y léanla en silencio.
MAESTRA: Lean la oración después de mí. "María pinta un sol grande."
NIÑOS: "María pinta un sol grande."
MAESTRA [Enseñándoles a los niños una tarjeta con la palabra *amarillo* escrita sobre ella]: Repitan la palabra después de mí: "amarillo."
NIÑOS: "Amarillo."

TEACHER [Showing the children a card with the word *who* written on it]: Repeat the word after me: "who."

CHILDREN: "Who."
TEACHER: Now look at the first sentence on the chalkboard and read it silently.
TEACHER: Read the sentence after me: "Who is painting?"
CHILDREN: "Who is painting?"
Teacher [Showing the children a card with the word *sun* written on it]: Repeat the word after me: "sun."
CHILDREN: "Sun."
TEACHER: Now look at the second sentence on the chalkboard and read it in silence.
TEACHER: Read the sentence after me: "María paints a big sun."
CHILDREN: "María paints a big sun."
TEACHER [Showing the children a card with the word *yellow* written on it]: Repeat the word after me: "yellow."
CHILDREN: "Yellow."

MAESTRA: Ahora miren la tercera oración en el pizarrón y léanla en silencio.

MAESTRA: Lean la oración después de mí. "Ella pinta un sol amarillo."
NIÑOS: "Ella pinta un sol amarillo."
[La maestra y los niños abren los libros y ven la primera página del cuento que van a leer. Hay un dibujo de María pintando un sol.]

MAESTRA: Miren el dibujo en la página veinte y nueve. ¿Quién pinta?
FELIPE: María está pintando.
MAESTRA: Sí, Felipe. María pinta. ¿Qué pinta María?
ANITA: Un sol.
MAESTRA: Sí, María pinta un sol. Y ¿de qué color es el sol?
NIÑOS: Amarillo.
MAESTRA: Ahora, escriban las tres palabras nuevas en sus cuadernos y escriban tres oraciones nuevas usando las tres palabras.

TEACHER: Now look at the third sentence on the chalkboard and read it in silence.
TEACHER: Read the sentence after me: "She paints a yellow sun."
CHILDREN: "She paints a yellow sun."
[The teacher and the students open their books and look at the first page of the story that they are going to read. There is a picture of María painting a sun.]
TEACHER: Look at the picture on page 29. Who is painting?
FELIPE: María is painting.
TEACHER: Yes, Felipe. María paints. What is María painting?
ANITA: A sun.
TEACHER: Yes, María is painting a sun. And what color is the sun?
CHILDREN: Yellow.
TEACHER: Now write the three new words in your notebooks and write three new sentences using the three words.

Analysis of *el método léxico* ◆ Few of the elements critical for effective reading instruction are present in the lexical method. Students are asked to read each sentence silently, but they do not read extended text on their own. As a result, they do not come to value reading or value themselves as readers. What students read is very carefully controlled. They are not given choices and do not read independently (beyond one sentence). The words they read are first presented in isolation and then put into sentences. These sentences seldom provide enough context to make the meaning of the words very clear. The sentences are not really even good examples of natural language. When the Felipe answers the teacher in a more natural way, "María is painting," the teacher has to restate the unnatural-text sentence, "María paints." In the sentence above that reads "*¿Quién pinta?*" (Who paints?), there is not any real context provided by the word *pinta* to help a reader infer the meaning of *¿Quién?*

The main emphasis of instruction in the lexical method is on recognizing individual words. Students are not encouraged to use the three cueing systems to construct meaning. Instead, they memorize words and then use them to decode sentences. Students connect the words to pictures, and this helps them construct sentence meaning, but the meanings are seldom related to their own background experiences or interests. Students do not discuss their reading. Instead, they simply answer teacher questions.

This method has been referred to in English as the whole-word method and is often confused with whole language. Normally, it forms part of most methods of teaching reading based on a word recognition view. Words that cannot be decoded using phonics rules are referred to as sight words. Teachers often use flash cards to teach these words as visual wholes. In some instances in English reading, as in the lexical method for Spanish, the approach used for sight words has been extended to all words. The whole-word method, used this way, has been contrasted with the phonics method. However, in most cases, teachers combine the two methods.

El método ecléctico o mixto *(The Eclectic or Mixed Method)*

The eclectic method contains features of several other methods. For that reason, it has also often been called *el método mixto* (Bellenger 1979). As in the visual concept method, students are given readiness activities to promote skills in spatial organization or visual-motor coordination. In addition, they may be given exercises to develop auditory discrimination, attention, memory, or oral language. Next, letter sounds are introduced, and students are encouraged to learn the sounds, the letter names, and the written symbols. After learning the letters and their sounds, students practice syllable sounds and combine them to form words or sentences. Students are also taught to take dictation, to copy words the teacher writes, to use letters from one word to create new words, to visualize the shapes of letters, to identify sounds represented by letters, and to practice penmanship. As this list suggests, an eclectic method may combine practices from both the synthetic and the analytic methods described earlier. Eclecticism characterizes many of the approaches to literacy that have been used in Latin America and in the United States. Methods of teaching reading in English have also often reflected this mixed approach. In fact, the eclectic method is probably the most commonly used method to teach reading in both Spanish and English.

Scenario for *el método ecléctico o mixto*

La lección se basa en unas páginas del libro de texto para enseñar la lectura, *Chiquilín* (Cabrera n.d.). Este libro se usa en Venezuela para enseñar la lectura en primaria. Los niños y la maestra están

The lesson is based on some pages from a reading textbook, *Chiquilín* (Cabrera n.d.). This book is used in Venezuela to teach reading in primary school. The children and the teacher

mirando la página titulada "pre-lectura" donde se encuentran las vocales y los dibujos de palabras que empiezan con cada vocal.

MAESTRA: Miren la página tres. Aquí miren los dibujos y las letras. Estas letras son las vocales. Cada letra está en mayúscula y en minúscula. Cada dibujo comienza con una de las vocales. Primero, pongan su dedo sobre la primera vocal, A, y repitan, "A, avión."
NIÑOS: "A, avión."
MAESTRA: Bien, ahora, pongan su dedo en la segunda letra, E, y repitan, "E, elefante."
NIÑOS: "E, elefante."
MAESTRA: Bien, ahora pongan su dedos en la tercera letra, I, y repitan, "I, imán."

NIÑOS: "I, imán."
MAESTRA: Bien, ahora pongan su dedo en la cuarta letra, O, y repitan, "O, ola."

NIÑOS: "O, ola."
MAESTRA: Bien, ahora pongan su dedo en la quinta vocal, U, y repitan, "U, uno."

NIÑOS: "U, uno."

are looking at the page titled "pre-reading," on which there are vowels and pictures of words that start with each vowel.

TEACHER: Look at page 3. Here you see the pictures and the letters. These letters are vowels. Each letter is in uppercase and lowercase. Each picture begins with one of the vowels. First, put your finger on the first vowel, A, and repeat, "A, airplane."
CHILDREN: "A, airplane."
TEACHER: Good, now put your finger on the second letter, E, and repeat, "E, elephant."
CHILDREN: "E, elephant."
TEACHER: Good, now put your finger on the third letter, I, and repeat, "I, magnet [imán]."
STUDENTS: "I, magnet."
TEACHER: Good, now put your finger on the fourth letter, O, and repeat, "O, wave [ola]."
CHILDREN: "O, wave."
TEACHER: Good, now put your finger on the fifth vowel, U, and repeat, "U, one [uno]."
CHILDREN: "U, one."

La maestra y los niños ven la próxima página y repiten otro ejercicio igual a la primera con más dibujos de palabras que empiezan con vocales. Esta vez las vocales (escritas en minúsculas) y los dibujos que representan el primer sonido aparecen en otro orden. Empiezan con la e de *enano*, sigue la o de *oso*, la i de *iglesia*, la u de *uña*, y la a de *asa*. Después de esta práctica, todos miran a la próxima página donde hay un dibujo de una mamá y su hija. Las sílabas *ma, me, mi, mo, mu* están escritas debajo del dibujo.

The teacher and the children look at the next page and repeat another exercise like the first one with more pictures of words that begin with vowels (written in lowercase). This time the vowels and the pictures that represent the first sound of each vowel appear in a different order. They begin with the *e* of *enano* (dwarf) and follow the *o* of *oso* (bear), the *i* of *iglesia* (church), the *u* of *uña* (fingernail), and the *a* for *asa* (cup handle). After this practice, everyone looks at the next page, where there is a picture of a mother and her child. The syllables *ma, me, mi, mo, mu* are written beneath the picture.

MAESTRA: Miren ustedes la página cinco. ¿Qué ven ustedes en el dibujo?

MARTA: Una mamá y su hija.

MAESTRA: Sí, Marta. Es una mamá y su hija. Debajo del dibujo ustedes pueden ver la palabra *mamá*. Vamos a aprender a leer esta palabra y otras. Ahora, miren las sílabas junto al dibujo, y repitan después de mí: "ma, me, mi, mo, mu."

NIÑOS: "Ma, me, mi, mo, mu."

MAESTRA: Bien. Ahora lean después de mí las palabras que están en la primera línea: "ama, mima, amo."

NIÑOS: "Ama, mima, amo."

MAESTRA: En la segunda línea, "eme, mimo, mía." Repitan.

NIÑOS: "Eme, mimo, mía."

MAESTRA: En la tercera línea, "mima, mimí, eme."

NIÑOS: "Mima, mimí, eme."

MAESTRA: Muy bien. Ahora vamos a leer una oración completa. Lean conmigo, "Mi mamá me ama."

NIÑOS: "Mi mamá me ama."

TEACHER: Look at page 5. What do you see in the picture?

MARTA: A mother and her daughter.

TEACHER: Yes, Marta. It is a mother and her daughter. Under the picture you can see the word *mother*. We are going to learn to read this word and others. Now, look at the syllables next to the picture and repeat after me: "ma, me, mi, mo, mu."

CHILDREN: "Ma, me, mi, mo, mu."

TEACHER: OK. Now, read the words in the first line after me: "ama [he/she loves], mima [he/she pampers], amo [I love]."

STUDENTS: "Ama, mima, amo."

TEACHER: In the second line, "eme [m], mimo [I pamper (someone)], mía [my]." Repeat.

CHILDREN: "Eme, mimo, mía."

TEACHER: In the third line, "eme [m], mimí [I pampered (someone)], eme [m]."

CHILDREN: "Eme, mimí, eme."

TEACHER: Very good. You are now ready to read a complete sentence. Read with me: "Mi mamá me ama [My mother loves me]."

CHILDREN: "Mi mamá me ama."

Analysis of *el método ecléctico o mixto* ◆ In this method one can see elements of several other methods we have already described. The lesson begins, like the alphabetic method, by teaching letters. The vowels are taught, as in the phonics method, by relating the beginning sounds to words that start with those sounds. This method then moves to syllables, and, like the syllabic method, uses syllables to teach words, although there is a mixture of unrelated words and the letter *m*. In addition, there are elements of the global method since the students' attention is directed at one point to a picture of a mother and her child. At the end of the lesson the students read a sentence related to the picture.

In the opening pages of this basic reading textbook, *Chiquilín* (Cabrera n.d.), the philosophy of teaching reading is laid out for teachers. The first two points of this explanation clearly show that this approach to teaching reading is a combination of the analytic and synthetic methods described previously:

La metodología de la enseñanza para la lectura del libro *Chiquilín* debe de seguir los siguientes pasos:

1. El niño debe leer y pronunciar los fonemas vocales asociándolos con la imagen que los origina. Ejemplo: "a" de "aro" "a" de "avión." Debe pronunciar cada sonido silábico, relacionándolo rápidamente con la palabra que lo contiene y la imagen que lo representa.

2. El niño debe leer frases, oraciones y pequeños párrafos, dentro de un contexto relacionado con una escena en particular. Luego el docente reforzará la lectura realizada con preguntas sencillas que permitan fijar el aprendizaje adquirido. (2)

Translation

The teaching methodology for reading in the book *Chiquilín* should follow these steps:

1. The child should read and pronounce the vowel sounds, associating them with the image of the word they come from. Example: "a" for "aro" [hoop] "a" for "avión" [airplane]. He [the child] should pronounce each syllabic sound, relating it rapidly with the word that contains the syllable sound and the image it represents.

2. The child should read phrases, sentences, and small paragraphs, within a context related to a particular scene. Then the teacher will reinforce the reading by asking simple questions that allow the learning to be retained.

Although the eclectic method may appear to combine the best of all other methods, it does not help students come to value reading or to value themselves as readers. A mixed method includes both part-to-whole and whole-to-part exercises whose goal is to have students identify words. The exercises seldom involve the reading of complete, authentic texts, so readers are not engaged in a process of using all the cueing systems to construct meaning. Students are given little choice in what they read, and teachers seldom read real literature to children. There is no teaching of strategy lessons or discussion of what was read.

Eclectic Approaches in Basal Readers

Under our discussion of eclectic methods and before closing this chapter on Spanish reading methods, we believe it is important to make a few comments about Spanish-language basal reading programs published for schools in the United States. Schools often use state funds to purchase these materials, and once they are adopted they become the reading program in many classrooms. It is important, then, to consider the methods reflected in these programs.

Before the 1980s Spanish basals were carefully controlled programs based on a combination of phonetic, whole-word, and syllabic approaches to teaching reading in Spanish. Freeman's study (Freeman 1987, 1988) of seven contemporary Spanish-language basal programs concluded that the materials reflected an eclectic approach to reading, and the programs were really more alike than different. She critiqued the adapted—and sometimes poorly translated—literature, the skills-based worksheets, the long lists of comprehension questions, and the teacher-centered approach to reading that the programs contained.

In the 1990s several publishers of Spanish-language basal programs responded to the earlier critiques (Freeman 1993). They produced new programs that included collections of quality children's literature organized around themes. Many of the selections were originally written in Spanish. They were accompanied by an appealing collection of expository support readings, either carefully translated or originally published in Spanish. One example of this was *Invitaciones*, a basal program for grades one through six (Freeman and Freeman 1997). Typical of all basals in the period, support activities contained exercises that reflected the alphabetic method, the phonics method, the syllabic method, the lexical method, and the global method. In reality, even though the literature and the themes reflected a sociopsycholinguistic approach, the activities looked more eclectic.

Basal publishers must remain competitive. Whether they are producing materials in Spanish or in English, publishers pay close attention to government mandates about reading. They note the demands of a conservative public calling for a move back toward the basics, and they listen to what teachers and administrators say. The message basal publishers are presently getting is that materials must be based on reliable, replicable research that supports the systematic and explicit teaching of skills and follows the five pillars discussed in Chapter 2. Unfortunately, the results are reading programs that include worksheets and scripted plans for every minute of the teaching time. The new basals clearly reflect a word recognition view of reading.

Principled Eclecticism

An eclectic method could be considered an attempt to blend new understandings about learning and teaching with the best of the old. While many educators today maintain that eclecticism is the best approach to teaching reading, we hold that it is important for educators to examine their beliefs about the reading process and learning and match their practice to those beliefs. We agree with Harste (1992) that "Eclecticism is a disease, not an educational philosophy . . . it is curable by taking a position" (5).

Eclectic methods commonly used to teach both Spanish and English combine some elements of synthetic and analytic approaches, and they focus on various levels of analysis or synthesis—the sentence, the word, or the syllable. Some attention is usually given to constructing meaning, but often with very limited texts. The basic problem with an eclectic approach is that teachers may combine techniques that reflect different views of how people learn to read. This sends a mixed message to students, and often they become confused about just what reading is supposed to be. Is it repeating after the teacher? Is it changing beginning and ending sounds in words? Is it completing worksheet exercises? Is it reading independently and responding?

An alternative is what we refer to as principled eclecticism. Teachers who follow a principled approach use a variety of techniques, but they make sure that the different activities reflect a consistent view of how people learn to read. The checklist for effective reading instruction can be used to ensure that classroom practices are consistent with a sociopsycholinguistic view of reading. In the next chapter we explain a method of teaching reading that reflects both principled eclecticism and a sociopsycholinguistic view of reading.

 Applications

1. We opened this chapter with a quote that described methods of teaching reading as *"mécanicos y rígidos"* (mechanical and rigid) and the view that reading had to be so difficult and painful that *"la letra con sangre entra"* (learning to read requires blood[shed]). Do you think this description is true of the methods used to teach reading in schools in your area? Why or why not? Give specific examples.

2. We categorized the methods used to teach reading into *métodos sintéticos* (synthetic methods) and *métodos analíticos* (analytic methods). Are methods used to teach reading at your school synthetic, analytic, or both? Why? If you do not teach currently, interview and/or observe elementary teachers at a local school to find out.

3. If you were not taught to read first in Spanish, interview someone who was. Did you or the person you interviewed use a *silabario* (silabary)? What was it like? What do you or the person you interviewed remember about being taught to read in Spanish?

4. *El método silábico* (the syllabic method) is by far the most common method used to teach reading in Spanish. Is this method used to teach Spanish reading at

your school? If it is not, do you see any evidence of the syllabic method in any of the materials? If you are not currently teaching, interview and/or observe elementary teachers at a school to find out.

5. What evidence of the whole-word method do you see in the teaching of reading in your school? Are any words taught that way? If you are not teaching currently, interview elementary teachers at a school to find out.

6. Many teachers use an eclectic approach to teach reading. What do we mean by "an eclectic approach"? Do you think you are eclectic in your approach to teaching reading? If you are not currently teaching, interview teachers to find out if they take an eclectic approach. Give specific examples of eclecticism in teaching.

7. Does your school use basal readers to teach reading? Which program is used? What methods are reflected in the basal reading programs? If you are not teaching now, interview elementary teachers at a school to find out about their basal reading programs.

A Principled Approach
to Teaching Reading

La enseñanza de la lectura y de la escritura sigue siendo el
rompecabezas para muchos maestros, y muy especialmente para los
que habiendo terminado la carrera normalista, se inician en la
docencia como profesores de primer grado de primaria. La falta de
experiencia profesional y el desconocimiento de las técnicas más
adecuadas para enseñar a leer y escribir a sus alumnos, los llena de
desasosiego y de incertidumbre y los conduce, no pocas veces, a
resultados menos que mediocres al término del año escolar.

Antonio Barbosa Heldt, *Como han aprendido*
a leer y a escribir los mexicanos

Translation
The teaching of reading and writing continues being a puzzle for
many teachers, especially for those who, having finished their
teacher education training, begin their teaching as first-grade
teachers. The lack of professional experience and the lack of

knowledge of adequate techniques for teaching reading and writing to their students, fills them with worry and uncertainty and leads them, quite often, to less than mediocre results at the end of the school year.

The quote above was written in 1971. The work in psycholinguistics and reading was just beginning. As Barbosa Heldt points out, many teachers did not know the best way to teach reading. As we noted in Chapter 5, many teachers adopt an eclectic approach. They use whatever seems to work. In this chapter we argue that teachers should take a *principled* approach. Principled teachers often use a variety of strategies, but their approach is consistent and reflects their beliefs about reading.

Approach, Method, and Technique

Anthony (1965) makes a useful distinction among *approach*, *method*, and *technique*. An approach consists of a set of beliefs about teaching and learning. In past writing we have also referred to this set of beliefs as an orientation. A method reflects how those beliefs are put into practice over time and constitutes the long-term plan or syllabus that the teacher develops. Techniques are specific classroom activities the teacher implements on a regular basis.

In previous chapters we distinguished between two approaches or orientations to teaching reading: the word recognition approach and the sociopsycholinguistic approach. We presented evidence for the validity of the sociopsycholinguistic approach. We believe that this approach is principled in that it is based on theory tested in practice. The checklist for effective reading instruction is based on this approach. Principled teachers follow practices that fit one approach consistently. On the other hand, an eclectic teacher might choose activities that fit either of the two approaches.

Principled teachers are consistent at the level of method as well. *Method* refers to the long-term plan for organizing curriculum. In this chapter we describe a method for organizing reading instruction that is consistent with a sociopsycholinguistic approach. This method is based on a model of teaching reading known as the gradual release of responsibility (Pearson and Gallagher 1983). The idea is for the teacher to begin by doing most of the work and then slowly release the responsibility for the task to the student.

Environmental Print Tasks with Bilingual Children

The gradual release model builds on the literacy experiences that students bring with them when they start school. Even before formal instruction begins, children growing up in a literate environment have started to form concepts about print. Before describing the gradual release of responsibility model, we would like to discuss what Spanish-speaking children already know about print and reading before they begin learning to read in school.

Yvonne invites her graduate students who are bilingual teachers to do a concepts of reading interview and an environmental print task (Goodman and Altwerger 1981; Romero 1983) with an emergent reader in order to help them understand a sociopsycholinguistic approach to reading and to see the importance of a principled method of teaching reading. Since Yvonne teaches in Spanish, her teachers choose a Spanish-speaking child who is not yet reading independently, usually a child around four years old. However, the interview could be done in any language. The teachers first conduct a child's concept of reading interview in Spanish with the child. This interview consists of a series of questions for the child such as "*¿Sabes leer?*" (Do you know how to read?) and, for those who answer yes, "*¿Cómo aprendiste a leer?*" (How did you learn to read?). For children who answer no, they ask, "*¿Cómo vas a aprender?*" (How are you going to learn?). The interviewer tries to get at what these young children think about reading by asking questions such as "*¿Es fácil o difícil leer?*" (Is it easy or hard to read?) and "*¿Es posible aprender a leer solo?*" (Is it possible to learn to read by yourself?).

Besides conducting the interview, the teachers also do a print awareness task to help them understand the child's concepts of reading and metalinguistic awareness. For this task the teachers gather four products (two in Spanish and two in English) that children would probably be familiar with in their south Texas border communities. Teachers choose products such as *Fabuloso*, a commonly used cleaner, *sopa de fideo*, noodle soup, or *Galletas Gamesa*, Gamesa brand cookies, a famous Mexican brand. For English, they choose anything from pizza boxes to Oreo cookies and Pampers diaper wipes. Over a period of four weeks, the teacher sits with his chosen child and asks questions about the four products. During the first interview, the teacher shows the child the actual product. So, for example, in the first week the teacher shows the child the bottle of *Fabuloso* or a package of *sopa de fideo*. Then the teacher asks questions like "*¿Has visto éste/ésta antes?*" (Have you seen this before?), "*¿Qué crees que dice?*" (What do you think it says?), and "*¿Qué te indica que dice . . . ? Indica con tu dedito donde dice . . .*" (What tells you that it says . . . Show me with your finger where it says . . .). These same questions are asked over the four-week period, but each time context is reduced. The second week, the labels are cut out and pasted on cardboard or construction paper. The third week the teacher shows the child a photocopy of the label. This removes any color cues. Finally, in the fourth week, the product name is simply printed on a card. Instructions and questions for these tasks can be found in the publications cited earlier, as well as in *Kidwatching: Documenting Children's Literacy Development* (Owocki and Goodman 2002) and in Application 2.

The power of this assignment comes clear as students write a paper analyzing their experience. The children's answers to the interview questions often surprise and excite the graduate students. Rosa, a second-grade bilingual teacher, first did the concepts of reading interview with her four-year-old daughter, Juliana, and wrote,

> Before I started this interview, I really wasn't sure what the outcome was going to be. I explained to my daughter that I needed to ask her a few questions. She felt so excited and important that she brought her little table and two small chairs so we could sit. The first question I asked was *"¿Sabes leer?"* (Do you know how to read?). Her immediate response was, *"Sí, mami, sí sé leer."* (Yes, Mommy, yes, I know how to read.) I stopped for a moment and thought that kids feel so enthusiastic about reading at a young age like my daughter. "So," I asked myself, "What happens at school that they lose this enthusiasm?" She went on to tell me she had learned how to read on her own and she said, *"Yo sé leer libros, cuentos, y eso que tú estás escribiendo y todo sé leer."* (I know how to read books, stories, and those words you are writing. I know how to read everything.) This was just the beginning of the interview questions, and I was enjoying it already.

Rosa then did the environmental print activity with her daughter over the four weeks using Pampers wipes and Knorr tomato bouillon for English and Suavitel, a fabric softener, and Yemina Conchas, a Mexican sweetbread, for Spanish. When she was shown the products, Rosa's daughter read "without hesitating what she believed was the print on the packages." When the labels were glued onto paper, she still read her version of the labels but this time tried to sound out the first letter of each word. On the third task, when color was removed, she hesitated more in identifying the products and could not identify the tomato bouillon without the red-colored tomatoes and decided the package said "oranges" instead. When Rosa showed her the words printed on cards, she was certain that all the cards said her name, Juliana Arisleidy Chapa. Among the things that Rosa wrote in summary was "I learned that print rich environments give the child an opportunity to learn the first step of reading without learning the sounds and letters first."

Another bilingual teacher, Nancy, also noticed how much context helps emergent readers and how frustrating isolated print is to young children. Nancy did this project with her four-year-old niece Nallely and described her niece's response to each stage:

Primera etapa: Nallely mencionó con mucho detalle cada uno de los artículos presentados. Su actitud era bastante emocionante y alegre. En su rostro reflejaba seguridad y mucha confianza en lo que contestaba.

Translation
First stage: Nallely mentioned a lot of detail about each of the articles shown her. Her attitude was happy and emotional. Her face reflected security and a lot of confidence in what she answered.

As Nancy worked with her niece, she noticed more hesitation and less confidence at each stage. The child's response to the final task, with only the words printed on the cards, tells a story about young children's responses to isolated words.

Cuarta etapa: En la etapa final donde sólo le mostré las letras de los productos, noté a Nallely muy inquieta. Ella pudo deletrear las letras pero sin poder tener significado de la palabra. No quería contestar mucho a mis preguntas, me decía que no sabía, como si quería que la entrevista se terminara pronto. Lo noté cuando me dijo, "No sé, tía" con un tono de voz bastante desesperante.

Translation
Fourth stage: In the final stage when I only showed her the letters of the products, I noticed that Nallely was very restless. She could spell the letters but without being able to tell the meaning. She didn't want to answer my questions very much and said to me, "I don't know, Auntie," with a kind of desperate note in her voice.

Many students who did this project with a young child found the experience to be a powerful one because through the interview they learned about children's views of reading and through the environmental print tasks they were able to see how important color and context are to emergent readers. They also learned how important it is to talk to children about reading and texts. For example, Yudith wrote:

After doing this project, I learned what children think about reading. In addition, I realized how important it is for children to encounter context clues and pictures when they read a book.

Anna commented:

Many children come from print rich homes, yet they get to school and we, the educators, dissect the words and teach without context. A simple study like the one I just conducted makes me aware that the young reader needs context to create meaning.

Paula observed:

My student was able to see the picture and make the connection to reading. She also used her previous experiences to relate to what she read. As teachers, we should allow time for children to talk about their experiences to make connections and to make the reading more meaningful to them. Instead some teachers isolate words and drill students without having them make connections.

Delia summarized what was perhaps the most important consideration for teaching reading:

Las consecuencias pedagógicas son pesimistas si se piensa en la escritura como "un sistema de signos que expresan sonidos individuales del habla" (Gelb 1978). Nos estamos refiriendo a la escritura alfabética. En cambio, si definimos la escritura en un sentido más amplio, tomando en cuenta sus orígines sociales, psico-genéticos y lingüísticos, como una forma particular de representar nuestro medio ambiente, le estaremos dando una visión sociopsicolingüística al proceso de la lecto-escritura. Entre las propuestas metodológicas y las concepciones infantiles, hay una distancia que puede medirse en términos de lo que la escuela enseña y el niño aprende. Lo que la escuela pretende enseñar no siempre coincide con lo que el niño logra aprender.

Translation
The pedagogical consequences are negative if one thinks of writing as "a system of signs that express individual speech sounds" (Gelb 1978). We are referring to alphabetic writing. On the other hand, if we define writing in a broader sense, taking into account its social, psychogenic, and linguistic origins, as a particular way of representing our environment, we are giving the reading-writing process a sociopsycholinguistic view. We can measure the distance between proposed methods and children's conceptual development in terms of what school teaches and the child learns. What school tries to teach doesn't always fit with what the child succeeds in learning.

Functions of Print Project

Another important project Yvonne's students carry out as they study about reading acquisition is a functions of print task (Owocki and Goodman 2002; Weiss and Hagen 1988). This task, like the environmental print task, can be done in any language. Drawing on the process suggested by Weiss and Hagan, students gather ten items that people often read, such as a magazine, a newspaper, a menu, a calendar, a birthday card or an invitation, a storybook, and a shopping list. This task is used with preschool through first-grade children. To carry out the task, the interviewer puts three of the items on a table and asks the child to choose one of them. So, if the interview is done with a Spanish-speaking child, for example, the interviewer might put a storybook, a newspaper, and a calendar on a table in front of the child and say, *"Enséñame el calendario"* (Show me the calendar). If the child picks out the calendar, the question that follows is *"¿Por qué lee la gente un calendario?"* or *"¿Por qué leemos un calendario?"* (Why do people read a calendar? or Why do we read a calendar?). The child's answers give the teacher/researcher insights into what children understand about the functions of different reading materials, even when no one has taught them.

As children watch adults reading, they make hypotheses about why people read different kinds of materials. Some particularly interesting responses from children are included below. It is clear from the responses children make that they do notice how adults use different texts and how they respond to texts. Figure 6–1 lists some of the questions and answers from children interviewed in Spanish with the task.

Question	Answers
¿Por que lee la gente libros de cuentos? (Why do people read storybooks?)	*Para pasar el exam de AR.* (To pass the Accelerated Reader test.) *Hay que leer muchos libros para poder pasar de grado.* (You have to read a lot of books to pass to the next grade.) *Para dormirse.* (To go to sleep.) *Para ser inteligente.* (To be intelligent.) *Para aprender cosas nuevas.* (To learn new things.)

(continues)

FIGURE 6–1. Functions of Print Responses

Question	Answers
¿Por qué lee la gente el periódico? (Why do people read the newspaper?)	Para saber quien murió. También para saber si hay algo en la Dodge Arena. Los juegos que van a ver. Si va a llover o no y si hay algún hotel. (To know who died. Also, in order to find out if there is something in Dodge Arena . . . the games they are going to see. If it is going to rain or not and if there is a hotel.) Para ver las personas que roban. (To see who has stolen things.) Para leer de la guerra. (To read about the war.)
¿Por qué lee la gente el libro telefónico? (Why do people read the telephone book?)	Para marcar a la pizza. (To call the pizza place.) Para buscar teléfonos y nombres de personas. (To look for the telephone numbers and names of people.) Para buscar el teléfono de los bomberos o la policía. (To look for the telephone number of the firemen or the policemen.)
¿Por qué lee la gente cartas? (Why do people read letters?)	Porque están enamorados. (Because they are in love.) Como el bil de la luz . . . cuando a mi hermano se le olvidó pagarlo y se quedó toda la noche sin luz. (It's like the light bill . . . when my brother forgot to pay it and we were without electricity all night.)
¿Por qué lee la gente el calendario? (Why do people read the calendar?)	Para ver cuando va a ser su cumpleaños. (To see when it's going to be your birthday.) Le íbamos a comprar flores a mi abuelita que ya está muerta y se le olvidó a mi mama. (We were going to buy flowers for my grand-mother who is dead now and my mother forgot.) Para saber si vamos a la escuela. (To know if we are going to school.)
¿Por qué lee la gente las revistas? (Why do people read magazines?)	Para ver las fotos y oler los perfumes. (To see the pictures and smell the perfumes.) Para poder hacer lo que hacen en las revistas. (To be able to do what they do in the magazines.) Pueden ver si alguien se casó. Son las personas de las novelas. (They can see if someone got married. They are the people on the soap operas.)

FIGURE 6–1. Functions of Print Responses (*continued*)

A final, telling question asked in the interview is *"¿Por qué lee la gente?"* (Why do people read?). Some children found that question difficult, but others had interesting answers. Some children knew it was necessary to read to succeed in school. One child said, *"Es importante porque si no lees no vas a pasar grado"* (It's important because if you don't read, you won't pass to the next grade). Another told her interviewer, *"Si no sabemos leer, no vamos a ir al colegio"* (If we don't know how to read, we aren't going to high school). Still another child saw reading as moving up the levels of reading books: *"Mi mamá siempre dice que aprenda mucho y por eso yo siempre leo. Ya voy en el libro verde y mi amiga todavía va en el libro pink"* (My mother always tells [me] to learn a lot and because of that I am always reading. I'm on the green book level and my friend is still in the pink book level).

However, some children did see the utility of reading for everyday tasks. One said, *"Si no saben leer no saben adonde van, o como pagar los biles, y no pueden leer con sus niños"* (If they don't know how to read, they don't know where they are going, or how to pay the bills, and they can't read to their children). One child even linked reading with her future: *"Para aprender muchas cosas. Para que aprendas inglés y español. Y cuando sea grande ir a trabajar. Cuando yo sea maestra voy a leer como tú"* (In order to learn many things. So you can learn English and Spanish. And when you are grown up in order to work. When I am a teacher, I'm going to read like you).

By conducting the reading interview and carrying out the environmental print task and the functions of print task, the teachers in Yvonne's class learned a great deal about what young children already know about reading, why they think reading is important, and how children begin to construct meaning from print even without formal instruction. In the following sections, we describe a model for reading instruction that builds on the understandings children develop even before they begin formal reading instruction in school.

Gradual Release of Responsibility Model

The gradual release of responsibility model reflects Vygotsky's (1962) concept of the Zone of Proximal Development. Vygotsky argued that we learn when we work collaboratively with an adult or a more knowledgeable peer. What we can do now with help we can do later independently.

Most of us have had learning experiences that confirm Vygotsky's hypothesis. At first, we may need help in running a new program on our computer, for example. Later, we can do it on our own. When it comes to reading, children need help. They can't read, so the teacher reads to them. Over time, the responsibility for

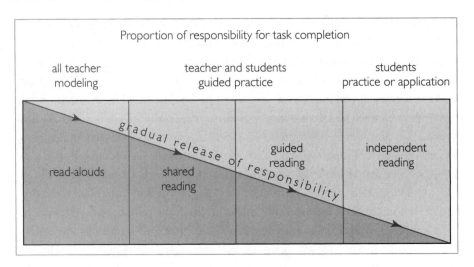

FIGURE 6–2. Gradual Release of Responsibility Model for Reading (Pearson and Gallagher 1983)

reading shifts from the teacher to the student. The goal is for the student to read independently. Of course, students may be able to read certain kinds of text independently and still need help to read more complex texts or different genres. The teacher's job is to judge the amount of help that is needed and provide that help. Figure 6–2 illustrates this gradual release of responsibility model.

The first stage shown in Figure 6–2 is reading aloud. At this stage, the teacher does all the work of reading. The second is shared reading. During this time, the students begin to share the task. The third stage is guided reading. Here, the responsibility shifts more to the students. Although the teacher provides strong support, the students have the primary responsibility for reading. The final stage is independent reading. At this point, the students take on the full responsibility for reading.

A principled teacher would plan instruction to include this sequence of instructional activities, repeating the sequence as students move on to more difficult reading materials or new genres. In this way, the gradual release of responsibility model becomes the method or long-term plan for a teacher who takes a sociopsycholinguistic view of reading. In the following sections, we describe each of these components of the gradual release of responsibility model in more detail.

Read-Alouds

Effective teachers we have worked with read aloud to their students every day. They do this whether they are kindergarten teachers or high school teachers. Most often, the teacher reads to the whole class. However, at times, the teacher may read to just a small group. With older students, the teacher may read aloud from a chapter book while the students simply listen. However, many picture books are appropriate for older students too. In addition to reading more complex books to older readers, teachers generally read for longer periods of time. Another difference between reading aloud to younger students and reading aloud to older students is that teachers often reread favorite books several times for younger readers. Since books for older readers are longer, the teacher reads a part each day, often a chapter, but does not reread the book.

There are several benefits of reading aloud to students. First, the teacher models fluent reading. It is important for students to hear a fluent reader, especially when the book is in their second language. This gives them a feel for the rhythm of the language as well as the pronunciation of words. In addition, a teacher can choose books to read aloud that help build background knowledge for a theme the class is studying. Hearing a good book can also pique students' interest in the topic and in reading. Further, reading aloud provides support for struggling readers and students still developing proficiency in a second language. Above all, when teachers read aloud, students enjoy the experience. Read-alouds help students come to value reading.

Jim Trelease has written extensively on the benefits of reading aloud to children. In his *Read-Aloud Handbook* (2001) he offers several useful suggestions. He encourages teachers to read as much as possible, but to have at least one set time each day for a read-aloud. Teachers often read to students after recess or lunch. This helps students settle down and transition from social to academic activity. Trelease suggests giving students a few minutes to adjust to thinking about the story. A good way to do this is to ask them questions about the previous day's reading.

Trelease reminds teachers to always say the name of the book, the author, and the illustrator. Over time students develop favorite authors and illustrators. He also suggests that teachers can stop periodically to have students predict what will come next. After reading the section, the teacher can come back to the predictions to see if they were right. This helps students, as they read on their own, make and confirm predictions.

If the book is a picture book, it is important to group students so they can see the pictures. The teacher can pause in the reading to be sure all the students see each picture. It helps for the teacher to be slightly above the students (sitting in a chair when the students are on a rug or sitting on the teacher's desk if students sit at theirs) so that all the students can see the teacher clearly and also see the book.

Since the teacher is doing the reading, the text can be beyond the students' reading level. Even when students can read many kinds of texts on their own, teachers can find read-alouds that challenge students, selections they would struggle with if they were asked to read them independently. Trelease also points out that if a chapter is too long to read in one session, it is a good idea to stop at a suspenseful point so student interest is maintained until the next reading period.

Finally, Trelease notes that good read-alouds require practice. Even proficient readers need to be prepared to do a good job. The reading can be enhanced by changing the voice for the dialogue of different characters. The teacher can speed up or slow down the reading to fit the pace of the text. It is also good to determine in advance places in the text at which the teacher might ask a question or have the students make a prediction. Careful planning results in a much more successful read-aloud.

In addition to his handbook, Trelease has written another book, *Hey! Listen to This: Stories to Read Aloud* (1992). This useful publication includes many short stories as well as passages from longer books that have been adapted for reading aloud. The selections are grouped thematically. For example, one group of stories centers on school days, another on food, and a third on gigantic creatures. *Hey! Listen to This* includes a number of classics, such as Ramona the pest. For busy teachers, it is especially nice to have one book with a wide selection of stories to use as read-alouds.

Shared Reading

To shift the responsibility for reading gradually from the teacher to the student, principled teachers move from reading aloud to shared reading. Shared reading is often a regular feature in lower-grade classrooms. Typically, teachers read and reread a big book. This is important for younger students who are just beginning to develop concepts of print and need to learn to match the words in the text with the teacher's oral language. Usually, the teacher moves a pointer under the words as she reads.

One of the benefits of shared reading for younger children is that hearing the teacher read stories, songs, and chants helps the child develop both phonological and phonemic awareness. Phonological awareness is the knowledge that the speech stream is broken up into units such as words and syllables. This awareness is most easily developed if the child follows along as the teacher reads from a big book and tracks the reading with a pointer. Children begin to realize that oral language is made up of discrete units and that these are separated in written language by blank spaces.

For children reading in Spanish, the key is to develop an awareness that oral language can be divided into syllables. For students learning to read in English, a further step is needed. Syllables are made up of individual phonemes. A phoneme is the smallest unit of sound that represents a change in meaning. English readers learn that a word like *dog* has three sounds. They develop phonemic awareness, which is the ability to recognize and manipulate phonemes in words. Spanish words can also be divided into phonemes, but the important unit for Spanish reading is the syllable, not the phoneme.

Students more easily develop phonological and phonemic awareness when they can see the written representations of words. They begin to connect sounds and letters. Opitz's book, *Rhymes and Reasons: Literature and Language Play for Phonological Awareness* (2000), is a wonderful resource for teachers looking for books in English to read aloud to help students develop phonological awareness. Opitz provides annotated bibliographies of books grouped into categories such as rhyming texts, alliterative texts, repetitive texts, poetry texts, song texts, and even goofy texts. For each book he gives a brief synopsis followed by suggestions for classroom activities a teacher can use to help students develop phonological awareness. For example, in his review of *Night House Bright House* (Wellington 1997), Opitz comments, "This book is loaded with examples of words that are created by phoneme substitutions. Each is accompanied by a rebus sentence. Example: ' "Tickle, tickle," said the pickle.' Provide children with the first set and ask how the first word was changed to create the second word" (62). Read-alouds with follow-up activities such as these help students develop the knowledge base needed for reading.

Alphabet books can also be used for shared reading to help students become aware of beginning letters and their sounds. Many alphabet books are written in rhyme, so teachers can also use them to teach ending sounds. Big-book versions of alphabet books are particularly useful since all the students can see the words. Teachers can stop to discuss the beginning sounds and letters and, if the book is a rhyming book, discuss different ways to spell the same sound. In both Spanish and English there is an abundance of alphabet books appropriate for students that are at different grade levels. In Chapter 7, we give specific examples of alphabet books in Spanish and English.

Although the teacher continues to do most of the work, students now share in reading by chiming in on repeated sections or reading familiar words. In Spanish a popular big book with a catchy refrain is *Fue David* (It Was David) (Menchaca and Menchaca 1997). In the story, Daniel does mischievous things such as taking all his mother's pots and pans out of the cupboards and messing up his brother's room. When asked who did these things, Daniel blames an imaginary friend with the repeated refrain, *"Yo no sé. Yo no fui. Pienso yo que fue David"* (I don't know. It wasn't me. I think it must have been David). Young children not only relate to the content of the story but love following along and repeating the refrain. In addition to joining in on reading big books, students enjoy reading along in shared reading experiences with songs, chants, or language experience writing that has enlarged print.

Most elementary teachers are familiar with big books. However, they are a fairly recent invention. Holdaway (1979) is credited for first developing big books in the 1960s. He wanted to take a developmental model of reading that begins with parents reading to their children and apply it to a classroom setting. He noted: "The major problem we have faced in applying a model of individual learning to the classroom is one of numbers . . . Another aspect of the problem of numbers concerns the visual intimacy with print which characterizes pre-school book experience" (64). Holdaway solved these problems by developing oversized books with large print that all the students in a typical class could see.

Holdaway and other teachers in New Zealand made the use of big books an important part of reading instruction. Many of their practices were later adopted in other countries. Publishers have responded to teachers' needs for big books, and now almost every elementary school has a supply.

The model of shared reading first developed by Holdaway has been applied as well in many second language settings. Elley (1998), in particular, has made shared reading a central component of the English teaching programs he has initiated in many different countries around the world. Teachers have learned to use big books for effective shared reading lessons to teach English in Fiji, Sri Lanka, and Singapore among other places. The students in the big-book programs learned to read English much more rapidly than similar students being taught using traditional ESL methods. Elley shows the gains in vocabulary and grammar that students make when teachers read a big book aloud three or four times during a two-week period and conduct follow-up activities with the students.

Shared reading provides many opportunities for teachers to demonstrate expressive, fluent reading and for students to participate. We discussed the onomatopeic method in Chapter 5. Although that method is restricted in its pure form, the reading of onomatopoeic books with children is an excellent way to get them involved in shared reading. Readers may remember Francisco's student, Salvador, who was attracted to a story in which the farm animals made noises that kept Don Vicencio awake.

Students love to participate in readings that include sounds. Books in Spanish often have *¡Cataplum!* as things crash down or explode. Big books like *El chivo en la huerta* (*The Goat in the Chili Patch*) (Kratky 1989a, 1992), *Pepín y el abuelo* (Pepín and His Grandfather) (Perera 1993), and the bilingual book *Listen to the Desert/Oye al desierto* (Mora 1994) are wonderful for shared reading with their repetitive phrases and animal sounds that students can say together or take on as parts for a kind of shared readers' theatre.

In English, the big book *One Red Rooster* (Sullivan Carroll 1996) is an excellent counting book that contains onomatopoeia. As we mentioned earlier, songs and poetry written on large charts make wonderful shared reading activities. (Most of the following references come in big book form.) They include the traditional songs like "Los pollitos dicen" (What the Little Chicks Say) (Fernández 1993) and "Vengan a ver mi granja" (Come See My Farm). During English time teachers can follow "Vengan a ver mi granja" with "Old MacDonald Had a Farm" and the children can pick animals and then all sing the animal sounds. Reading poems that include onomatopoeia is also an enjoyable shared reading activity. Several traditional poems with animal sounds include *"Los sapitos"* (The Little Toads) (Houghton Mifflin 1997), *"Alborada"* (Dawn) (1993; Houghton Mifflin 1997), and *"Las hormigas marchan"* (The Ants March) (Houghton Mifflin 1997).

Like read-alouds, shared reading offers many benefits. Teachers can model strategies. For example, a teacher could cover some words in a predictable book with sticky notes. Then as she reads, the teacher can pause and ask the students to predict the hidden word. The teacher can also uncover the word one letter at a time to help students learn to use graphic cues to confirm their predictions.

Shared reading also allows teachers to demonstrate how good readers think by using think-alouds. For example, the teacher might think aloud to show how she connects the current book to one read previously, or the teacher might demonstrate rereading to make sense of a passage or reading on to get more information.

Shared reading offers many useful teaching points. Parkes (2000) explains how teachers can use shared reading for both implicit and explicit instruction. As they follow along and participate in the reading of a big book, students develop book and print conventions. They learn about punctuation, letter-sound relationships, words, syntax, and semantics. Much of this learning is incidental, but teachers can also target each of the three cueing systems with specific lessons during shared reading. For example, a teacher could focus on syntax by covering the pronouns in a passage and then having students discuss the kinds of words that could fit into each blank and talk about why one pronoun, such as *she*, sounds better than another one, like *her*.

Parkes' book is a very useful resource, especially for teachers of younger students. In addition to explaining how to use shared reading for implicit and explicit instruction, Parkes shows clearly how to conduct an effective shared reading lesson and lists the resources a teacher needs for shared reading, such as high-lighter tape, pocket charts, and a pointer. She also gives examples of good shared reading lessons using both narrative and informational texts. She suggests follow-up writing activities and includes a useful chapter on how to choose books for shared reading.

Although shared reading is used most commonly with younger students, it also is essential for many older students, especially those who still struggle to read grade-appropriate texts. Since most big books are written for younger children, the content and pictures are usually not appropriate for older students. Often, though, teachers share reading by reading aloud from a class text as students follow along in their individual copies. The teacher stops periodically to ask questions about the reading or to have students make predictions. Teachers can also model how proficient readers make sense of texts by using a think-aloud.

Teachers may also put a reading selection on a transparency and project it so that all the students can read it, or they may scan in some pages and project them in a PowerPoint presentation. Like younger students, older readers also benefit from alternative formats for shared reading such as buddy reading and listening to a taped reading of a book.

In her book *On the Same Page: Shared Reading Beyond the Primary Grades*, Allen (2002) provides many examples of how teachers of older students can use shared reading effectively. For example, shared reading passages can lead to productive vocabulary study. Allen also discusses how to grade shared reading experiences. Like Parkes, Allen explains how to use shared reading for explicit strategy instruction. Through the use of shared reading, teachers can help older struggling readers move toward independence.

Interactive Reading: A Bridge to Guided Reading

A kind of intermediate stage between shared reading and guided reading is interactive reading. Students are given more responsibility because they now read to and with other students. Students can be paired in such a way that each pair has a stronger reader to support a more struggling one. As a less proficient reader works with a more proficient reader, the less proficient reader can begin to chime in and pick up the intonation pattern of the language. In bilingual and dual language classes, students often work in bilingual pairs. Depending on the language of instruction, the native speaker becomes the more proficient reader. When instruction switches to the other language, the student who was less proficient now becomes the more proficient reader. This provides a good balance so that each student has a chance to take the lead.

Reading pairs can be organized within a classroom or across different classrooms. Samway, Whang, and Pippit (1995) have written about the benefits of buddy reading as part of a cross-age tutoring program in a school with many English language learners. As they demonstrate, both the older readers and their young partners benefit from engaging in buddy reading.

Another way to form a bridge between shared and guided reading is to use listening centers. Students can follow along as they hear fluent readers read texts. They can also read along with the readers on the tapes. Both these options can help struggling readers begin to read more fluently and expressively.

Guided Reading

The third stage of the gradual release model is guided reading. Here, the responsibility shifts much more to the students. During guided reading, students do more reading on their own under the guidance of their teacher and with her support. Guided reading allows students to apply the skills they have developed during shared reading. Typically, the teacher works with a small group of students who have similar instructional needs. The teacher uses short books during the guided reading lesson. Often the teacher uses leveled books. These are small books that are organized by various criteria, such as the number of words, the syntactic complexity, and the text-to-picture match. The students may reread a familiar book first. Then the teacher introduces a new book and guides the students as they read it with her. Afterward, students read the book on their own. They may also do writing related to the book. Throughout the lesson, the teacher uses the text to teach reading strategies in context.

There are several differences between shared and guided reading. Shared reading is most often done as a whole-class activity. Guided reading involves small groups of students. In shared reading the teacher often uses a text all the students can see, although teachers of older students may read a normal-sized book while the students follow along in their books. For guided reading, each student has a copy of the book. The key difference between shared and guided reading is that in shared reading the teacher does most of the reading, and the students occasionally chime in, while in guided reading the students do most of the reading with support from the teacher. Both shared and guided reading provide opportunities for implicit and explicit teaching.

During a guided reading lesson the teacher models good reading strategies and students learn both strategies and skills. Lessons are designed to ensure student success. This builds confidence and independence. By working with small groups, teachers can carefully monitor students' use of strategies and provide responsive instruction that matches the needs of the reader. The goal of guided reading is to propel students toward independent reading.

The key to success with guided reading is flexibility. Teachers need to adjust instruction to meet the needs of their students. This requires considerable professional skill. A good resource for teachers who want to implement or refine guided reading is *Reaching Readers: Flexible and Innovative Strategies for Guided Reading* (Opitz and Ford 2001). The authors begin by outlining the roles of the teacher and students and the goals of guided reading. Then they discuss how to group students, how to select texts, how to conduct the guided reading session, and how to manage the rest of the class while working with a small group. In the chapter on conducting the lesson, the authors include scenarios from classes at different grade levels so readers get a clear picture of what makes up a good lesson. *Reaching Readers* provides answers to many of the questions teachers may have about guided reading.

Independent Reading

In 1966 Dan Fader published a remarkable book documenting his success with helping boys in a reform school improve their reading ability and develop a love of reading by simply providing them with books and magazines that they enjoyed reading and also providing time each day to read them. Ten years later, Fader (1976) published a second edition of this book. In it, he explained that many of his former students were able to break out of a cycle of poverty and crime as the result of getting hooked on books. The key was finding books the students wanted to read. *Hooked on Books,* as well as other work by Fader and others, made educators aware of the benefits of independent reading.

In most schools students are given some time for independent reading on a regular basis. The time period varies. Generally, older and more proficient readers are given more time to read on their own. Often, the reading period is referred to as DEAR time (drop everything and read) or SSR (sustained silent reading). *Silent* is a relative term. Especially in lower grades, students may read aloud to themselves or with a partner. In some schools everyone reads at the same time each day, and in other schools individual teachers schedule the time for independent reading. Although in many cases students read by themselves, this can be a time for students to read with partners. In many dual language schools, teachers organize bilingual pairs, and the two students support one another when reading in either language.

During independent reading, students select and read books or magazines for enjoyment or information. One key for successful independent reading sessions is for students to make good choices of texts to read. For that reason, teachers usually spend time teaching students to choose appropriate books, and teachers monitor student choices so that students won't be bored by easy books or frustrated by hard ones. Teachers may also organize the books in the room to make choosing the right book easier.

We have developed a checklist teachers can use as they select books for guided and independent reading (see Figure 6–3). This checklist includes factors that support readers. For example, if books are predictable and culturally relevant, they are easier for students to read. In the same way, books with a good text-to-picture match provide important cues for younger or less proficient readers. In addition, books should be authentic and engaging. This is particularly important for books students read independently.

As they read independently, students can apply the strategies and skills they have learned during read-alouds, shared reading, and guided reading. Teachers may organize the class into literature circles or information circles so that students who read the same book may discuss it together.

---

1. Are the materials authentic? Authentic materials are written to inform or entertain, not to teach a grammar point or a letter-sound correspondence.

---

2. Is the language of the text natural? When there are only a few words on a page, does the limited text sound like real language, something people would really say? If the book was translated, how good is the translation?

---

3. Is the text predictable? Books are more predictable when students have background knowledge of the concepts, so teachers should activate or build background. For emergent readers, books are more predictable when they follow certain patterns (repetitive, cumulative) or include certain devices (rhyme, rhythm, alliteration). For developing readers, books are more predictable when students are familiar with text structures (beginning, middle, end; problem-solution; main idea, details, examples, etc.). Books are more predictable when students are familiar with text features (headings, subheadings, maps, labels, graphs, tables, indexes, etc.).

---

4. For picture books, is there a good text-to-picture match? A good match provides nonlinguistic visual cues. Is the placement of the pictures predictable?

---

5. Are the materials interesting and/or imaginative? Interesting, imaginative texts engage students.

---

6. Do the situations and characters in the book represent the experiences and backgrounds of the students in the class? Culturally relevant texts engage students.

FIGURE 6–3. Checklist of Text Characteristics That Support Reading

Krashen (2004) has summarized the research on what he terms free voluntary reading. Almost without fail, studies have shown that students make gains in reading comprehension when they are given time to read. The few studies that do not show gains were usually very short-term studies. It takes time to establish a routine for independent reading. Students need to learn how to make good choices of books. When teachers give students time to read on a regular basis for at least a semester, the students show clear gains in their reading comprehension.

Although independent reading is an essential component of an effective reading program, it works only if it is implemented correctly. Pilgreen (2000) lists eight key elements of a good SSR program for second language learners. First, students need access to appropriate books. Nothing can sink an SSR program more quickly than a lack of books. If students don't find something interesting to read, they won't get hooked on books. Instead, they will interrupt other students who are trying to read. Along the same lines, the books must be appealing. Teachers have found different ways to display books and magazines so that they attract students. For example, they may line them up on the chalkboard or find another way to display them so that the covers are easily visible. Organizing books by topic can also help students find books of interest. In addition, teachers can include as many books as possible on the current theme they are teaching.

Besides access and appeal, Pilgreen lists a conducive environment as one of the factors that characterizes successful programs. At the very least, the room should be quiet (or relatively quiet, with students reading in pairs) during SSR. Students should know not to interrupt other readers. Teachers also create conducive environments by bringing in a couch or beanbag chairs for students to sit in as they read. One teacher even created a reading loft. Her students could climb up a ladder to the loft and read their books. Pilgreen also points out that teachers should encourage students to read. Struggling readers often need encouragement. Even when the teacher provides books a struggling reader can read, the student's past experiences might make him or her reluctant to try reading, and for such students, an extra nudge may be needed.

In many districts whole schools have adopted SSR programs. In some cases the programs have failed because the teachers were simply told to plan some time each day for SSR, but they were not given any training in how to develop a good program. Staff training is a key factor in creating effective programs. It helps for all teachers to follow similar procedures. Of course, teachers all need the right books and time in the schedule for SSR.

One factor that Pilgreen lists surprises many people: nonaccountability. By this, she means that students should not be tested or made to write a book report on every book they read. If students have to take a quiz every time they finish a story, SSR quickly loses its appeal. In fact, we have seen schools that have adopted programs that provide books but also provide computerized systems with quizzes and a way to compile student points. In these schools, a class might earn a pizza party if the students earn enough points by reading books and passing tests. The problem is that students stop reading for pleasure or information. Instead, they read to pass a quiz. Good readers choose easy books that they can read quickly to pile up points. Although these programs are attractive to administrators because they provide books and a computerized management system, they are actually dangerous. Students who are rewarded with points or prizes for reading may not read without those external rewards. The programs can subvert the development of a love of reading.

Even though Pilgreen says that students should not be held accountable for each book they read, she also states that teachers should engage students in different kinds of follow-up activities. She lists a number of these. Students can give oral reports on books or make a poster for a book they liked. They can write a blurb to advertise a book or record an ad for the book. They can create a diorama to represent key ideas in a book. Students who have read the same book can develop a class presentation on the book. Teachers can hold a short conference with a student who has finished a book to talk about what the student learned or what she liked or disliked about the book.

One teacher we know created a database program where his fifth graders could log in, read other students' comments on a book, and then add their own. Students enjoyed giving their opinion on the books they read, and in the process they provided evidence that they had read and understood the book. The follow-up activity could also reflect the content of two or three related books. For example, students could create a Venn diagram showing how the books or some of the characters are alike and different. After reading a book, students like to talk about it or share what they have learned, and effective teachers provide students with various ways to do that.

Finally, Pilgreen points out that a good SSR program must provide students with distributed time to read. Just reading for an hour on Friday isn't enough. By the next week, students will have forgotten what they were reading. Instead, students need a set period of time each day or every other day for reading. When students know the schedule for SSR, they begin to look forward to that time, and they make better use of the SSR period. In all, Pilgreen lists eight factors that are important in establishing a good independent reading period: access, appeal, conducive environment, encouragement, staff training, nonaccountability, follow-up activities, and distributed time to read.

⬛ Techniques

We have said that principled teachers choose a method that is consistent with their view of reading. We have described the gradual release of responsibility model, which includes a series of routines that constitute the method for a principled teacher. During reading instruction, teachers also employ a number of techniques. *Technique* refers to a classroom strategy or activity. Principled teachers use a variety of techniques to help their students learn to read. They check that the techniques they use are consistent with their method and approach. They make sure that the focus stays on constructing meaning from text. As long as an activity has comprehension as the goal, a principled teacher will use it. The specific techniques a teacher uses are varied, but they are not eclectic because they are guided by this overarching focus on constructing meaning.

An example of a technique that a principled teacher might use is one that helps students make and confirm predictions. This technique builds the students' knowledge and use of the semantic cueing system. The teacher chooses a real object that she thinks the students don't know about. For example, a bilingual teacher could build a lesson around a concept such as *hallacas*.

First, the teacher reveals the title *Hallacas* on the overhead projector and asks students to brainstorm what they think *hallacas* might be. Since *hallacas* are real things, the teacher asks any student who knows the answer not to tell the class. Then the teacher reveals one line at a time. After each line, students add new guesses and also decide if they should remove any earlier guesses. For example, if students guessed that *hallacas* were some kind of geographical feature such as a mountain range, they would take that guess off the list when they read that one can buy them. If students guessed that *hallacas* were some kind of art or craft, they would remove that guess when they read that they are *sabrosas* (delicious). Below we provide the full *hallacas* strategy lesson.

Hallacas
- A todo el mundo le gustan hallacas.
- La palabra *hallaca* es una combinación de dos palabras, *allá* (España) y *acá* (El Nuevo Mundo). Hallacas representan la influencia de los españoles y de los indígenas.
- Se pueden comprar o hacerlas en la casa.
- Muchas familias las hacen juntas.
- Son más sabrosas hechas en casa.
- Son el plato típico de Las Navidades.

- Hay que juntar muchos ingredientes para prepararlas.
- Se usa una masa especial de harina de maíz.
- Esta masa se pone bien delgada en forma redonda y luego se rellena con una preparación a base de pollo, carne de puerco, tomates, pimentones rojos, cebollas, ajos, y otras especies que le dan sabor al guiso.
- Se dobla la masa con este relleno y se envuelve en hojas de banana o de plátano. Se amarran con hilo y luego se ponen a cocinar en agua caliente por una hora aproximadamente.
- Los venezolanos comen hallacas durante todo el mes de diciembre, pero durante la Nochebuena de Navidad y de Año Nuevo es el plato que nunca falta en la mesa.

Translation

Hallacas
- Everyone likes hallacas.
- The word *hallaca* is a combination of two words, *there* (Spain) and *here* (the New World). Hallacas represent the influence of the Spanish and the indigenous people.
- They can be bought or made at home.
- Many families make them together.
- They are more delicious made at home.
- They are a typical Christmas dish.
- It is necessary to gather a lot of ingredients to prepare them.
- A special dough made of corn flour is used.
- This dough is made very thin and formed in a circle and then is filled with a mixture of chicken, pork, tomatoes, red peppers, onions, garlic, and other spices that give the dish flavor.
- The dough is doubled over with this filling inside and wrapped in banana or plantain leaves. It is tied with a string and then put in hot water to cook for approximately an hour.
- Venezuelans eat hallacas during the entire month of December, but on Christmas and New Year's Eve it is a dish that is never missing from the table.

Students enjoy these lessons. What is important is for students to discuss with classmates why they made certain predictions and which clues helped them confirm their predictions or helped them decide they had not made a good guess. Less proficient readers are helped to see that even the good readers don't know all the words. They also come to understand the process good readers use to make guesses about words they don't know. Finally, they start to see the importance of reading on for more information instead of stopping to wait for help. Of course, they also understand that sounding out words like *hallacas* won't help them make sense of text.

Linda Hoyt has written a series of books that contain excellent strategy lessons (1999, 2000, 2002, 2005). These lessons are consistent with a sociopsycholinguistic view of reading because they focus on comprehension. The books are wonderful resources for techniques that principled teachers can use. Another very good resource is Kucer and Silva's book *Teaching the Dimensions of Literacy* (2006). This book also contains many useful strategies for teachers. All the strategies can be used as techniques by a principled teacher.

 ## Conclusion

Teaching reading can involve teachers and students in many different kinds of activities. Too often those activities give students conflicting messages about what the goals of reading really are. It is important for teachers to take a principled approach to the teaching of reading. By taking a principled approach, teachers align the methods and techniques they select with their view of reading.

In this chapter we have outlined a method, based on the gradual release of responsibility model, that is consistent with a sociopsycholinguistic view of reading. We have also given one example of a technique that fits this view. The sociopsycholinguistic view of reading builds on the understandings about reading that children bring to school. The interview, the environmental print task, and the functions of print task that we described can all provide important insights into how young children view reading.

In the first six chapters, we have discussed reading in Spanish and in English, including two views of reading, the history of reading instruction, the methods used, and a principled approach. In the next two chapters we discuss writing. It is important for bilingual teachers to understand writing development in both Spanish and English in order to help students become truly biliterate.

 ## Applications

1. In this chapter we distinguished among *approach*, *method*, and *technique*. Looking at the list below, work with a partner or in a small group to determine which are approaches, which are methods, and which are techniques. Be pre-

pared to defend your responses. Some items on the list might fit more than one category depending on how they are implemented.

> reading the chapter and answer the questions at the end
>
> social constructivism
>
> using big books
>
> teaching reading using syllables
>
> doing a literature study
>
> organizing around themes
>
> behaviorism
>
> looking up vocabulary words
>
> teaching reading using a basal reader series
>
> sociopsycholinguistic view of reading
>
> Accelerated Reader
>
> comprehension questions
>
> Reading First
>
> using a variety of reading strategies to help students construct meaning
>
> using flash cards
>
> giving students phonemic awareness exercises
>
> word recognition view of reading
>
> using a gradual release of responsibility model to teach reading

2. With a preschooler, do a series of environmental print tasks over several weeks. Choose several products the child might be familiar with. Following are some questions you might ask, listed in Spanish and in English. Write up your results and be prepared to discuss what you learned by doing this task.

Reconocimiento de la escritura en el ambiente
Print Awareness in the Environment

Preguntas de muestra	Sample Questions
¿Has visto esto antes?	Have you seen this before?
¿Dónde?	Where?
¿Qué piensas que es esto?	What do you think that is?
¿Qué crees que dice?	What do you think it says?

Preguntas de muestra

¿Cómo sabes?

¿Por qué dijiste eso?

¿Qué te hace pensar eso?

¿Qué te indica que dice eso?

Indícame con tu dedito dónde dice . . .

¿Qué más dice esto?

¿Cómo sabes?

Sample Questions

How do you know?

Why did you say that?

What makes you think so?

What tells you what it says?

Show me with your finger where it says . . .

What else does this say?

How do you know?

3. Do the functions of print task with a preschooler in Spanish or in English. What did you learn? What interesting answers did the child give? Why did the child answer in that way?

Funciones de la Escritura en el Ambiente

Introducción

Esta entrevista informal se hace individualmente con niños de cuatro a siete años. Antes de hacer la entrevista hay que coleccionar los objetos sugeridos en la lista de abajo o escoger entre los de la lista y otro tipo de texto. Por ejemplo, algunas personas han escojido una tarjeta de cumpleaños o la cuenta de electricidad.

Direcciones para la entrevista
Diga al niño/a la niña: "Te voy a enseñar algunas cosas que probablemente hayas visto en la escuela o en tu casa."
Ponga enfrente del niño/de la niña los tres primeros elementos de la lista: el libro de cuentos, la tarjeta de cumpleaños, y el periódico.

Diga al niño/a la niña: "Enséñame el libro de cuentos."

Functions of Environmental Print

Introduction

This informal interview is done one on one with children between four and seven years old. Before conducting the interview, collect the objects suggested on the list below or choose among those on the list and another type of text. For example, some people have chosen a birthday card or an electricity bill.

Directions for the Interview
Say to the child: "I am going to show you something that you have probably seen at school or at home."
Put the first three items on the list in front of the child: the storybook, the birthday card, and the newspaper.

Say to the child: "Show me the storybook."

Pregunte: "¿Por qué leemos libros de cuentos?"
Escriba lo que el niño/a conteste.

Quite el libro de cuentos y reemplácelo con otro artículo de la lista. Esté seguro/de tener siempre tres objetos enfrente del niño/de la niña.

Al final pregunte "¿Por qué leemos?" Se puede introducir esta idea diciendo, "Hemos hablado de varias cosas que la gente lee. Vamos a fingir que estás hablando con alguien que no sabe nada de la lectura. Esta persona te pregunta, '¿Por qué leemos?' ¿Qué contestarías?"

Ask: "Why do people read storybooks?"
Write what the child answers.

Take the storybook away and replace it with another item on the list. Be sure to always have three items in front of the child.

At the end, ask, "Why do people read?" You can introduce this idea saying, "We have talked about several things that people read. Let's pretend that you are talking to someone who doesn't know anything about reading. That person asks, 'Why do people read?' What would you answer?"

Entrevista
Interview

Nombre _____ Edad _____
(Lo reconoció?)

Objeto	¿Lo reconoció?	Respuesta
Item	**Recognition**	**Response**
1. Libro de cuentos Storybook	sí	no
2. Tarjeta de cumpleaños Birthday card	sí	no
3. Periódico Newspaper	sí	no
4. Libro/guía de teléfonos Telephone book	sí	no
5. Revista Magazine	sí	no
6. Lista de compras Shopping list	sí	no

Objeto **Item**	¿Lo reconoció? **Recognition**	Respuesta **Response**
7. Carta Letter	sí	no
8. Cuenta (de electricidad, etc.) Bill (electric, etc.)	sí	no
9. Calendario Calendar	sí	no
10. Direcciones Directions	sí	no

¿Por qué leemos?
Why do people read?

Effective Writing Instruction

Pablo is a fourth-grade student in a dual language school where he receives part of his day's instruction in Spanish and part in English. Pablo does lots of reading and writing in both Spanish and English in a wide variety of genres. Figure 7–1 is taken from one section of Pablo's long report titled, "My Grandfather and Me." For this report Pablo interviewed his grandfather and then wrote about what he found out and how he felt about his grandfather's life. Pablo describes his grandfather's adult life and records details that seem especially interesting, including killing a pig for his wedding celebration. In his conclusion (see Figure 7–2), which follows after several pages, Pablo shows his respect for his grandfather with the end of his last sentence, "he worked hard to have a nice family and life."

Pablo's writing sample in Spanish (see Figure 7–3) is the first chapter of a four-chapter story about the adventures of King Cobra. In this opening chapter we see that Pablo has imagination and an understanding of how to set up a plot. In his story King Cobra must overcome an evil character. His story's ending (see

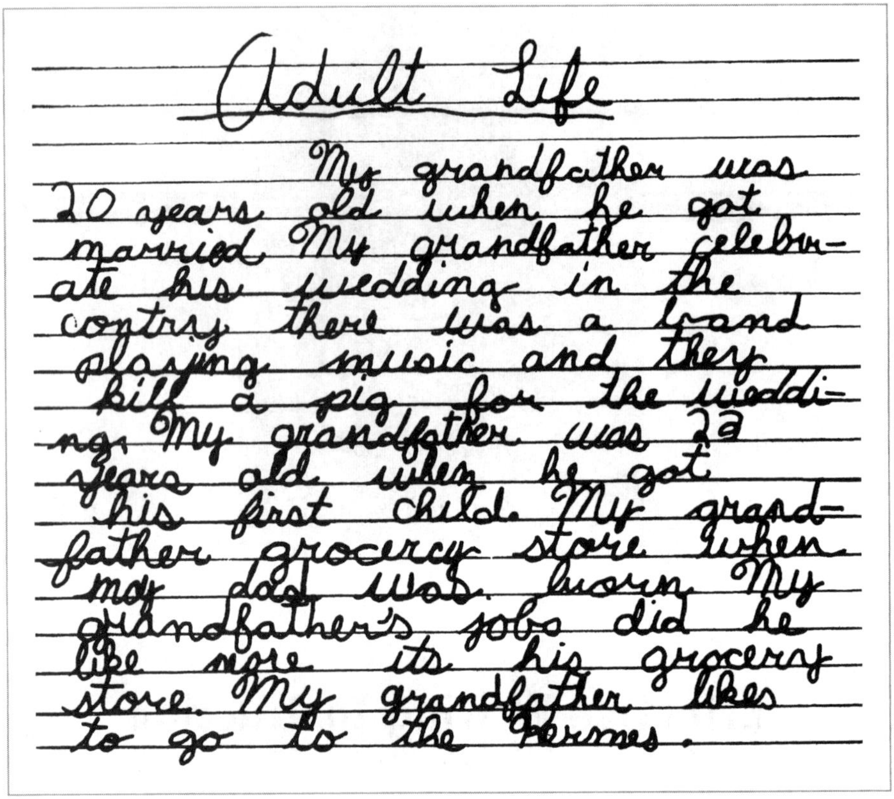

Adult Life

My grandfather was 20 years old when he got married. My grandfather celebrate his wedding in the contry. there was a band playing music and they kill a pig for the wedding. My grandfather was 22 years old when he got his first child. My grandfather grocercy store when my dad was born. My grandfather's jobs did he like more its his grocery store. My grandfather likes to go to the Hermes.

FIGURE 7–1. Pablo's Grandfather Story

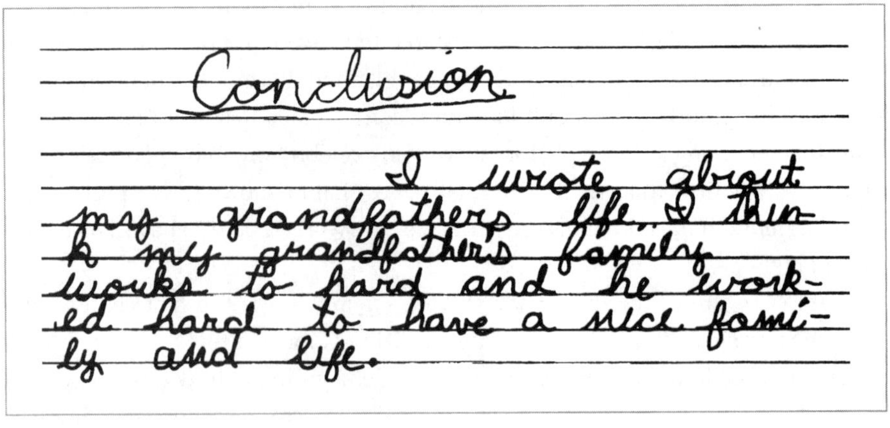

Conclusion

I wrote about my grandfathers life. I think my grandfather's family works to hard and he worked hard to have a nice family and life.

FIGURE 7–2. Conclusion to Grandfather Story

King Cobra.

Había una vez
un señor que se llama
King Cobra. Y el peleaba
con las personas malas
y las mataba. Un día su
hermano vino y se llama
King Snake. El también
sabía pelear. Y una vez
ellos se metieron en prob-
lemas y ellos estaban en
la corte con el lider
de los malos. El hermano
de King Cobra. Y el lider
de los malos estaba
diciendo mentiras de que
ellos querían robar su
esposa" pero no le
creyeron a King Cobra
lo que dijo. Entonces
los metieron a la
carsel a el y a su
hermano. Ellos estaban
triste.

1 pg

King Cobra
Once there was
a man who was called
King Cobra. And he fought
the bad guys
and they treated him badly. One
day his
brother came and his name was
King Snake. He also
knew how to fight. And one time
they had some problems
and they were in
court with the leader
of the bad guys. The brother
of King Cobra and the leader
of the bad guys were
saying lies that
they wanted to steal his
wife, but they didn't
believe what King Cobra
said. Then
they put them in jail,
him and his brother.
They were sad.

FIGURE 7–3. Pablo's King Cobra Story

Figure 7–4) is also quite predictable. The last line shows that the heroes win in the end and that *"ellos vivieron muy felices"* (they lived very happily).

Pablo's writing contains errors. However, he expresses himself clearly in both English and Spanish. In addition, he writes both nonfiction and fiction comfortably. At fourth grade Pablo is well on his way to becoming a confident writer in two languages. How did Pablo arrive at this stage? It is important that bilingual teachers understand how to support students writing in two languages. This includes providing a variety of rich writing experiences and knowing how to evaluate and support emergent writing.

In earlier chapters we focused on reading. In this chapter and the next we turn to writing development to show how teachers can help students learn to write effectively in two languages. Even though we discuss reading and writing development in different chapters, we recognize that they are interrelated processes. As we have discussed views of reading and methods of teaching reading, we have described lessons in which reading and writing are linked. As we discuss writing development, we give examples that come from classrooms rich in opportunities for

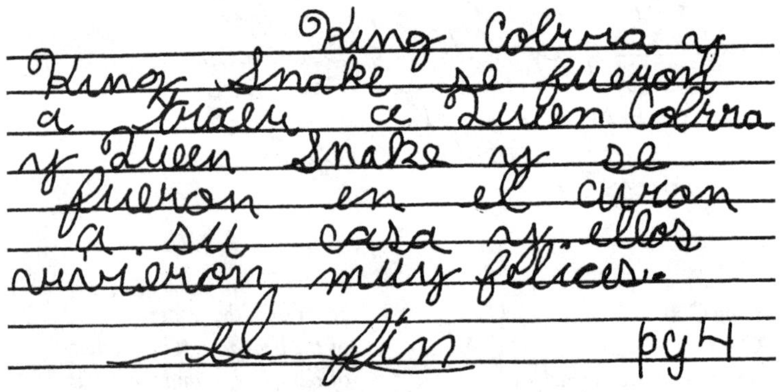

King Cobra and King Snake went
to get Queen Cobra and Queen Snake and
they went by plane
to their house and they
lived very happily.
The end.

FIGURE 7–4. Conclusion to King Cobra Story

meaningful reading and writing. The teachers in these classrooms understand that a good literacy program always connects reading and writing.

We begin our discussion of writing by presenting different approaches to teaching writing. In the same way that there are two views of reading, there are also two views of writing that we refer to as a traditional approach and a process approach. We contrast these two views and then present a checklist of effective writing instruction. After describing the elements of a successful writing program in general, we turn to the details of writing development. We focus on the natural development of writing in both English and Spanish in classrooms in which teachers take a process approach. For each developmental stage, we suggest classroom activities and give examples of good teaching that supports students and moves them to higher levels of writing.

Two Views of Writing

Just as there are two views of reading, there are two distinct views of writing. The first view of writing, the traditional view, parallels the word recognition approach to teaching reading. The second view, process writing, parallels the sociopsycholinguistic view of reading. Figure 7–5 shows the differences between the traditional approach and the process approach.

Like the word recognition view of reading, the traditional view of writing begins with small units and builds up to wholes. Teachers often start by having students copy letters and words. The teacher directly instructs students on how to form the letters and how to combine letters into words and sentences. The teacher tells students what to write about. The topics may or may not relate to students' lives. Students are expected to produce certain kinds of writing in specified time periods. For example, they might copy sentences from the board or complete a worksheet during a twenty-minute writing period.

Writing assignments in traditional classes are generally exercises in penmanship and spelling at early stages. Later, students learn to write complete sentences and paragraphs with a topic sentence and details. Eventually, they move to a five-paragraph essay. The audience for all this writing is really the teacher. The teacher's job is to assign the writing, provide direct instruction in the elements of writing to be learned, and then correct what the students produce. Students seldom share their writing with one another, although good papers may be posted on the board. The focus of writing instruction is always on the final product, and the goal is for students to develop the skills needed to produce writing that follows conventions of spelling, punctuation, and grammar.

Traditional Writing Classrooms	Process Writing Classrooms
Focus on the product.	Focus on the process and product.
Begin with parts and build to whole messages.	Begin with the messages and then focus on the parts.
Teacher directly instructs on how to form letters, then words, and combine words into sentences.	Teacher creates conditions for authentic written responses.
Teacher gives topics.	Teachers help students learn to choose good topics.
Topics may or may not relate to students' lives.	Topics come from students' backgrounds and interests.
Time for writing is restricted and inflexible.	Time for writing is open and flexible.
Few resources are available for writers.	Many resources are available for writers.
Writing product must be conventional.	Writing moves naturally from invention to convention.
Students write for the teacher.	Students write for a real audience.
The teacher corrects.	Classmates and others respond.
Writing is private and individual.	Writing is shared and social.

FIGURE 7–5. Two Views of Teaching Writing (based on Pearson and Gallagher 1983)

In contrast, with process approaches to writing, the focus is always on communicating a meaningful message. Students start with a message and teachers help them put their message in a written form that others can read. The early work of Graves (1983, 1994) and his colleagues (Calkins 1986; Hansen 1987) helped teachers understand how to implement classroom writing instruction modeled on the process professional writers go through. Teachers and teacher educators have continued to publish useful books on how to implement process writing approaches (Calkins 2003; Fletcher 1992; Harwayne 2000; Routman 2000).

Teachers who take a process approach understand that writing develops naturally in stages as students move from inventing spellings toward producing conventional forms of the language. The teacher's job in a process writing class is to create situations in which writing is a natural way to communicate. For example, teachers might take students on a field trip and then have them write about the experience. For young writers, the teacher may act as scribe, using a language ex-

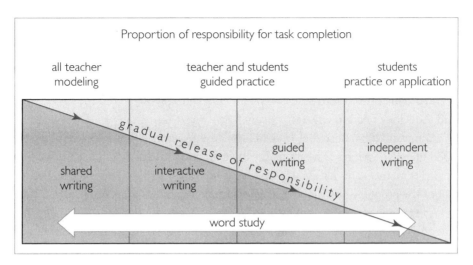

Proportion of responsibility for task completion

all teacher
modeling

teacher and students
guided practice

students
practice or application

gradual release of responsibility

shared
writing

interactive
writing

guided
writing

independent
writing

word study

FIGURE 7–6. Gradual Release of Responsibility Model for Writing (based on Pearson and Gallagher 1983)

perience approach. Gradually, students take over the responsibility for writing. Just as in reading, there is a gradual release of responsibility in writing. Figure 7–6 shows the stages in the gradual release of responsibility in writing model.

 ## Gradual Release Model for Writing

The first stage, shared writing, parallels a read-aloud because the teacher does all the writing. This stage is referred to as shared writing because the students contribute ideas. During a language experience activity, for example, the students tell the teacher what to write, and he acts as the scribe. Interactive writing, the second stage, is similar to shared reading. Students begin to take responsibility for the writing as they share the pen with the teacher. This often occurs during the morning message or the daily news. Students contribute information and also come up to write sentences or words. The teacher may also ask students to add punctuation to a message. An excellent resource for teaching various conventions of writing during interactive writing is *Getting the Most Out of the Morning Message and Other Shared Writing* (daCruz-Payne and Browning-Schulman 1998).

The third stage, guided writing, is like guided reading. The students now take on the main responsibility for writing, but the teacher is there to support and guide the process. During guided writing, the teacher also gives many minilessons on specific aspects of writing (Atwell 1987, 1998). The goal of writing instruction is the final stage, independent writing. Students are given time to compose on their own. Then they share their results with classmates, often sitting in an author's chair.

Word study runs through the entire writing program. At early stages, during word study teachers help students notice and focus on letters and words. Teachers may create word walls and involve students in creating alphabet books. At later stages, students may carry out linguistic investigations on spelling patterns and word histories. Word study helps provide young writers with the knowledge and tools they need to write effectively.

Akhavan (2004) describes in detail how the teachers at her K–5 school developed effective writing workshops for their many English language learners. She provides many examples showing how the students' writing improved as the result of the process approach her teachers implemented.

As students move on to writing different genres, they often go through the stages of writing again. At first the teacher provides almost all the support. Gradually, the responsibility shifts to the students, and they write independently. Instruction is focused on the process of writing as well as on the final product. Students learn how to choose good topics, to revise drafts, and to edit what they write.

 ## Checklist for Effective Writing Instruction

The checklist for effective writing instruction reflects the three general components of good process writing classes: prewriting activities, writing activities, and postwriting activities. A great deal has been written about process writing for native English speakers (Calkins 1986, 1991; Fletcher 1992). Additional books and articles focus on process approaches for students writing in a second language (Gibbons 2002; Hudelson 1986, 1989; Rigg and Enright 1986). Ferreiro, Pontecorvo, and colleagues (1996) researched how young Spanish-, Portuguese-, and Italian-speaking children develop writing in each language by analyzing and comparing a version of *Little Red Riding Hood* written by the children in their native languages. Freeman and Bonett-Serra (2000) detail what an effective writing program for Spanish-speaking children would look like, and more recently, Castedo and Waingort (2003) have written a two-part article detailing the story writing of seven-year-olds in Argentina. Bruno de Castelli and Beke (2004) describe how the writing process helped older writers of Spanish become more comprehensible and more effective writers. We encourage readers to consult these books and articles for a more complete discussion of process writing. Here we only comment briefly on the checklist questions. Then we examine in detail the normal developmental patterns teachers may expect when working with young writers in bilingual and dual language classes.

To help teachers as they plan for teaching writing, we have developed a checklist for effective writing instruction (see Figure 7–7). We encourage teachers to use this checklist as they set up and then refine their own writing program. The checklist is based on a process approach to teaching writing that follows the gradual release of responsibility for writing model.

In traditional approaches to writing, teachers usually give students their topics. They may do this by making a specific assignment, providing a list of topics to choose from, or putting a story starter on the board. When teachers give students the topic, they miss an essential component of writing: writers choosing their own topics. Good writers make good choices of what to write about. When students choose their own topics, they take ownership of the writing and write for authentic purposes. That is, they write to express ideas that are important to them, instead of simply writing in response to an assignment.

Teachers help students make good topic choices by modeling the process of deciding what to write about and what not to write about. For example, a teacher might think aloud for the class: "Today I thought about three things I might write about." Then the teacher could list all three and discuss why one is better than the other two. Some teachers brainstorm with students how to choose topics, and they keep a list of possible topics up in the room.

---

1. Do teachers model the steps they go through to choose topics? Do they help students go through these same steps as they choose topics to write about?

2. Are students encouraged to draw on their own experiences when they choose topics? Do they write for authentic purposes?

3. Do students make connections between their reading and writing? Do they see that reading provides ideas for writing?

4. Do students keep and update a list of topics that they have written about and that they plan to write about?

5. Do students see writing as a process, and do they understand the various activities they should engage in as they move a piece of writing toward its final form?

6. Does the classroom have ample accessible literature, content, and resource books for students to reference as they write?

7. Are students allowed to invent spellings, drawing on their internal phonics hypotheses and their pictures of words derived from their reading experiences?

8. Do students have opportunities to share their writing with others? Is there authentic response, which is both critical and sensitive to the writer's needs?

FIGURE 7–7. Checklist for Effective Writing Instruction

Effective Writing Instruction

The best writing comes when students choose topics that tap into their own experiences and interests. Many teachers have students keep a personal list of possible topics. Students can keep an updated list of things they have written about and things they want to write about. Teachers discuss these topics with students in whole-class settings and in individual conferences, and they have students share possible topics with one another. Students also get ideas for writing from their reading (Hansen 1987) or write to report on topics they have investigated in social studies, math, science, or other subjects.

Besides helping students learn how to choose topics, teachers in process writing classrooms give students ample time for researching topics and for writing drafts, instead of assigning topics and giving a definite time period for the writing to be completed. In a process writing classroom most teachers create a kind of workshop setting, a large block of time each day devoted to reading and writing. Of course, teachers also have to help children understand how to use their time well. Not only do students have to start to see writing as a process, but they have to come to understand the process itself by being immersed in it during the workshop time.

Good writers don't start with all their ideas in their heads. Instead, they learn as they write. For this reason, writers need to know how to use a variety of resources. Teachers discuss with students possible resources for developing ideas and often encourage students to read more to get ideas and to look at other resources such as video or computer data banks to research topics. They also encourage students to talk to classmates, parents, and others as they plan their writing. In traditional classrooms, writing is private and individual, while in process classrooms, writing is shared and social.

Often, young writers have good ideas, but they become frustrated by their lack of control over writing conventions when they try to put their ideas on paper. They may have trouble forming letters, spelling words, or punctuating their messages. Teachers encourage these emergent writers to invent spellings and punctuation to represent their thoughts. However, these teachers also monitor student development and nudge them gradually toward more conventional forms. In addition, they help students edit their work for publication when appropriate.

In classrooms where students share their writing with others in a supportive environment, they become more aware of the need for using conventional writing forms that classmates, parents, and the teacher can understand. Control over standard forms takes time, but when students write for authentic purposes— when they have a real message and a real audience—they gradually refine their inventions and move toward writing that others can read.

![icon] Writing Development

Goodman and Goodman (1990) have described learning to read and write as finding a balance between invention and convention. Young writers invent spellings to express their ideas. They also invent words and punctuation marks. As they read, they become aware that the community of readers and writers has established certain conventional forms for writing. Different communities have established different conventions. In Spanish punctuation, for example, questions are signaled by a mark at the beginning of the question as well as one at the end. In English, on the other hand, the only cue comes at the end of the sentence. In Spanish, proper adjectives (like *español*) are not capitalized, but in English, they are. Children need to learn these conventions.

Children begin by producing scribble writing. Schickedanz and Casbergue (2004) explain that at first the scribbles children make are evidence of the discovery that they can make marks. Then, after several months, young children begin to notice that the marks remind them of something and identify it. This is probably not intentional, but more what the authors describe as "a happy accident" (9). Once children start to think they would like to re-create something they have scribbled, there is a change. However, as Schickedanz and Casbergue point out, "the sheer joy of creating marks dominates the child's marking for many months" (10). Still, there are more and more moments when children's scribble becomes more deliberate, and they want to say something with their marks.

Children's scribble writing gradually takes on purpose. Children's scribbles become first attempts at representing letters, which are easily distinguishable from a child's drawing. These first letters, referred to as mock letters by Schickedanz and Casbergue, are important in the development of writing. "Mock letters, which display many characteristics of alphabet letters, contain the segments that are the building blocks of actual letters" (18). A good example of mock letters in scribble writing comes from Anthony. His teacher, Blanca, asked her students to write about their Thanksgiving celebrations. Anthony drew a picture. Then he scribbled mock letters under it (see Figure 7–8). He told Blanca that his writing said, "I went to my grandma's on Thanksgiving." Blanca wrote his message using conventional letters and spellings and read it back to him. It is easy to distinguish Anthony's drawing from his writing. His letters are not yet well formed, but they are clearly intended to represent writing, not drawing.

Blanca is helping her students move toward conventional writing. In order to facilitate the writing development of emergent writers, teachers need to understand the normal patterns of writing development. With that knowledge, teachers can

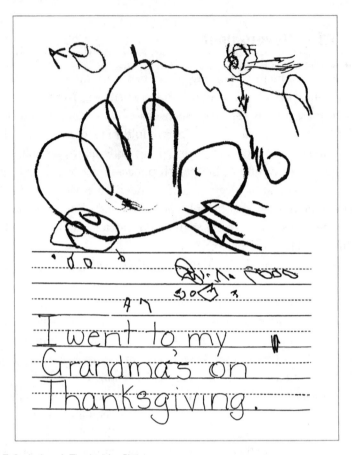

FIGURE 7–8. Anthony's Thanksgiving Picture

interpret and support students' written inventions while at the same time moving them toward conventional forms. If invention goes unchecked, nobody can read a child's message. However, if too much convention is imposed too early, children may lose the sense of writing as a process of constructing their own meanings. Bilingual teachers, as always, have even more to learn. They need to understand patterns of writing development that occur in English and in Spanish as well as what might be expected of Spanish speakers growing up in an environment dominated by print in English.

Early research by Read (1971), Chomsky (1970), and others has provided important insights into the natural process that children learning to write in English go through as they move from invention to convention. Continued investigations into children's spelling development (Hughes and Searle 1997; Laminack and Wood 1996; Schickedanz and Casbergue 2004; Wilde 1992) show both the natural patterns and the ways teachers can help students move from invention to convention. In

Spanish, the seminal work in children's writing development comes from Ferreiro and Teberosky (Ferreiro, Pontecorvo, et al. 1996; Ferreiro and Teberosky, 1979, 1982).

Before discussing this research, we wish to point out that while we use the term *stage* to describe different points of students' progress in writing, this is just a convenient way of discussing behaviors that really fall along a continuum. Children move in and out of stages. There is no neat, linear progression. However, the categories we refer to as stages reflect our understanding of the major insights that children generally achieve as their writing becomes progressively more conventional.

When it comes to writing development, it is experience with writing rather than age that counts. In some cases, very young children exhibit advanced stages of development. Paty, a graduate student, decided to test what she was learning about writing development with her four-year-old son, Flavio. When she asked him to write *cat* in Spanish, he represented the Spanish word for *cat*, *gato*, by writing "GTO," and then he wrote "CT" for cat in English. He was able to form conventional letters and surprised even his mother. He included both consonants and, for Spanish, a vowel. At four, he is already moving toward a fairly advanced stage of writing.

Five-year-old Leslie produced nearly conventional spellings in Spanish (see Figure 7–9) even though she didn't yet put spaces between her words. Other than

FIGURE 7–9. Leslie's Writing in Spanish

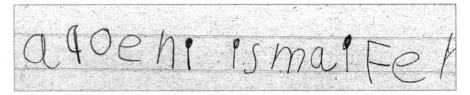

FIGURE 7–10. Leslie's Writing in English

reversing a *p*, she spelled each word correctly: "las amigas se pelearon" (The friends were fighting). Her writing in English was not quite so advanced, but after reading about Apple Annie, Leslie produced the writing shown in Figure 7–10. She must have liked this character, since she wrote, "Apple Annie is my friend." These two young writers have progressed to advanced stages of spelling in two languages. It is their experience with written language rather than their age that has allowed them to do this.

Stages of Writing Development

It is important for teachers to understand normal patterns of writing development for bilingual students. This knowledge can help teachers validate what children know. It can also guide teachers in providing the kinds of encouragement and instruction that will help their students become more effective writers. The following discussion draws on work done by Buchanan (1989) in her excellent book *Spelling for Whole Language Classrooms* as well as Fereirro and Teberosky's *Los sistemas de escritura en el desarrollo del niño* (1979) and the English translation, *Literacy Before Schooling* (1982).

Buchanan divides children's spelling development into four major stages: prephonetic, phonetic, phonic, and syntactic-semantic. She bases the stages on her observations of children's writing in English. For each stage she discusses the major concepts that the child has developed, and she suggests ways teachers can help children progress toward the next stage. Buchanan encourages teachers to keep samples of student writing so that they can identify patterns in the writing and keep track of students' progress.

The stages that Buchanan identifies for English correspond to five levels that Ferreriero and Teberosky describe for Spanish. Ferreiro and Tebersoky are Piagetian scholars who have worked extensively in Argentina and Mexico. Their findings are based on research in which they dictated words or sentences to children or asked children to complete certain tasks. Using these methods, Ferreiro and Teberosky were able to probe children's understandings of written language.

The results of the research by Buchanan and Ferreiro and Teberosky provide complementary insights into the understandings about print that children bring with them as they start school. When teachers understand how children conceptualize written language, they can plan lessons that build on these understandings. As we describe each stage of writing development in this chapter and the next, we use examples from Ferreiro and Teberosky and writing samples we have collected from children in bilingual classrooms. Figure 7–11 summarizes the characteristics of each stage of writing described by Buchanan and each level identified by Ferreiro and Teberosky.

Stage (Buchanan)	Level (Ferreiro and Teberosky)	Characteristics
prephonetic	1	There is no connection between letters and sounds. Writing is egocentric. It is not used to transmit information. The size of the letter string equals the size of the object.
	2	Writers assume that there is a fixed number of letters in a word and that there is a variety of letters (one letter is not repeated). Writers use the letters of their name.
early phonetic	3	There is a connection between the physical aspects of producing a word and the spelling of the word. Each letter stands for one syllable in the word.
late phonetic	4	Each element of sound production in the pronunciation of a word should have its own graphic representation. Writers move from a syllabic to an alphabetic hypothesis.
phonic	5	Sound is the key to spelling. However, writers may overgeneralize phonics rules. They realize that one sound may be represented by more than one letter and that the same sound may be represented by different letters or groups of letters.
syntactic-semantic		In the spelling of words, meaning and syntax provide important cues that in many cases take precedence over sound cues.

FIGURE 7–11. Stages and Levels of Writing Development

The Prephonetic Stage

The first stage is referred to as prephonetic because children are using symbols to represent things, not a word for the thing. A mark on the paper might represent a stuffed bear, not the word *bear*. As children in this early stage move from scribble writing to recognizable letters, they frequently mix letters and numbers. They often rely on the letters of their own name as they write. And they may not understand the difference between being asked to write and being asked to draw, even though their marks on paper show that they can do both.

Ferreiro and Teberosky's levels 1 and 2 correspond to Buchanan's prephonetic stage because at this level children do not associate writing and sounds. An example of level 1 writing comes from five-year-old Alexis (see Figure 7–12). He told his teacher that his writing said *"mi papá."* Alexis is beginning to form recognizable letters, and like many young writers, he uses letters from his name. The writing is prephonetic because there is no correspondence between the letters Alexis writes and the sounds in *mi papá*.

Ferreiro and Teberosky expand our understanding of this stage. They found three characteristics of children's writing at level 1: First, the writing is egocentric. That is, children do not realize that they have a responsibility for writing something that others might be able to read. Sometimes they know what they are writing, but they do not expect others to read it, nor do they expect to be able to read what others write. Even within level 1, though, children begin to develop a sense of audience and start to expect that others can read what they write.

Second, children believe the size of the written word should correspond to the size of the object the word represents. For example, children at this level would expect the word *papá* (father) to be bigger than the word *hermano* (brother) because for most young children, their father is bigger than their brother.

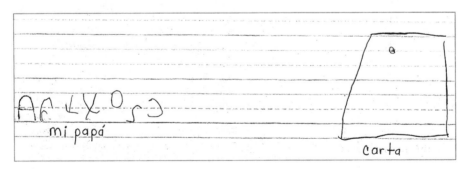

FIGURE 7–12. Alexis' Writing

When Ferreiro and Teberosky (1979) asked four-year-old Gustavo to write *pato* (duck), he drew some wavy lines. The dialogue between Gustavo and the researcher that follows shows Gustavo's thinking:

Researcher:	Gustavo:
¿Podés escribir "oso"?	
¿Será más largo o más corto?	Más grande.
¿Por qué?	[Gustavo comienza a hacer una escritura enteramente similar, pero que resulta más larga que la anterior, mientras silabea.]
	O-so. ¿Viste que sale más grande?
Sí, pero ¿por qué?	Porque es un nombre más grande que el *pato*. (242)

Translation

Can you write "bear"?	
Will it be longer or shorter?	Bigger.
	[Gustavo begins to write some thing similar but longer than what he wrote before while he sounds out in syllables.]
	O-so. Do you see that it comes out bigger?
Yes, but why?	Because it is a bigger name than *duck*.

Gustavo reasons that since bears are bigger than ducks, the written representation for *bear* should also be bigger. Two other examples from Ferreiro and Teberosky (1979) clarify how children relate quantifiable aspects of words to quantifiable aspects of meaning. A five-year-old in Mexico visiting her doctor told him that this time he had to write her name longer because her birthday had been the previous day. She was now bigger, so her name must be bigger too!

An additional example shows another way that level 1 children connect writing and size:

una niña mexicana de 5 años, llamada Verónica, escribe su nombre así: VERO; pero piensa que cuando sea grande lo va a esribir "con la be grande" (es decir, BERO, ya que en México la V es llamada "be chica" y la B es la "be grande"). (243)

Translation

A five-year-old Mexican girl named Verónica writes her name like this: VERO; but thinks that when she is older she is going to write it "with the big B" (that is, BERO, because in Mexico the V is called "small b" and the B is the "big b").

A third characteristic of writers at level 1 is that they do not distinguish clearly between what we call writing and drawing. For example, if a parent tells a child to write "mother," she might, instead, draw a mother. On the other hand, a child might say he will *draw* something and then write letters. In a study that replicated parts of Ferreiro and Teberosky's research discussed earlier, Freeman and Whitesell (1985) found this same confusion of terms among English-speaking preschool children in Tucson, Arizona. Children appear to distinguish writing from drawing, but they may not consistently use the words *write* and *draw* to describe what they are doing. They also frequently mix numbers and letters.

Ferreiro and Teberosky also point out that young writers often reverse characters, both letters and numbers, and that *"en este nivel y en niveles subsiguientes, señalemos que no puede ser tomada como índice patológico (preanuncio de dislexia o disgrafia), sino como algo totalmente normal"* (at this level, and in subsequent levels, we wish to point out that this [reversal of letters and numbers] cannot be taken as a pathological indication of a problem [announcing dyslexia or dysgraphia] but instead as something totally normal) (248).

We use Vicente, a level 1 writer, as an example of this phenomenon. Vicente drew a picture of the sun and some playground toys (see Figure 7–13). Then he wrote on his picture. Vicente told his teachers that his writing said, *"Había mucho sol y jugué afuera muchos días"* (There was a lot of sun, and I played outside many days). He appears to have reversed the number *4* and the letters *n, S,* and *R,* though the small *r* and both the *n* and the *R* were also written conventionally. He also inverts *v* in two places. It is important to realize that reversals like these are a natural part of writing development.

It's not that children *see* the letters backward. Instead, they are making hypotheses about the directionality of letters and numbers. They have to decide which way they face. Most letters of the alphabet can be thought of as facing toward the right. However, letters like *d* face to the left. Other letters, such as *g* may face either way, depending on the font, although capital *G* faces right. Numbers, on the other hand, face left except for *5* and *6.* Young children usually look for consistency and overgeneralize as they make their hypotheses. They expect that all the letters should face the same way. Unfortunately, the system isn't completely consistent. Children are constructing an underlying rule, not simply imitating surface forms. Since the rule they need is complex, this takes time. Unfortunately, some young children are not given the time they need. They are labeled as dyslexic early in their schooling even though their reversals are a natural part of development.

Ferreiro and Teberosky found that many of the Argentinean children they studied had a few words fixed in their repertoire. These children may have learned

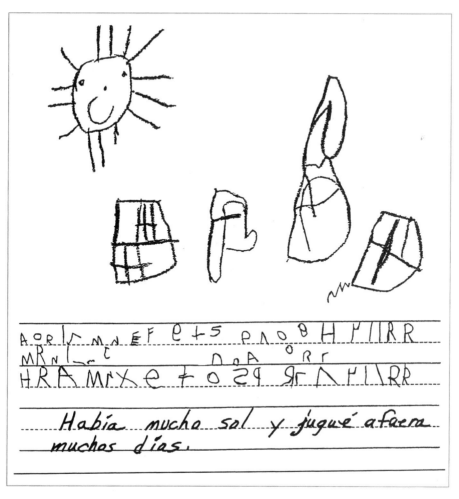

FIGURE 7–13. Vicente's Picture of the Sun

the words from a family member, or they may have seen the words often. Laura, for example, could write four words: *mamá*, *papá*, *oso*, and *Laura*. Ferreiro and Teberosky report Laura's explanation, "Laura *me enseñó mi mamá, y* papá*, oso y* mamá *aprendí yo de un librito para empezar a leer*" (*Laura* my mom taught me and papá*, oso*, and *mamá* I learned myself from a little beginning reading book).

Young writers may also copy words from around the room. As a language experience activity, Rhonda had her students choose a favorite story, illustrate it, and then tell her what was happening. Figure 7–14 shows Anita's drawing and labeling of *La bella durmiente* as well as Rhonda's writing of her summary. Even though Anita was at an early stage of writing, she did recognize the story title and was able to copy it quite accurately. Anita had a bit of trouble writing the article

No invitaron a la hada mala a la fiesta
de la princesita. Se enojó la hada olvidada
y su regalo que le dió fue que se picara
el dedo y morirá.

> They didn't invite the bad fairy to the party
> of the little princess. The forgotten fairy got mad
> and her gift that she gave was that she would prick
> her finger and die.

FIGURE 7–14. Anita's Drawing

straight on the title. She first wrote a crooked *L* and then erased it. When she showed her paper to Rhonda, together they decided the *a* was missing from her straightened *L*, and Rhonda added an *a*. As students copy letters, they begin to form the letters more conventionally. Anita was also learning that writing can be used to tell a story.

Ferreiro and Teberosky divide the prephonetic stage into two levels. In level 2 they found that the graphic forms children made were more defined and more conventional. Most of their letters were recognizable, although some reversals still occurred. A good example of level 2 writing comes from Ramón, a student in Pricila's kindergarten class (see Figure 7–15). Like many young writers, he relies on the letters from his name. At this point, there is still no correspondence between the letters and the sounds of the words they represent.

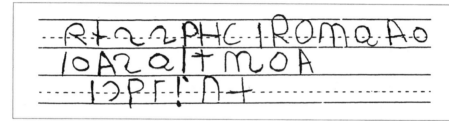

FIGURE 7–15. Ramón's Writing

Ferreiro and Teberosky also found that children at this stage hypothesize that words must have a certain, fixed number of characters and that words require a variety of characters. They drew these conclusions from a study in which they gave children cards with letters, numbers, words, and nonsense words. They asked children to sort the cards into two piles. One pile was "for reading" and one was "not for reading." They asked the children why they placed each card in a particular pile. The researchers found that young children hypothesize that words must be a certain length and have a variety of characters to be "for reading." So words like *un* (the Spanish article for *a* or *an*) were often rejected by the Spanish-speaking children because they were too short or there were "just a few." When given cards with repeated letters like *AAAA*, the children also put them in the "not for reading" pile because there was not a variety of letters.

For example, when Ferreiro and Teberosky asked Romina to write three words and a sentence, she wrote the following, using letters from her name:

R I O A

O A I R

A R O I

O I R A (251)

Like many other children that Ferreiro and Teberosky studied, Romina believes that words must have at least four letters. She also knows that different words have different sequences of letters. Romina mixes the letters from her name to accomplish this. It's interesting to note that for Romina there is no difference between the number of letters in a word and the number in a sentence. Her last line, which was a dictated sentence, has the same number of letters as the dictated words. Terms like *word* and *sentence* are quite abstract for young writers, and they may not distinguish between the two at first.

Freeman and Whitesell replicated this study with English-speaking preschoolers, and found the children used the same criteria. So, for example, five-year-old Tracy told the researchers, "*P* was not to read because 'It doesn't have any more letters . . .' and *a* was 'nothing'" (1985, 23). When five-year-old Beth was shown a card with *BBBB*, she put it in the "not for reading" pile because they were "all *B*'s."

Writing samples from bilingual kindergarten children in the United States help confirm Ferreiro and Teberosky's conclusions. José is a kindergartner in Blanca's classroom, where children are encouraged to write daily. José drew a picture and wrote a message that his teacher put into conventional form. His writing (see Figure 7–16) shows that he believes that words or sentences must have a minimum number of letters and also must have a variety of letters. He writes ten letters on each line and, although letters are repeated, the order of the letters is varied. It is interesting to note that he is beginning to rely on letters that are not in his name.

José is writing in Spanish, but his letter strings reflect his exposure to English environmental print. For example, he begins with *sk*. Spanish does not start words with *s* followed by a consonant, and *k* appears only in borrowed words. He also includes double consonants, such as "ss" or "pp" that do not occur in Spanish.

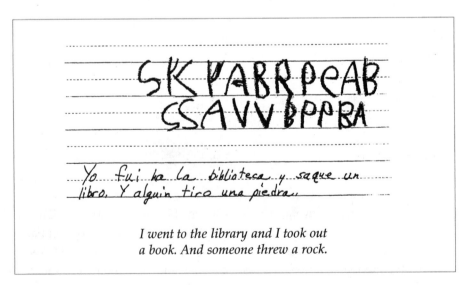

SK PABRPEAB
SSAVV BPPBA

Yo fui ha la biblioteca y saque un
libro. Y alguin tiro una piedra.

*I went to the library and I took out
a book. And someone threw a rock.*

FIGURE 7–16. José's Writing

Many students like José in bilingual or dual language classes produce spellings that show the influence of the two languages they are learning.

These insights into children's writing development have implications for teaching them to read. When children notice print, they focus on the bigger, more salient words. Most signs for stores or names of products, like breakfast cereals, have several letters. Children often ignore short words. In both English and Spanish writing, the content words (nouns, verbs, adjectives, and adverbs) are generally longer than the function words (articles, conjunctions, prepositions, and so on). It is natural for children to focus on those bigger, more important words.

Even though children come to school more aware of long words than short words, and even though their own writing shows that they think words should have a minimum number of letters and should have a variety of letters, books for beginning readers often feature short words with repeated letters (*ball, is, oso, la*). The idea is that if we use short, simple words with only a few letters, we make reading easier for children. However, children may not believe that these short words are really for reading since they come to school already having made hypotheses about words based on the words they see around them every day. At first, children notice these bigger chunks, or wholes, and only later do they attend to the smaller parts. If reading materials start with the parts, this makes reading harder for children, not easier.

Writing Instruction for Prephonetic Students

Buchanan (1989) points out that the most important thing teachers can do for children at the prephonetic stage is to encourage them to continue writing. Teachers should make a variety of writing materials available. Some children like to use markers rather than pencils. Children can also choose different sizes and colors of paper. Many teachers have a writing center in the room with these materials for children to use.

Teachers should respond to student writing, asking the students what they have written and commenting on the message. This helps students understand that written language can communicate ideas. At this stage, though, it is important not to correct student writing since children have not yet made the connection between letters and sounds. The teacher can put students' names on their papers, and soon, students will start to write their own names. Teachers can also put students' names on their desks. Often, teachers create a name center. Students can arrange classmates' names in different ways (longest to shortest, boys' names and girls' names, names that start with the same letter).

In addition, teachers should ensure that children are surrounded by meaningful print. Many teachers put alphabet letters up around the room. They read to children frequently using big books so that children can see the print easily. Teachers also use the language experience approach. They involve students in an activity and then write the experience up on butcher paper as the students recount the events. Language experience allows teachers to model writing and helps students begin to make connections between written words and the sounds of oral language.

A good example of a teacher in a dual language class who provides appropriate support for his prephonetic-stage students comes from Jeff.

Animal Lessons with Writing—Kindergarten ◆ Jeff teaches kindergarten in a rural community with a high Hispanic population. In his dual language program, he teaches native Spanish speakers and native English speakers academic content in both languages. Jeff involves his students in a number of activities that gradually move them into writing. He scaffolds his instruction, providing the support his young students need as they begin to learn about written languge.

Early in their kindergarten year, Jeff's students study animals. Although they are interested in all kinds of animals, the children are especially intrigued by wild African animals. One way that Jeff introduces concepts and print about wild animals is through a lion hunt chant. Jeff uses pictures of animals in the chant, including a lion, an elephant, a monkey, a zebra, and a giraffe. He tracks the words on a chart as the children chant with him:

¿Dónde está el león?	Where is the lion?
¿Está bañándose en el río?	Is he taking a bath in the river?
No, el elefante está bañándose en el río.	No, the elephant is bathing in the river.
¿Está jugando en el árbol?	Is he playing in the tree?
No, el mono está jugando en el árbol.	No, the monkey is playing in the tree.
¿Está pastando en el prado?	Is he grazing in the meadow?
No, la cebra está pastando en el prado.	No, the zebra is grazing in the meadow.
¿Está comiendo hojas de los árboles?	Is he eating the leaves of the trees?

No, la jirafa está comiendo hojas de los árboles.	No, the giraffe is eating the leaves of the trees.
¿Está deslizándose hacia arriba en el árbol?	Is he wiggling up in the tree?
No, la boa constrictora está deslizándose hacia arriba en el árbol.	No, the boa constrictor is wiggling up in the tree.
¿Está cazando animales para comer?	Is he hunting animals to eat?
Sí, está cazando animales para comer. Sh . . . Sh . . . Sh . . .	Yes, he is hunting animals to eat. Sh . . . Sh . . . Sh . . .

In addition to having students chant the words, Jeff writes the basic expressions of the chant on strips for two pocket charts. For example, a strip might read *"un elefante bañándose"* (an elephant bathing) or *"un león cazando"* (a lion hunting). In one chart the words are in order. In the other chart the words are mixed up. Working in pairs or small groups, the students put the words in the second chart in the same order as the model.

Jeff also uses the lion chant as a model for small books the students take home to read to their families. He makes and illustrates his own book based on the chant. The first page asks, *"¿Dónde está el léon?"* (Where is the lion?). Under the words is the picture of a lion. Each of the following pages focuses on one of the other animals in the chant. The pages have a repetitive pattern. For example, the second page (see Figure 7–17) has a picture of an elephant and says, *"¿Está bañándose en el río? No, el elefante está bañándose en el río."* The student books are exactly like the teacher's model. Jeff collates and staples the student books ahead of time since his kindergarten students have difficulty doing this task on their own without considerable adult supervision.

As Jeff creates these books, he models the writing and sometimes does a directed drawing on each page with the children. To create each page, Jeff works with small groups of six to nine students. For example, when working on the page that says, *¿Está bañándose en el río? No, el elefante está bañándose en el río* (Is he bathing in the river? No, the elephant is bathing in the river), Jeff clips a copy of *¿Donde está el león? (Where Is the Lion?)* on an easel so that all of the students in the group can see it easily. Jeff and the children write the word *elefante* (elephant) at the bottom of the page. Jeff models the correct letter formation, says the name of the letter, and helps the students hear the letter sound as each letter of the word *elefante* is written. In this way he can teach the mechanics of letter formation and

¿Está bañandose en el río?
No, el elefante está bañandose en el río.

elefante

FIGURE 7–17. Elephant Page from the *Lion Hunt Chant* Book

letter sounds and names in meaningful context. The students then read the elephant page chorally with Jeff as they track the words from left to right and from top to bottom with their fingers using a sweeping motion.

Jeff also works with the students to make a second kind of take-home book. This is created at an independent writing center. At this center the students can make their own original books from sheets of photocopy paper that are folded and stapled between colored construction paper. Students use felt pens, regular pens, colored pencils, and crayons to write and illustrate their books, which they will later read to their peers during author's chair.

Hanging on the wall next to the writing center is a word bank that reflects the theme that the class is currently working on. The word bank is a pocket chart that has pictures of things that students might want to write about. Next to the pictures are the words for the pictures, which are color-coded in Spanish and in English. For example, next to a picture of a lion is the word *lion* written in orange and *león* written in green. The children know that the orange words are English and the green words are Spanish. As they write their books, the children can choose to copy words from the word bank, or they can use scribble writing, random letters, initial letters, or invented spelling, depending on their developmental stage.

The students spend much class time talking and reading about animals. Many of the books Jeff reads can be found in the animal bibliography for young children in Chapter 3 (see Figure 3–3). During these activities, Jeff's students are developing academic concepts as well as literacy. Using an opaque projector, Jeff shines pictures of animals such as elephants and lions onto large pieces of butcher paper. The projector allows Jeff to blow up the pictures to large sizes. He then uses the pictures to draw outlines of the animals. The children paint the animals and draw in the proper background settings. These murals are kept up on the walls throughout the unit. When students are working on projects, a cassette tape of wild animal sounds plays in the background to develop that sense and stimulate further discussion among the children.

As an additional activity, students in small groups sort pictures of animals into different categories such as *los que viven en la selva* (those that live in the jungle), *los que viven en el prado* (those that live in the grassland), *los que comen prado* (those that eat grass), and *los que comen carne* (those that eat meat). Together the class makes charts to record what the children have learned. For example, after students sort pictures of animals by their outer covering, Jeff puts up a chart with several columns. At the top of each column is a piece of material that resembles one kind of covering—fur, scales, leather, or feathers. Students place their animal pictures under the appropriate heading and then label each picture.

Some teachers might not consider any of the activities we've described so far as writing in the usual sense, but the activities do represent early stages of writing. Students are associating words with pictures. The books they read and make help them recognize the letters in the words. They are putting words together into patterns. They are learning how pages are assembled into a book. In all of these activities, students are actively constructing meaning using print. These experiences are the important first steps toward independent writing.

As a final activity, the children work in small groups to create a class big book called *Animales salvajes* (Wild Animals). This book is also modeled on the lion chart. It features the same animals and focuses on where they live. Each page has one of two pattern sentences with a blank space: "____ *viven en la selva*" (____ live in the jungle) or "____ *viven en prados*" (____ live in the grasslands). Using animal stencils, the students trace and then cut out the animals from the chart and decide on their setting. If their animal is a grasslands animal like an elephant, it is pasted on yellow paper. If it is a jungle animal like a monkey, it is pasted on light green paper. (Jeff has the students use light green because the trees and grass will be dark green.) The illustrations are particularly striking if they are done entirely from colored construction paper. The students cut the animals, trees, grass, rivers, sun, and so on from construction paper and glue the items onto the twelve-by-eighteen-inch construction-paper background (yellow or green, depending on the animal's habitat). This becomes a page of the book. It is the same sheet that has the pattern sentence written on it.

After their pages are assembled, the children write the name of the animal on each page. They use the books, charts, and labeled pictures around the room to help them spell the animal names. Each student in a group that creates a page signs it. Once the book is finished, it is laminated and stays in the classroom for students to look at and read together.

These activities are the beginning of writing development for the children. The students in Jeff's class continue to develop their writing as the year progresses. They share their writing with their classmates and are encouraged at all stages to express their ideas using drawings and invented spellings. Because the words they want to write are available on the classroom walls and in big and little books, Jeff's kindergartners can begin to write from early in the year, and they start to make the important connection between reading and writing. In the process, they begin to move from the prephonetic stage toward more advanced stages of writing development. In the next chapter, we describe these more advanced stages.

 ## Applications

1. If you are in a dual language school or have access to one, collect writing in Spanish and in English from one student at the third-grade level or higher. What do you conclude generally about that student's writing in Spanish? In English? Can you tell which language is the dominant language for the student? Is there evidence of transfer from one language to another? Explain and give specific examples from the writing.

2. Watch a teacher doing the morning message or the daily news. You may use your own classroom if you do either regularly. What language skills are taught in the context of the writing? What skills are the students learning as they do this activity on a daily basis? List and be specific.

3. Collect some scribble from a three- or four-year-old child. What do you notice about the scribble? Does the child distinguish between drawing and writing? Can you make out mock letters?

4. Find some writing samples of a child who is writing at the prephonetic stage. Does the child intend to write in Spanish or in English? Go back to the examples and discussion in the chapter and analyze your writing samples.

Stages and Levels of
Writing Development

We begin our examination of the more advanced stages of writing development with three pieces that were written by second graders in a Spanish-English bilingual classroom in a rural school. Many of the students in this school are migrant children, and most families work in agriculture. Since the class had been studying about dinosaurs, Carolina, their teacher, asked the children to write what they had learned as one of the selections for their school-required portfolio. Although all three children are in the same classroom, their writing samples show that they are at very different stages of writing development in Spanish.

Alejandra's piece (Figure 8–1) is at an earlier stage of development than the writing of her peers. She does form letters into words, and some of the words can be understood. For example, Alejandra told Carolina that the title was *"Los dinosaurios comen mucho"* (Dinosaurs Eat a Lot) and the first sentence read, *"Unos comen hojas"* (Some eat leaves). Few words beyond *los* and *y* appear to be spelled conventionally. Alejandra does not use capital letters and puts a period only after the first sentence. In addition, she draws pictures and numbers her sentences

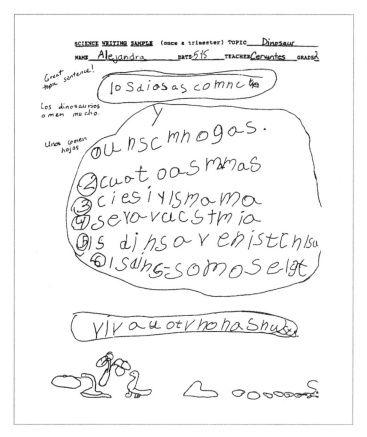

FIGURE 8–1. Alejandra's Dinosaur Piece

rather than using paragraph form. She circles the parts of her paper (title, body, and conclusion) rather than indenting. This convention is one that many writers use in the early stages. At this point, Alejandra's writing is characterized more by her inventions than by her awareness of the standard conventions for writing.

By contrast, Joel's piece (Figure 8–2) has only three errors. He spells *especiales* (special) without the *c* in the fifth sentence, and he does not add the *n* to the verb in the seventh. In the last sentence, he misspells *pescuezo* (neck), a difficult word. Sentences start with a capital letter and end with a period. The piece lists characteristics of dinosaurs using the same sentence structure for each of the first six sentences and then only changing the verb from *son* (are) to *tienen* (have) in the last two. While this piece is almost completely correct, it lacks variety and imagination. Joel is not taking risks with his writing. Rather than inventing new ways of expressing his ideas, Joel is following a conventional pattern carefully.

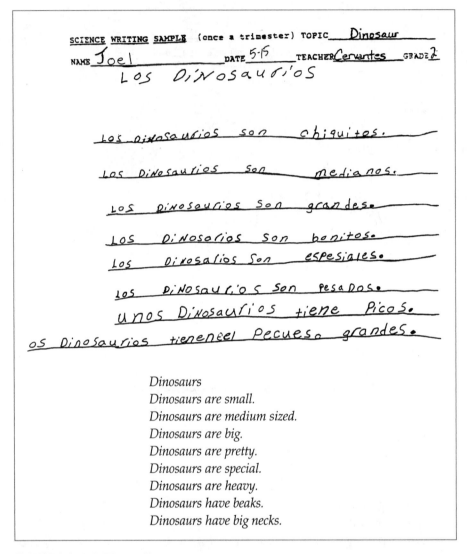

SCIENCE WRITING SAMPLE (once a trimester) TOPIC __Dinosaur__

NAME _Joel_ DATE 5-15 TEACHER_Cervantes_ GRADE 2

LOS DINOSAURIOS

Los Dinosaurios son chiquitos.

Los Dinosaurios son medianos.

Los Dinosaurios son grandes.

Los Dinosorios son bonitos.

Los Dinosalios son espesiales.

Los Dinosaurios son pesados.

unos Dinosaurios tiene Picos.

os Dinosaurios tieneneel Pecueso grandes.

Dinosaurs
Dinosaurs are small.
Dinosaurs are medium sized.
Dinosaurs are big.
Dinosaurs are pretty.
Dinosaurs are special.
Dinosaurs are heavy.
Dinosaurs have beaks.
Dinosaurs have big necks.

FIGURE 8–2. Joel's Dinosaur Piece

There is a danger that if teachers place too much emphasis on correctness, students may not take the risks needed to grow as writers. Their concern with producing conventional writing stifles the inventive force. They produce writing that is correct but dull. Students who play it safe will not try out new expressions or advanced vocabulary. They need to be encouraged to develop their voice and express themselves using more vivid language.

The third piece (Figure 8–3) shows a writer who is experimenting with more complex sentence structure, vocabulary, and ideas. José begins by relating the

Los dinosaurios.

ase mucho Tiempo
cualo LaTiera era
mas Caliete quela de
nosoTros avia muchos

dinosaurios avia unos
gordos, Otros Flacos
Otros Largos oTros chico
OTros grandes al unos
en Forma de dinoser
Te oTros Forma de
cocodrilo.

Dinosaurs
A long time ago
when the earth was
hotter than
ours there were many
dinosaurs there were some
fat ones, others thin
others long others small
others big there are some
in the shape of a dinosaur
and others in the shape of a crocodile.

FIGURE 8–3. José's Dinosaur Piece

Stages and Levels of Writing Development

time and setting in which dinosaurs lived and making a comparison with the present. He then goes on to describe different kinds of dinosaurs. Although there are examples of unconventional spelling and punctuation, José does a good job of not only demonstrating his command of the structure and the vocabulary of Spanish but also showing what he has learned about dinosaurs. José's writing shows a good balance between invention and convention.

All three writers attempt to express what they learned from readings and discussions in Carolina's classroom. Their pieces show that they know some important things about the conventions of writing. They are at different stages in their development, and they show varying degrees of willingness to risk inventing new forms to express their meanings. It is only through the process of inventing written forms and receiving meaningful feedback that writers develop. In the following sections we describe the stages writers go through once they advance beyond the prephonetic stage.

The Early Phonetic Stage

Over time, children move into the phonetic stage. The major concept for students in this stage is that "there is a connection between the physical aspects of producing a word and the spelling of a word" (Buchanan 1989, 135). Children in the phonetic stage are not yet connecting sounds to spellings. Instead, they are linking sound production with spelling. Spelling development moves gradually from concrete to abstract, and the physical actions involved in producing a sound are more concrete than the physical qualities of the sound itself.

Young children are good phoneticians. They are very aware of how and where sounds are produced in their mouths. Read (1971), for example, showed that what appeared to be very odd spellings simply reflected children's reliance on sound-production mechanisms. For example, one young child spelled *truck* with the letters *chrak*. Substituting *ch* for *t* seems strange to many adults, but if you say "truck" and then "chruck," you'll notice that the actions you use and the movement of your tongue are nearly the same. The convention in English is to use a *t* before *r* to represent this sound rather than a *ch*, but from the point of view of sound production, a linguist (or a small child) could justify either choice equally well.

Buchanan's early phonetic stage for English writing development parallels Ferreiro and Teberosky's level 3 writing for Spanish. In level 3, children begin to assign a sound value to letters and sound out words for themselves. Up to this point, children think that letters represent objects directly, as we discussed with the example of Gustavo, who thought the word *oso* (bear) should be bigger than *pato* (duck) because bears are larger than ducks. At level 3 children now realize that the letters connect to the sounds of the words we use to name the objects. Actually, as we pointed out, children focus more on the physical actions required to produce the sounds than on the sounds themselves.

Early Phonetic Writing in English

In the early phonetic stage, children usually use one letter for each word. Later in the phonetic stage they use one letter for each syllable. In English they may also include final consonant sounds in words. Two samples of Rosalinda's writing (see Figures 8–4 and 8–5) show her use of initial and final consonants. In the first sample she writes *house* as "hs" and *rainbow* as "rbl." The *l* may be the result of her pronouncing the word more like "rainbowl." Children often sound out words as they write, and sometimes they overenunciate. In the second example, Rosalinda spells *ladybug* as "ldbg" reversing the *g*. Here she writes the initial consonant of each syllable plus the final consonant. As she writes, Rosalinda is aware of how she is producing the sounds, and the initial consonants of each syllable along with the final consonants are the ones she notices most.

Children writing in English like Rosalinda most often represent the syllables with consonants. That's because the correspondence between consonant sounds and the letters used to represent them are more consistent in English than the

FIGURE 8–4. Rosalinda's *Rainbow* and *House* Spelling

FIGURE 8–5. Rosalinda's *Ladybug* Spelling

correspondence between vowel sounds and the letters used to represent vowels. The sound of /b/, for example, at the beginning or end of a word is almost always represented by the letter *b*. On the other hand, the long vowel sound /ey/ can be spelled several ways: *a* in *ladybug*, *ai* in *wait*, *ay* in *way*, *a_e* in *late*, and even *ei* in *weight*. Young writers in English begin with consonants because the sound-letter correspondences are more consistent.

Level 3 Writing in Spanish

Emergent Spanish writers in Spanish-speaking countries generally write vowels first. The appearance of vowels in Spanish writing can be attributed to the fact that there is a consistent correspondence in Spanish between the five vowel sounds and the five letters used to represent them. On the other hand, Spanish speakers raised in an environment dominated by English print may show a mixture of vowels and consonants. Here we will share examples that show young Spanish-speaking writers in the United States developing in a similar way to those of the Argentine study, where vowels are definitely most used, as well as an example that shows the influence of English.

In the Argentinean study, the children were asked to write words and sentences dictated by the researchers. Mariano first wrote his name correctly. Like many children, he had learned to write his own name, and he used the letters from his name to represent other words. When asked to write *sapo* (toad), he wrote *AO*. He was able to use letters from his name to write the vowels from the two syllables of *sapo*. Then, when the researchers asked him to write *"Mi nena toma sol"* (My baby girl sunbathes), he wrote every vowel in the sentence: *"IEAOAO."* He also wrote *"PO"* when asked to write *pato* (duck), showing that consonants are not always deleted. This finding that Spanish writers frequently begin with vowels is especially important information for bilingual teachers. While in the past, strings of vowels on a child's paper may have been interpreted as random letter practice, teachers can now recognize that those vowels could relate directly to a message the child intended to write.

Efraín's writing provides a good example of a child using vowels to represent the syllables in his words (see Figure 8–6). Carolina, his teacher, wrote the words when he read his story back to her, matching them to his writing. This type of

When the boy was in the water
the submarine . . .

FIGURE 8–6. Efraín's Writing

record keeping is an excellent practice because it provides teachers with valuable information they can use as they chart students' progress in writing. Unless a teacher listens to a child and writes down what he or she says, it is very difficult to figure out the writing later. When a teacher listens to a child in this way, it also helps the child understand the communicative nature of writing.

The first line of Efraín's writing includes all the vowels from the words in order. The only exception is that the letters *d* and *a* appear after the *ea* for *está*. He may have repeated the last syllable of the word to himself as he wrote and added the consonant and repeated the final vowel. He writes the consonant as *d*. Both *d* and *t* are produced in the same place in the mouth, and children at this stage rely on such features of physical production. In the second line, Carolina wrote only the first two words. Efraín adds an extra *o* after the *e* for *el* and then includes two consonants in *submarino* (submarine). He also includes three additional consonants in the remaining letter string. This shows that he is beginning to become aware that writing contains both consonants and vowels. This may reflect the English print in the environment. However, in most of his writing he still uses one vowel for each syllable.

Another student in Carolina's class, Rosa, showed Carolina her picture and told her, *"La niña está en la casa. Tiene mucho frío"* (The girl is in the house. She's cold). Carolina wrote on Rosa's paper: *"¿Por qué tiene frío?"* (Why is she cold?). Carolina read the question, and Rosa wrote back *"OEAELO"* to represent *"porque hay hielo"* (Because there is frost) (see Figure 8–7). Here she represented each syllable with one vowel consistently for the first two words. She uses *e* for *ie*. Like Efraín, she shows a beginning awareness of consonants by including the *l* in *hielo*.

Whether they use vowels, consonants, or some combination, writers at level 3 operate on a syllabic hypothesis. They generally write one letter for each syllable in a string of words. It is more difficult for teachers to read children's writing when it consists entirely of vowels. However, if teachers ask students to read what they have written (as soon as possible after they complete the writing), they will note the close correspondence between the letters the children write and the vowels in the words of their message. Children at this level have made an important conceptual leap: they have begun to connect letters and sound production, and it is important for teachers to recognize and support this advance.

A final example of level 3 writing comes from Ariana, a first grader in Sam's bilingual class. She had seen the words *Valentine* and *San Valentín* written all around the classroom. When she went to make her valentine card, she wrote *"sanvavenn."* This spelling includes consonants, but she probably copied them from the environmental print around the room. At this point, her copying is not exact. She seems to have lost her place after *sanva* and then started again with *venn*.

Inside the card drawing:

¿ Por que
tiene frío?
OEAELO

Rosa

Porque hay
hielo.

FIGURE 8–7. Rosa's Writing

Then she wrote her own message on the card. She carefully sounded out her intended message, *"¿Cómo está su familia?"* (How is your family?) and represented the words with the letters *ooeauaiaif*. She has both vowels for *cómo*, the *ea* for *está*, and the *u* of *su*. For *familia* she reversed the last two vowels and then added the initial *f*.

 ## Late Phonetic Stage and Level 4 Writing

Buchanan divides the phonetic stage into an earlier and a later phase. The early stage is characterized by using one letter for each word or syllable. At the advanced phonetic stage students begin to connect the production of each sound with a letter. They move from a syllabic hypothesis to an alphabetic hypothesis. Their inventions still don't match conventional spelling, since our spelling system isn't based solely on sound production. But now they begin to use both vowels and consonants.

FIGURE 8–8. Rosa's *Butterfly* Spelling

A third example from Rosalinda (see Figure 8–8) shows her progression toward the advanced phonetic stage. She reverses the order of *l* and *f* when she writes "*BRLF*" for *butterfly*. This is not a cause for concern. Often children work hard at pronouncing a word and writing the letters. If they forget a letter, they add it where there is space. What is more significant is that Rosalinda adds a final *i* here, using letter-name spellings. She may be moving into the later phonetic stage, where children begin to use both consonants and vowels. A fourth sample from Rosalinda's writing (see Figure 8–9) shows this progression more clearly. Her spelling of *star* as "stor" shows her awareness of the vowel production along with the consonants. It is common for students to have trouble with vowels before *r* because the *r* changes the sound of the preceding vowel.

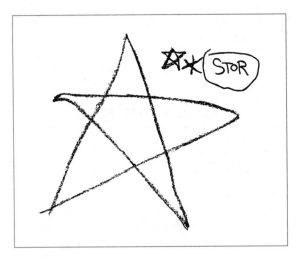

FIGURE 8–9. Rosalinda's *Star* Spelling

Students at the advanced phonetic stage will often assume that the name of a letter is the same as the sound it makes. Rosalinda represents the /ay/ sound with the letter *i* in *brlfi*. Another clear example of letter-name spelling comes from María, who also uses *i* for the sound /ay/ and the letter *r* for *are* (see Figure 8–10).

Students whose first language is not English may also rely on letter names during spelling, but they may think that the names for letters in English are the same as their sounds in their first language. A good example comes from a bilingual kindergartner writing to her father (Daddy) (see Figure 8–11). She writes *take* as "tec," *me* as "mi," and *please* as "plis." In each word, the vowel she uses has the right name in Spanish for the sound she wants to represent. As this example shows, students may use letter-name spelling from either one of the languages they know.

FIGURE 8–10. María's Writing

FIGURE 8–11. Kindergartner's Note to Dolly

The advanced phonetic stage in English corresponds to level 4 writing in Ferreiro and Teberosky's analysis. Spanish writers begin with vowels. However, they begin to notice that both vowels and consonants are used in environmental print. If teachers read them big books, children also start to notice that the words have more than vowels. This leads them to the alphabetic hypothesis, that each sound in a word should be represented by a letter.

In Rhonda's kindergarten, other children were still writing only their names or strings of vowels, but after hearing the story, Susi drew a picture of the ugly duckling hatching and labeled it on her own using both vowels and consonants (see Figure 8–12). Her spelling *"el ptito feo"* (the ugly duckling) is nearly conventional *"el patito feo."* She gets all the consonants and leaves out just one vowel. This example shows again that it is experience with writing rather than age that influences a student's writing stage.

Phonetic Stage Strategies

Children at an early phonetic stage benefit from the same strategies as those in the prephonetic stage. Children can play with alphabet cards or magnetic letters.

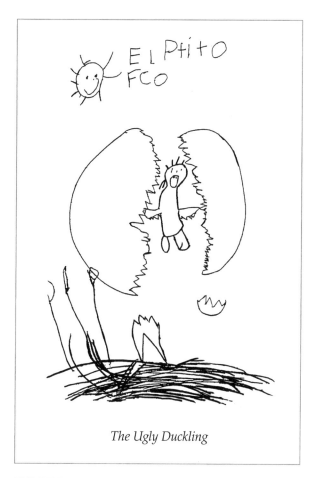

The Ugly Duckling

FIGURE 8–12. Susi's Writing

Teachers should read to them, do language experience activities, and ensure that there is lots of print up around the room.

In addition, teachers can effectively use alphabet books. Many alphabet books for young readers focus on initial sounds. *Annie, Bea, and Chi Chi Dolores* (Maurer 1996) contains names of things associated with school activities, such as *J* for "jumping rope," *K* for "kicking a ball," and *L* for "lining up." A similar book in Spanish is *ABC ¡Ya me lo se!* (The ABCs, I Know Them Now!) (Canetti 1997). In this colorfully illustrated alphabet book, student names are combined with verbs that describe activities students do at school. The text alliterates a child's name and a school activity, such as *"Darío dibuja"* (Dario draws) and *"Elena estudia"* (Elena studies). Another book for beginning readers, *ABC and You* (Fernandes 1996), has student names and characteristics on each page, from "Amazing

Amanda" to "Zippity Zack." All three of these limited-text books provide good models for students to follow in creating their own alphabet books.

Poetry alphabet books can help teachers focus students on both beginning and ending sounds in words. A poetry alphabet book in Spanish, *ABC animales* (Broeck 1983), can help students focus on the beginning sound highlighted on the page and on the spelling of the rhyming words. Each page of the colorful *ABC animales* describes a different animal:

D de delfín	*D* for dolphin
alegre saltarín	happy jumping animal
que cruza los mares	that crosses the seas
de muchos lugares (9)	from many places.

In English, *It Begins with an A* (Calmenson 1993) presents students with a series of riddles to solve. Each rhyming page gives clues and asks, "What is it?" For example, the *A* page reads, "You travel in this. It begins with an *A*. It starts on the ground, then flies up, up away! What is it?" The *C* page reads, "This takes your picture. It starts with a *C*. Get ready, get set. Now smile for me! What is it?" (6). Students enjoy solving the riddles, and young children increase their vocabulary knowledge and can start to focus on beginning sounds. Figure 8–13 is a bibliography of alphabet books in Spanish and in English for young children.

The same activities that are helpful in earlier stages continue to aid children in the advanced phonetic stage. They need to be read to, to be read with, and to write. Using poem and song charts or big books, teachers can start to point out different ways to represent sounds, and as long as children continue to read and write every day, they will continue to move toward conventional spelling. Hughes and Searle (1997) carefully document how teachers worked with students who wrote many words conventionally but still struggled with tricky words. They offer useful suggestions for working with students at the advanced levels. At this point, some direct instruction can help students start to recognize spelling patterns that work quite consistently.

It is important for teachers to keep track of students' progress and then to work with individuals or small groups who don't seem to notice that their spellings are irregular. In general, though, more reading and writing is the key, especially if children are writing for real purposes. They will move toward conventional spelling if they have a message they really want classmates to read. They will revise their spellings when their messages are not clear to their intended audience.

Broeck, Fabricio Vanden. 1983. *ABC animales*. Colección piñata. México, DF: Editorial Patria.

Calmenson, Stephanie. 1993. *It Begins with an A*. New York: Scholastic.

Canetti, Yanitzia. 1997. *ABC ¡Ya me lo sé!* Big book ed. Boston: Houghton Mifflin.

Detwiler, Darius, and Marina Rizo-Patron. 1997. *Mi libro del ABC*. Boston: Houghton Mifflin.

Drew, David. 2000. *Food Alphabet*. Big book ed. Crystal Lake, IL: Rigby.

Ehlert, Lois. 1989. *Eating the Alphabet*. New York: Scholastic.

Fernandes, Eugenie. 1996. *ABC and You*. Boston: Houghton Mifflin.

Grande Tabor, Nancy M. 1992. *Albertina anda arriba*. New York: Scholastic.

Horenstein, Henry. 1999. *A Is for? A Photographer's Alphabet of Animals*. New York: Scholastic.

Maurer, Donna. 1996. *Annie, Bea, and Chi Chi Dolores*. Big book ed. Boston: Houghton Mifflin.

McPhail, David. 1989. *Animals A to Z*. New York: Scholastic.

Perea Estrada, Altamira. 1996. *Un abecedario muy sabroso*. New York: Scholastic.

Sempere, Vicky. 1987. *ABC*. Caracas, Venezuela: Ediciones Ekaré-Banco del Libro.

Shannon, George. 1996. *Tomorrow's Alphabet*. Hong Kong: South China Printing.

FIGURE 8–13. Alphabet Books for Younger Students

 ## The Phonic Stage

Buchanan calls the next stage in spelling development the phonic stage. It is at this point that children realize the importance of the sounds themselves. In the phonetic stage they are concerned with the physical actions involved in producing the sounds, and in the phonic stage they are more focused on the sounds that result. Many of their misspellings at this stage show they are overgeneralizing about relations between sounds and spellings. For example, they might spell all /s/ sounds with an *s* and use *c* to represent the /k/ sound.

Buchanan notes that students in the phonic stage make two important discoveries: one sound may be represented by more than one letter, and the same sound may be represented by different letters or groups of letters. Young writers in English begin to realize that a letter like *c* sometimes represents the /k/ sound, as in *candy*, and sometimes represents the /s/ sound, as in *center*. At the same time, a sound like /f/ can be represented in different ways: *f*, *ph*, and even *gh* at the end of a word. During the phonic stage, students may begin by using the same letter for each sound and then move toward the conventional spelling.

Benita's writing (see Figure 8–14) has many of the characteristics of the phonic stage. For example, she writes *phone* as "fon." Both *ph* and *f* can represent the /f/ sound, and Benita hasn't sorted out when to use which spelling. She chooses the more common spelling, *f*. She may have been influenced by her knowledge of Spanish here. She also writes *so* as "sow." Again, she knows that the long *o* sound can be spelled in different ways, and she hasn't yet figured out which spelling she should use for this word. In the same way, she spells *know* as "now," leaving out the silent *k*. She is also beginning to be aware of the final silent *e*. She even adds an unneeded *e* to *can* at one point. Benita's writing still shows some features of the advanced phonetic stage. She hasn't worked all the vowels out, and she uses letter-name spelling, as in "mi" for *my*.

Another good example of the phonic stage comes from Kelly, a first grader who is our one example from a native English speaker (see Figure 8–15). Her story contains many conventional spellings, but she still needs to work out how to represent certain vowels. For example, Kelly spells *town* as "tone," and *they* as "thea." The *ea* digraph can have the /ey/ sound, as in *steak*, but that spelling is not used at the end of a word to represent the long *a* sound. On the other hand, she uses *a* for the long *a* sound in *great* where she should have used *ea*. In addition,

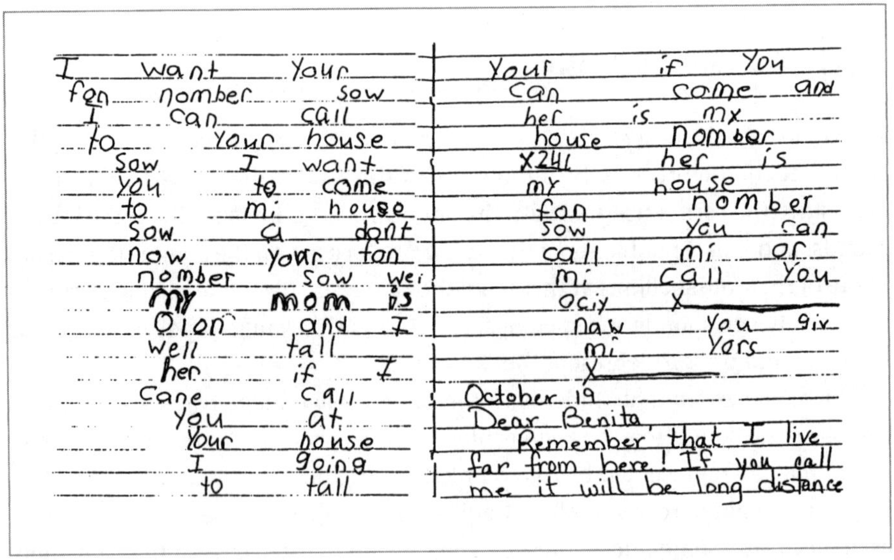

FIGURE 8–14. Benita's Writing

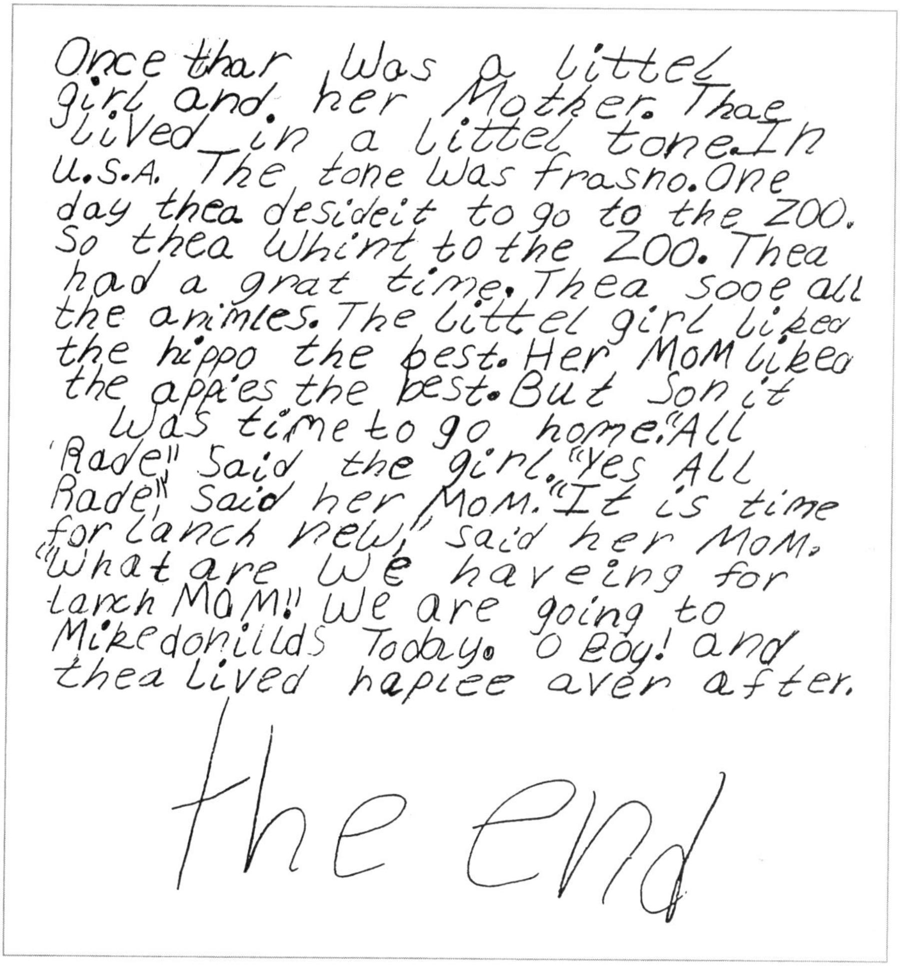
Once thar Was a littel
girl and her Mother. Thae
lived in a littel tone. In
U.S.A. The tone Was frasno. One
day thea desideit to go to the ZOO.
So thea Whint to the ZOO. Thea
had a grat time. Thea sooe all
the animles. The littel girl liked
the hippo the best. Her MoM liked
the appes the best. But Son it
Was time to go home. "All
Rade" Said the girl. "Yes All
Rade," Said her MoM. "It is time
for lanch new," said her MoM.
"What are We haveing for
lanch MOM!" We are going to
Mikedonilds Today. O boy! and
thea lived haplee aver after.

the end

FIGURE 8–15. Kelly's Writing

she assumes that *little* will be spelled as it sounds, *littel,* with the vowel before the final consonant. With continued reading and writing, Kelly will begin to control some of these conventions, and, like the little girl in her story, live "haplee aver after."

Students in dual language classes show writing development in both languages. Alexis, a native Spanish speaker in second grade, wrote about going to Sea World in both English and Spanish. Her English writing contains some predictable errors typical of a student at the phonic stage (see Figure 8–16). She leaves out the *h* of *Wen* (when), probably reflecting her pronunciation. She reverses the *o* and *r* in *wrold* (world). Alexis may be relying on visual memory that there is an

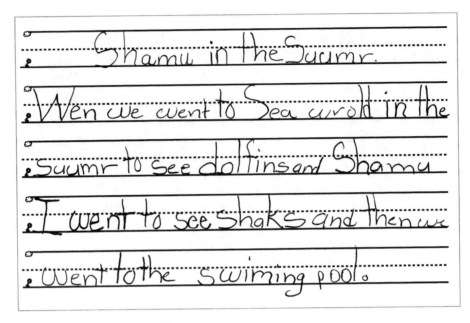

FIGURE 8–16. Alexis' English Writing

o in the word. Similarly, she leaves out the *e* before the *r* in *suumr* (summer) and doubles the *u*. She uses *f* for the *ph* in *dolfins* (dolphins), a common error for Spanish speakers, and leaves out the *r* in *shaks* (sharks). Finally, she puts just one *m* in *swiming* (swimming). This may also reflect her knowledge of Spanish since Spanish doesn't double consonants to signal short vowel sounds as English does. Despite these errors, most of the words are spelled conventionally, and the message is easy to read.

Another bilingual student, seven-year-old Citlaly, also writes in both Spanish and English. Her English writing also shows certain predictable errors (see Figure 8–17). She is trying different spellings for the long vowels in the words, *flawr* (flower), *may* (my), and *laic* (like). Long vowel sounds can be represented by different combinations of letters in English, and it takes students some time to develop conventional spellings of these sounds. Citlaly also substitutes *o* for *ea* before the *r* in *hearts*. Young writers often have difficulty deciding on the correct spelling of vowels before *r*. In addition, *ea* is seldom used in English to represent the sound it has in *heart*. More commonly, *ea* before *r* has the sound heard in *bear* or *dear*. Although she still needs to work out some vowel spellings, Citlaly is at a phonic stage in English spelling.

> Citbly   1 de enero 21
> Today   is Wednesday January
> 21 2004. I did a flawr for
> may mom and I did a
> trok for may Dab. I
> Laic the Horts and the
> flawr.

FIGURE 8–17. Citlaly's English Writing

Level 5 Writing

The final stage that Ferreiro and Teberosky identify is level 5. At this stage children refine their alphabetic hypothesis. They use both consonants and vowels to represent all the sounds in each word more consistently. Level 5 is the equivalent to Buchanan's phonic stage. Most words are spelled conventionally. Errors come as young writers grapple with different ways to spell a sound. For example, a writer might not be sure whether to use *s* or *z* in *mesa*.

Alexis, whose English writing we just analyzed, also wrote about her trip to Sea World in Spanish (see Figure 8–18). She reverses the letters in *Wrold* (world), perhaps relying on her English spelling. Most of her other errors come from a confusion between *b* and *v*, two sounds that are very similar in pronunciation in Spanish. She substitutes *b* for *v* in *berano* (verano) and *faborita* (favorita). She substitutes *v* for *b* in *vallenas* (ballenas) once and then spells it correctly with a *b*. She also uses *v* in *tamvien* (también) and *vonita* (bonita). Her spelling of *leones* as *liones* may reflect the influence of English. She also leaves out accent marks, which is common. Alexis spells most words right, but she still has trouble with some letters that could represent the same or a very similar sound.

Citlaly also writes at level 5 in Spanish (see Figure 8–19). As in English, her errors are predictable. She substitutes *s* for *c* in *parsialmente* (parcialmente), *v* for *b* in *vien* (bien), and *s* for *c* in *haser* (hacer). She has difficulty spelling the word for *first* in *first communion*. She spells it *primes* instead of the conventional *primera*. Citlaly's teacher, Delia, hypothesized that she might have been thinking of taking communion for the first time (*primera vez*) and then combined the two words.

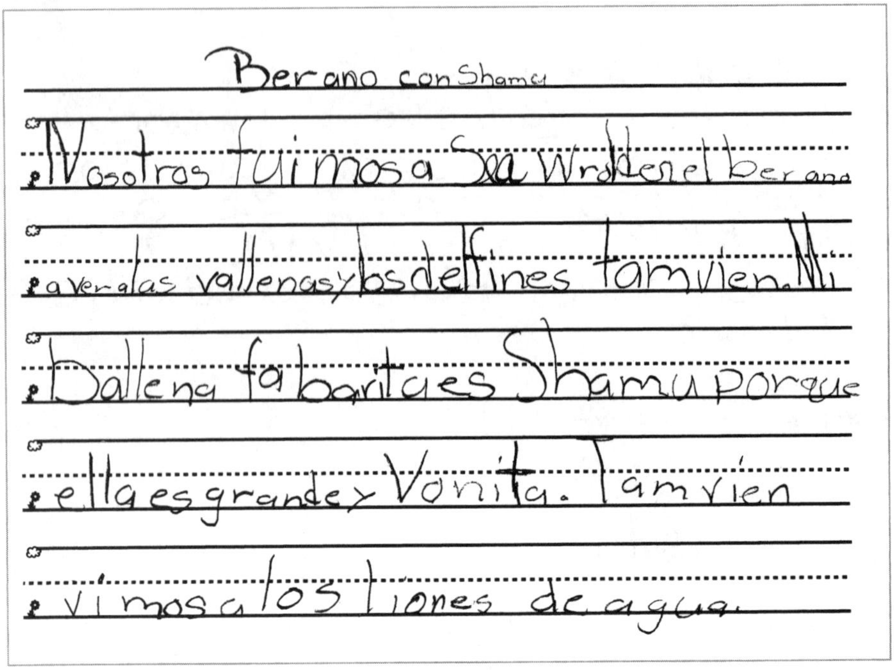

Berano con Shamu

¿Nosotros fuimos a Sea Wroltenel berano

¿a ver a las vallenas y los delfines tamvien. Mi

¿Dallena favorita es Shamu porque

¿ella es grande y Vonita. Tamvien

¿vimos a los liones de agua.

FIGURE 8–18. Alexis' Spanish Writing

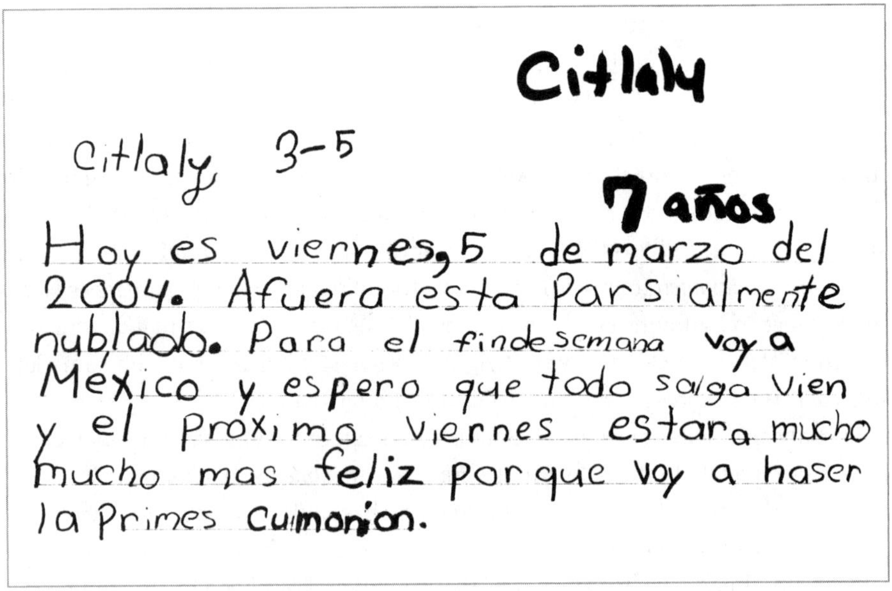

Citlaly

Citlaly   3-5

7 años

Hoy es viernes, 5 de marzo del
2004. Afuera esta Parsialmente
nublado. Para el findesemana voy a
México y espero que todo salga vien
y el próximo viernes estara mucho
mucho mas feliz porque voy a haser
la Primes Cumonion.

FIGURE 8–19. Citlaly's Spanish Writing

Despite these errors, her writing in Spanish is quite advanced for a student in March of her first-grade year.

A delightful example of level 5 characteristics comes from Ana, near the end of her kindergarten year (see Figure 8–20). There are still some problems with spacing, although she has a good sense of syllable boundaries. For example, she writes *"megus ta bi nira"* for *me gusta venir a* (I like to come to). Almost all of her misspellings are alternative representations of a particular sound. She consistently represents the sound of /y/ with *ll* when convention requires a *y*. She also substitutes *b* for *v* in *venir*, *c* for *s* in *se*, and *s* for *c* in *cien*. Ana is indeed *"perparada para ir al primero"* (prepared to go to first grade).

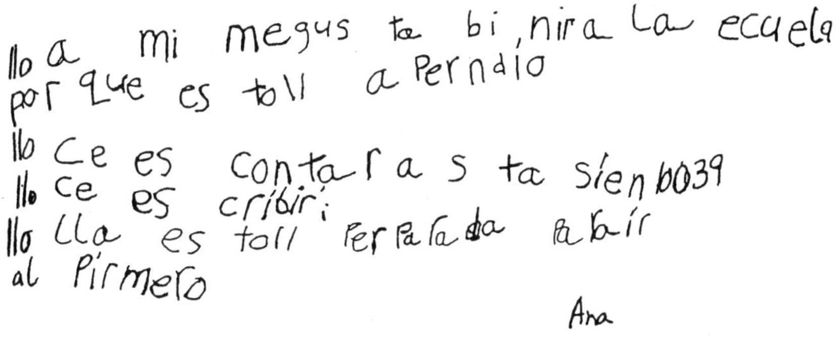

Conventional Spanish
Yo a mí me gusta venir a la escuela
porque estoy aprendiendo
Yo sé es contar hasta cien
Yo sé escribir
Yo ya estoy preparada para ir al primero

Translation

I like to come to school
because I am learning
(What) I know is to count to one hundred
I know how to write
I am now ready for first grade

FIGURE 8–20. Ana's Writing

Phonic Stage Strategies

Teachers can help children who have moved to the phonic stage by having them find words that follow a certain pattern that they are having trouble with. A child might make a list of words in English where *ea* makes the long sound of *e*, as in *tea*. A good way to make children more aware of a pattern is to put a key word up on butcher paper and then have children add other words that follow the same pattern. For example, a teacher could begin with *tea*, and children could add other words as they notice them during class reading and writing activities.

It is especially helpful to talk with students about the idea that one sound can be represented by more than one letter or letter combination, and one letter or letter combination can represent different sounds. Teachers can have children make hypotheses and then collect and categorize words to test their hypotheses. For instance, a teacher could ask children to collect words with *ea* and categorize their words by the different sounds associated with the digraph. Then students could try to form a rule to account for the patterns they see.

Similar activities could be used with Spanish speakers. Students could make class word walls with words ending in *ción*, as in *nación* (nation) and *canción* (song). They could also make lists of words that cause common spelling problems, including words with *v* and *b*, such as *bonito* (pretty) and *ver* (to see); words that start with a silent *h*, such as *hay* (there is/are); words with *y* or *ll* spellings, including *ayer* (yesterday) and *ella* (she); and words with *s* and *c* such as *cien* (one hundred) and *sé* (I know).

Alphabet books for older learners can be used to help students focus on these kinds of spelling issues as well as to help them play with language and be creative. For example, the Venezuelan publication *ABC* (Sempere 1987) is an illustrated animal alphabet book that uses alliteration. For the letter *V*, which causes so much spelling confusion with *B*, the author writes:

A volar me llevó el viento	The wind carried me so I could fly
y todo chiquito lo vi:	everything looked very small:
veinte ovejas, diez venados	twenty sheep, ten deer
y una vaca con violín. (3)	and a cow with a violin.

Students could write their own alliterative verses and share with classmates.

Each page of *De la A a la Z por un poeta* (From A to Z by a poet) (del Paso 1990), an alphabet poetry book in Spanish appropriate for older learners, offers students examples of the relationships between sounds, spellings, and meaning. For ex-

ample, part of the page on the letter *H* reads: *"La H no suena en 'hilo' ni en 'hombre'*
. . . Mas tú la puedes hallar-y aunque te diga que es muda-incluso en el verbo 'hablar' "
(The *h* is silent in the words *hilo* [thread] and *hombre* [man] . . . But you can find
it, even though I tell you it is silent, even in the word *hablar* [talk]). In the same
way, part of the *D* poem points out that

La *d*, ya lo verás,	The *d*, as you are going to see,
un tanto desordenada:	is a little disorganized:
está en todo y está en nada,	it is in everything [*todo*] and in nothing [*nada*]
está delante en detrás. (8)	it is in front [*delante*] in [the word] behind [*detrás*]

Another complex alphabet book for older learners that would support spelling
development is the onomatopeic alphabet storybook *Carlota, reina de las letras, o
El rapto de la ñ* (Carlota, Queen of the Letters, or The Rapture of the Ñ) (Monreal
1995). The story opens on a stormy night with two sounds that begin the alphabet, *"Una sombra apareció repentinamente invadiendo la habitación. —¡Ahhh!—gritó
Carlota. El susto de Carlota estalló junto con el trueno: —¡¡Braum!!"* (A shadow appeared suddenly invading the room. "Ahh!!" shouted Carlota. Carlota's fear ex-
ploded together with the thunder: "Boom!!") (2). Later the Spanish letter *ñ* comes
into play, *"¡Ohhh! ¡¡¡Es la ñ!!!" —dijeron asombrados Óscar y Carlota al tiempo. "Te
estábamos buscando." "¡Niño pequeño! ¡Pequeña niña! Añoraba compañia y cariño."*
("Oh! It's the ñ!" said the frightened Oscar and Carlota. "We were looking for
you." "Little boy! Little girl! I was yearning for your company and affection.")
Students could write similar stories using letters of the alphabet to play with the
sounds and spellings.

The alphabet provides a natural organizational scheme for class-made books.
Teachers can begin by reading an alphabet book related to the content area theme
they are studying or to reinforce important concepts such as culture. A favorite alphabet book is Alma Flor Ada's *Gathering the Sun* (Ada 1997b), with vivid illustrations by Simón Silva. This bilingual book has a poem in English and one in
Spanish for each letter of the alphabet. The poems center on objects and events in
the life of migrant farm workers. The *D* page, for example, has a poem about
"Duraznos" (peaches) and the *C* and *Ch* pages commemorate the life of César
Chavez. Ada's poetry and Silva's art help readers understand and respect the life
of Hispanics whose roots are Mexican and whose livelihood comes from the soil.
Students can then make their own bilingual cultural alphabet books.

During an extended ocean theme with his third graders, Francisco read *The Ocean Alphabet Book* (Pallotta 1986). Each page features an ocean animal. For example, the *J* page reads, "J is for Jellyfish. Jellyfish are soft, gooey and see-through. Their dangling arms can sting if you touch them" (10). Francisco's students used this book as a resource for group investigations into different ocean animals. As their final project for the ocean unit, the students decided to make their own class ocean alphabet book. They followed the model of Pallotta's book. They discussed what ocean animal to put on each page. They drew pictures of their sea animals and then wrote what they had learned about each ocean creature. They read their finished book to the class. It became a favorite resource book in Francisco's classroom library. At the same time, because this was an alphabet book, it provided a review of all the alphabet letters and sounds. As students looked for specific animals in the book, they also practiced their alphabetizing skills.

Another fascinating alphabet book for older students is *The Butterfly Alphabet* (Sandved 1996). The author, Kjell Sandved, spent more than twenty-five years photographing butterflies whose wing patterns contain the letters of the alphabet. Each page is a close-up of one wing with the name of the butterfly, and at the end of the book, the author includes additional information about each butterfly. The text on each page is a two-line rhyming poem with the key word printed in the color of the butterfly wing that is pictured. Books such as *The Butterfly Alphabet* not only expand students' vocabulary but help them think about words that have the same ending sounds even when spelled differently. For example, for the page showing the butterfly wing that looks like the letter *N*, Sandved writes, "Butterflies enchant the hours / Sipping *nectar* from the flowers" (27). Here, students see two spelling patterns for one sound: *our* and *ower*. Similarly, for the page with the letter *T*, the author writes, "Nature's angels fill the sk<u>ies</u> / In *twinkling* butterfly disgu<u>ise</u>" (39). This book offers two models for a group or class alphabet book: students can write poetry for each letter around some theme and/or they can highlight certain words within their poems. As students create their books they continue to develop content knowledge along with awareness of alphabet letters and different spelling patterns associated with various sounds. For a list of alphabet books for older students, see Figure 8–21.

The best way to help students who are in this stage advance is to give them time to read and write. Word games, playing with words and sounds, and activities like those described previously can help bring spelling patterns to conscious awareness, but many of the insights children gain are subconscious and come from their reading and writing. However, the more interest teachers show in words and spellings, the more children are apt to take a similar interest, especially if the teacher takes the approach that this is a topic worth investigating rather than

Ada, Alma F. 1997. *Gathering the Sun*. New York: Lothrop, Lee and Shepard.

Alshalabi, Firyal M. 1995. *Ahmed's Alphabet Book*. Kuwait: Rubeian.

Calmenson, Stephanie. 1993. *It Begins with an A*. New York: Scholastic.

Cassen Mayers, Florence. 1990. *The Wild West*. New York: Harry N. Abrams.

Chin-Lee, Cynthia, and Terri de la Peña. 1999. *A es para decir América*. New York: Orchard.

del Paso, Fernando. 1990. *De la A a la Z por un poeta*. México, DF: Grupo Editorial Diana.

Drew, David. 2000. *Food Alphabet*. Big book ed. Crystal Lake, IL: Rigby.

Drucker, Malka, and Rita Pocock. 1992. *A Jewish Holiday ABC*. New York: Trumpet.

Monreal, Violeta. 1995. *Carlota, Reina de las letras*. Madrid, Spain: Grupo Anaya.

Pallotta, Jerry. 1986a. *The Icky Bug Alphabet Book*. New York: Scholastic.

———. 1986b. *The Ocean Alphabet Book*. New York: Trumpet.

———. 1993. *The Extinct Alphabet Book*. New York: Scholastic.

———. 1996. *The Freshwater Alphabet Book*. New York: Trumpet.

Pratt, Kristin J. 1993. *Un paseo por el bosque lluvioso/A Walk in the Rainforest*. Nevada City, CA: Dawn.

Samoyault, Tiphaine. 1998. *Alphabetical Order: How the Alphabet Began*. New York: Viking.

Sandved, Kjell B. 1996. *The Butterfly Alphabet*. New York: Scholastic.

Singer, Arthur. 1973. *Wild Animals: From Alligator to Zebra*. New York: Random House.

Wilbur, Richard. 1997. *The Disappearing Alphabet Book*. New York: Scholastic.

FIGURE 8–21. Alphabet Bibliography for Older Students

information that should be memorized. For additional ideas for helping students investigate language and discover patterns in spelling, see *Essential Linguistics* (Freeman and Freeman 2004).

 ## The Syntactic-Semantic Stage

Buchanan adds one additional stage in English spelling. In the syntactic-semantic stage, children become increasingly aware that spelling systems reflect more than sounds. Spelling is also shaped by syntax and meaning. Students at this stage spell most words correctly, but they may have trouble with homophones or homographs. For example, a student may confuse *your* and *you're* or *there, their,* and *they're*. Lessons that mix these similar words seem to only further confuse students. Normally, the words appear in different contexts, and students do best when they use syntactic and semantic information to decide which form to use.

Students who have reached this stage benefit most by increased reading and writing. However, they can also become more aware of spellings by investigating word histories. Many students also enjoy wordplay. Most puns are based on the use of homophones or homographs. If students maintain a lively interest in words, they begin to spell words more conventionally. In addition, at this stage students are often writing for wider audiences and are more aware of the need to move toward conventional spelling in order to communicate effectively.

 ## Conclusion

In this and the previous chapter, we have looked at the stages of spelling development in Spanish and in English. When teachers are aware of the normal developmental stages children go through as they learn to write, they can better support young writers. A good example of the importance of teacher knowledge about writing development comes from Manuel, a second grader who had arrived recently from Mexico. Manuel's class had been studying a unit on animals. Below are Manuel's invented spellings for the ten words his teacher dictated for a spelling test (in parentheses).

1. an (animal)
2. bs (birds)
3. bn (bison)
4. fs (feathers)
5. fs (furs)

6. gn (gone)
7. kl (kill)
8. ls (laws)
9. on (ocean)
10. ps (plants)

Unfortunately, Manuel's teacher did not know about writing development and did not recognize that Manuel was at the early phonetic stage. She marked all the answers wrong since they were not spelled conventionally. As we can see, Manuel represented the beginning and ending sounds of most of these words correctly. His spelling was developing quite well for someone just learning English. Fortunately, his student teacher at the time, Denette, was studying early literacy and recognized Manuel's strengths. Denette was able to point out to the teacher that Manuel was developing important hypotheses about English spelling and suggested activities that would help him continue to move toward conventional spelling.

In addition to knowing about normal development, it is important for teachers to help students develop self-confidence in their ability to communicate through writing. We end this chapter with an example from Katie's class. Katie teaches pre-first-grade students. These are students who have gone through kindergarten but are not yet ready for first grade. Many of Katie's students are English language learners.

Katie is a wonderful teacher. Her students write each day. The students read their messages to Katie, and she writes a response to model conventional spelling. The room is filled with print. Katie not only helps her students develop their writing abilities but also builds their confidence in themselves as writers.

Figure 8–22 is an example of Linda's writing. Linda drew a picture of herself and two of her friends. She wrote their names on their desks, and then she wrote a message for Katie. Linda is in the late phonetic stage since she represents both consonants and vowels and also focuses on sound production. For example, she uses "kt" for the *gd* of *good*. Both the *k* and the *t* are produced at the same place in the mouth as the *g* and the *d*. As Linda read the message, Katie wrote the words under Linda's spelling. Linda makes it clear that she values good spelling and values herself as a writer. This is the most important lesson a young writer could learn.

FIGURE 8–22. Linda's Writing

Applications

1. Collect a writing sample in Spanish and in English from three or four first-grade children. The writing should be a story or a summary of something they have learned. Compare the writing samples as the dinosaur samples were compared at the beginning of the chapter. What can you tell about strengths and challenges for each writer?

2. Collect a writing sample in Spanish and one in English of a child from first to fifth grade. If the student's writing is not easy to read, write beside the student's writing what was intended. Analyze the writing samples using the stages and levels described in the chapter. Be prepared to share the samples and your analysis.

3. In this chapter there was a discussion of different alphabet books and how they could be used. Bring to class two or three alphabet books and share with a group how these books could support student learning.

4. Denette discovered that the student who took the spelling test really did understand some features of English spelling. The student could hear and write beginning and ending sounds. Bring in some writing samples of children you see doing this same thing in either Spanish or English to discuss with your classmates.

5. In class, brainstorm words that have different sounds associated with one spelling in English (such as *ea*) and words with different spellings for one sound in Spanish (such as *ll* or *y*).

Thematic Teaching to Develop Biliteracy

In bilingual and dual language classes, principled teachers help all their students become biliterate. They keep the focus of both reading and writing instruction on constructing meaning. These teachers scaffold instruction by following the gradual release of responsibility model. They understand normal developmental processes in both reading and writing and support their students who are becoming proficient users of two languages.

Principled bilingual teachers also understand that language is best learned as students investigate big questions, drawing on resources from the different content areas. They teach language through academic content and organize their curriculum around integrated themes connected to the content standards. Creative teachers can engage bilingual students in inquiry projects even when districts mandate the use of basal reading programs (Edelsky, Smith, and Faltis in press).

One benefit of organizing around themes in bilingual classes is that the same academic concepts are studied in each language. The content is not repeated, but a concept that is introduced in one language is further developed as students continue their study in a second language. Thematic instruction provides a natural sequence of preview, view, and review because the same topic is developed in each language and in each subject area.

Students preview a subject when they study it in their first language. They view the subject when it is further expanded on in a lesson in their second language. Then they review the subject when it is discussed again in a later lesson in their first language. When curriculum is integrated in this way, all students can develop high levels of literacy and learn academic content in two languages (Freeman and Freeman 2005).

In this chapter we describe lessons from two teachers who organize their curriculum around themes to provide a natural preview, view, and review. These teachers combine reading and writing activities to help all of their students reach high levels of biliteracy.

From the Field to the Table

Rosa teaches second grade in a bilingual classroom in a district in the Rio Grande Valley of South Texas. Her students are almost all Latino. Some are dominant in English; some are dominant in Spanish. Most of the students come from families that are involved in agriculture. Several are from migrant families who move with the crops. Although the philosophy of the district is to transition students to English by third grade, Rosa is doing graduate studies in bilingual education and understands that the stronger the base her students have in their first language, the more proficient users of English they will become. Rosa needs to give her students a strong foundation in their first language and also prepare them for the high-stakes third-grade tests they will take the following year in English.

Rosa works with other second-grade teachers in her school to be sure that the academic content they teach builds on the students' background and is based on the state standards. A theme the teachers have agreed upon is From the Field to the Table. This theme connects to the students' lives and encompasses many of the TEKS (Texas Essential Knowledge and Skills) standards. In the TEKS language art standards, for example, students are required to identify relevant questions for inquiry, use multiple sources for gathering information, and read and interpret graphic sources including charts, diagrams, and graphs. Students are expected to write to record ideas, reflect, and discover. They are to use different forms of writing including making lists, taking notes, and showing connections through graphic organizers. The math TEKS require students to measure and record information on graphs. According to the science TEKS students are to learn what plants need to grow and to identify functions and parts of plants. In the social studies standards two key concepts are the dependence of humans on the environment and the relationship between production and consumption. The health TEKS call for students to study the food groups and what makes healthy and unhealthy eating. Technology is a separate standard, and students are to incorporate technology in their learning including finding and reading information on the Internet and writing and editing reports on a computer.

Rosa and the other teachers review these standards and brainstorm ideas for activities that they can use to help students meet them. They also decide on the available materials they will share as they teach. Although each teacher will implement the theme differently, this initial planning time during which they connect their teaching to their students' backgrounds and the content standards is essential.

Big Questions

Rosa begins by brainstorming with her students some big questions that they will investigate as they conduct their theme study. On an overhead transparency she lists some big questions the students raise: What makes a seed grow into a plant? How long do seeds take to grow into plants? What plants can we eat? How do plants we grow, such as wheat, become foods we eat, like bread? What makes some food healthy or unhealthy?

Once the class has identified several big questions, Rosa carries out an activity designed to find out what her students already know about seeds. During science time, she shows them a large jar of seeds and asks, *"¿Qué son estas cosas en el frasco?"* (What are these things in this jar?). Her students answer enthusiastically, *"¡Semillas! Pepitas!"* (Seeds! Seeds [another word for seed]!). Then Rosa asks them if they can identify any of the seeds: *"¿Reconocen algunas de estas semillas?"* (Do you recognize any of these seeds?). Some children recognize *maíz* (corn); others recognize *frijol* (bean), *calabaza* (squash), and *sandía* (watermelon). Some children even recognize lettuce seeds and pepper seeds, explaining that their mothers plant those seeds in their family garden.

Seed Growth

During Spanish language arts, Rosa reads four short picture books: *Semillas y más semillas* (Seeds and More Seeds) (Cutting and Cutting 1995), *¿Qué sale de las semillas?* (*Seeds*) (Kratky 1995c, 1997), *Plantas y semillas* (Plants and Seeds) (Walker 1995c, 1992a), and *De las semillas nacen las plantas* (Plants Grow from Seeds) (Lucca 2003, 2001). These limited-text books show different kinds of seeds and the plants that grow from them. Rosa has the students form groups of four. They push their desks together and she gives each group a plastic bag with a variety of seeds. She tells them, *"Pongan las semillas que son iguales juntos"* (put the seeds that are the same together). The children group similar seeds and talk about the seeds as they work. When they are finished, Rosa puts another transparency up on the overhead. She draws a circle in the center and writes *semillas* (seeds) in it. Then she asks the students if they can identify some of the seeds in their bag. She begins with one group. They know which are the lettuce seeds. Rosa draws a line from *semillas* and makes a smaller circle in which she writes *lechuga* (lettuce). Each group identifies one type of seed. The most difficult is the tiny carrot seed. As each group responds, Rosa adds to the graphic.

During English language arts, Rosa reads additional books about plant growth. She begins with *Growing Colors* (McMillan 1988), a book of colorful photos showing various fruits and vegetables. The students and the teacher identify the plants and talk about the colors, shapes, and textures. They decide, for example, that an orange is round, orange, and bumpy; an ear of corn is long, oval, and bumpy; and raspberries and blackberries are red, black, oval, or round and prickly. Rosa writes some of these descriptive words on the board.

Next, she hands out a blank chart with the word *seed* written at the top of the first column and the words *color, texture,* and *shape* heading the other columns. Working in their groups, the children examine their seeds again. They write the name of each type of seed on the chart and then fill in a description for each kind of seed.

After each group fills in their chart, Rosa collects the seeds and the charts. Now that the students have started to develop vocabulary and concepts related to seeds, Rosa moves on to the topic of seed growth. She reads *Growing Radishes and Carrots* (Bolton and Snowball 1985), a content pop-up book that contrasts how long it takes radishes and carrots to grow. This predictable text provides information on plant care. It also shows how plant growth can be measured. Rosa reminds her class about a story they read together in kindergarten in both English and Spanish, *The Carrot Seed* and *La semilla de zanahoria* (Krauss 1945, 1978). This is the story of a boy who patiently waits for his carrot seed to grow despite the doubts of his family. She and her students read the big-book version, and they discuss how long carrot seeds take to grow.

The following day during Spanish language arts time, Rosa takes out another big book, *Una semilla nada más* (Just One Seed) (Ada 1990). She and the students first discuss the cover, showing a boy with a seed and hand hoe. The students predict that he will plant the seed and take care of it. They also make guesses as to what kind of seed he has. One student thinks it looks like a sunflower seed. Rosa reads the book, and the students chime on the refrain, *"Espérate y lo versa"* (Wait and you will see), as the boy patiently waits for his seed to grow even though family members doubt that it will. With the help of a bird, the boy tends the seed, and it grows into a large plant. Rosa's students respond excitedly when a huge sunflower pops up on the last pages.

The story is quite similar to *The Carrot Seed*. In each story there is a boy with a seed and several family members who doubt it will grow. However, there are also differences, so Rosa gives each group a paper with a Venn diagram and asks them to write down how the stories are the same where the circles intersect and how they are different on the two sides. When they finish, the groups share their responses and Rosa makes a composite Venn diagram on the overhead.

During science, Rosa reads three additional books about plant growth: *Las semillas crecen* (*Seeds Grow*) (Walker 1995b, 1992b), *¿Cómo crece una semilla?* (How Does a Seed Grow?) (Jordan 1996), and *Pon una semilla a germinar* (Get a Seed Germinating) (Solano Flores 1988). Drawing on the information in these books, Rosa and the students list the steps that are necessary to grow a plant from a seed. Then Rosa asks the students what they think their next project will be. *"¡Vamos a plantar semillas y crecer plantas!"* (We're going to plant seeds and grow plants!) they answer.

The next day Rosa wants to review in English some of the key concepts the students have studied in Spanish. During English language arts, she and the students recite the poem *Growing* (Bogart 1995), about a sunflower growing. Then she reads *I'm a Seed* (Marzollo 1996), a story told from the point of view of two different growing seeds, one a flower and the other a pumpkin. The students discuss the stages of growth again, and they also discuss the literary device personification, since the seeds actually talk to each other. In small groups the students write their own seed stories. They choose a seed and imagine the plant telling about the stages of growth. In order to do this, they need to know what the seed grows into and have an idea of what the seed looks like. They also need to know the stages of the plant's growth. Rosa suggests they use seeds from their plastic bags. She has books around the room so students can look at pictures of seeds and seed products. The groups will read their stories to the others in the class the following day.

Later that day, Rosa reminds the students that they are going to grow their own plants. She reads two books in English, *How Does It Grow?* (Morrison 1998) and *Growing a Plant: A Journal* (Jenkins 1998). The first book explains how a plant grows. It shows the steps for making seeds sprout. It contains a description of an experiment students can do with plants to show root absorption. The book also describes how to grow bean seeds. Rosa tells the students they will choose some seeds from their plastic bags and grow their own plants. Then Rosa reads the big-book version of *Growing a Plant: A Journal*, and students discuss how they will keep a plant journal as their seeds grow. Rosa gives them construction paper to make their journals.

During science time in Spanish the next day, the students choose their seeds, wrap their seeds in wet paper towels, and put them in plastic bags. Rosa has some groups put their seeds on a windowsill where they will get sun and has other groups put their seeds in desks in the dark. Still others are placed in the refrigerator in the classroom. The students will conduct an experiment to find out how these different conditions will influence plant growth.

Over the next several days, students record in English in their plant journal the date and the number of days since the seed was put in the wet paper towel. They also draw a picture to record how the seeds are sprouting. In addition, they write up their observations of the plant growth. After several weeks, they measure the growth of the sprouts and graph them, comparing the growth in different environments: sun, dark, and cold. Rosa's students eventually plant the healthy sprouts in dirt to watch them grow over the coming month.

What Plants Give Us

Rosa's students have been answering the questions What makes a seed grow into a plant? What are the stages of plant growth? and How long do seeds take to grow into plants? Rosa wants to move her theme to the next major concept, answering the questions What plants can we eat? and How do plants we grow, like wheat, become things we eat, like bread?

Since her students are all from Mexico, Rosa begins by reading *La tortillería* (Paulsen 1995a), a beautifully illustrated and written book also available in English, *The Tortilla Factory* (Paulsen 1995b). This book describes the cycle of tilling the land, planting the corn, growing the corn, harvesting the corn, grinding the corn to make *masa* (dough), making the tortillas, eating the strength-giving tortillas, and then planting more corn.

Rosa has her students in their groups draw a big circle on a large piece of paper and chart the story's plot as a cycle, recording the events in sequence, beginning with *"En la primavera la tierra negra es labrada por manos morenas que siembran semillas amarillas"* (In the spring, the dark soil is worked by dark hands that plant the yellow seeds) (9 and 11). This activity introduces the important concept of natural cycles. The graphic helps the students understand how the events in the story begin and end at the same point.

To introduce poetry, Rosa reads *Songs to the Corn: A Hopi Poet Writes About Corn* (Lomatewama and Reyes 1997b) during English language arts. This book, which is also available in Spanish (Lomatewama and Reyes 1997a), contains a series of poems. Each poem is accompanied by a short explanation written by the author, Ramson Lomatewama, a Hopi artist, teacher, and poet. He gives interesting facts about the way the Hopi regard corn and its importance to their culture. He also explains features of the poems. For example, after the first poem, he writes, "Poetry doesn't have to be long or fancy. It can be simple and short—like this one. This poem shows how I feel about each kind of corn" (6). Rosa and her students discuss why people write poems and the differences between poetry and stories.

During Spanish science time, the students look at a poster that shows the planting of a corn seed and the growth of a corn stalk. The parts of the plant are all labeled. Using the poster as a model, the students draw and label their own corn stalks. As the students work in their groups, Rosa overhears their conversations about their own experiences with corn. Many of the students have harvested corn or have helped to shuck corn that would be ground into corn flour.

Over the next few days, students read books about other products that come from plants, including *Girasoles* (*Sunflowers*) (Boland 1998a, 1998b), *Las diferentes cosas que vienen de las plantas* (The Different Things That Come from Plants) (Walker 1993b), *Alimento que obtenemos de las plantas* (Food We Get from Crops) (Walker 1993a), *Plants We Use* (Shulman 2004a), *A Seed Is a Promise* (Merrill 1973), and *Crops* (Ignacio 2000).

With this background knowledge, students work in pairs on the next activity. They choose a plant and conduct an Internet search to find out about where the plant is grown, how it is harvested, and the products the plant produces. The pairs research different plants including corn, cotton, potatoes, oranges, and wheat. They are surprised at the variety of products that come from the plants. Corn is especially interesting to them, so Rosa reads *El maravilloso maíz de México* (González-Jensen 1997a). This book, which is also available in English, *Mexico's Marvelous Corn* (González-Jensen 1997b), tells about the many products that come from corn. Another book that Rosa uses is *El maíz* (Buckley 2002), also available in English as *Corn* (Buckley 2001). This book has clear photographs showing how corn grows and also showing the many products that come from corn, including ethanol and gasoline. Rosa's students find that many common plants are used in products they did not expect.

Bread, Bread Everywhere

From the discussion about the products that come from plants, Rosa moves to concepts related to health. She begins by asking students in English what their favorite breakfast is. As the students volunteer answers, she writes them on an overhead transparency. Students call out everything from tacos with *chorizo* (sausage) and egg to pancakes. She then reads to them some pages from *Good Morning, Let's Eat!* (Badt 1994), a book about what people eat for breakfast around the world. So, for example, Rosa reads that in Vietnam, the most common breakfast food is rice, while in Israel the traditional breakfast is cheese, tomatoes, cucumbers, salad, yogurt, pickles, and boiled eggs. As the class talks about what people eat in each country, one student records what is eaten on a card and then puts that card up on the world map next to the country.

Rosa then asks the class, *"¿Qué comieron ustedes esta mañana de desayuno?"* (What did you eat this morning for breakfast?). Students list what they ate. The list includes tacos as well as toast, donuts, and cereal. Rosa then points out that usually people eat some type of bread. She shows them a poster labeled *"Los panes del mundo"* (The Breads of the World) (Scholastic 1993). The students recognize the sweet breads of Guatemala, the bread from France that we call French bread, and the hamburger buns. They think the nam bread of India looks like tortillas. The class locates where each kind of bread comes from on their world map.

Next, Rosa reads the big book *Bread, Bread, Bread* (Morris 1989) and has students find the countries on the world map where the different breads come from. She also reads *Pass the Bread!* (Badt 1995). Using this book, Rosa leads the students in a discussion of differences among breads. She helps students notice that some breads, like tortillas, are flat, while others are raised. Students also point out that some breads are homemade while others are store-bought. Certain breads are used to celebrate special occasions, like the *Rosca de reyes* (Ring [Crown] of the Kings), which is eaten on January 6 in Mexico to celebrate the coming of the Wise Men.

This leads Rosa to the next activity. First, she and the class read chorally. In Spanish they recite the poem *Tortillas* (González-Jensen 1994). Then she shows the students three different kinds of bread, a flour tortilla, a corn tortilla, and a hamburger bun. She asks the students, *"¿Cómo son iguales? ¿Cómo son diferentes?"* (How are they the same? How are they different?). The students discuss this in pairs and then report back. They point out that the shapes are the same and all three are a kind of bread. However, the ingredients are different. They also bring up an idea they had discussed earlier. The tortillas are flat, but the hamburger bun is a kind of raised bread because it contains *levadura* (yeast). Once the students bring up *levadura*, Rosa takes out another big book, *Pan, pan, gran pan* (Bread, Bread, Huge Bread) (Cumpiano 1990). In this story two children help their grandmother make bread, but a large can of yeast accidentally falls into the dough. The rest of this fanciful story has the characters as well as the community trying to control the bread, which is spreading throughout the town.

This book, which talks of different community members such as the policeman and the teacher, introduces a social studies theme. Rosa continues this theme by pointing out how some breads, like tortillas, are used as a utensil. Then she reads the humorous bilingual story *A Spoon for Every Bite/Una cuchara para cada bocado* (Hayes 2005), which tells of a rich man who is infuriated when his poor neighbors tell him that they know a man so rich that he uses a different spoon for every bite of food he takes. The rich man buys more and more spoons and spends all his fortune, only to find out that the poor man uses a tortilla as his spoon, and so the poor man never uses the same spoon twice.

Since the students enjoy this book so much, Rosa reads two other books. The first one, *Abuelito Eats with His Fingers* (Levy 1999), tells the touching story of a little girl who comes to appreciate her grandfather when she discovers how well he can draw. She makes tortillas with her grandfather's help and is delighted to discover that he eats tortillas with his fingers just like she does. This story sparks discussion about the importance of grandparents. Many of Rosa's students have grandparents living with them at home.

A second bilingual story, *Magda's Tortillas/Las tortillas de Magda* (Chavarría-Cháirez 2000), tells of another little girl, Magda, who tries to make perfectly round tortillas like her grandmother does. Magda is embarrassed that her tortillas come out in all sorts of funny shapes. She can't make neat, round ones, but then all her family members want to try her tortillas because they are so unusual. Magda feels proud because her grandmother calls her a "tortilla artist." Rosa and the students discuss making tortillas at home. Almost all the girls and most of the boys in the class know how to make tortillas. They explain that a meal would not be complete without fresh, hot tortillas to eat.

To continue the social studies theme of family traditions, Rosa asks the students how many of them eat *pan dulce* (Mexican sweetbreads). The children share their favorite kinds, each of which have a special name, including *empanadas* (turnovers), *conchas* (shells), and *orejas* (ears). Rosa then reads the big book *Del padre al hijo* (*From Father to Son*) (Almada 1997a, 1997b), the true story of how the tradition of making the *pan dulce* is passed along in one family from generation to generation. She also tells the students that the small version of the book in both Spanish and English as well as other books about family bakeries are in the classroom library. These include the bilingual book *The Bakery Lady/La señora de la panadería* (Mora 2001), which tells how grandchildren learn to make Mexican bread from their grandparents, and *Jalapeño Bagels* (Wing 1996), the story of a boy finding his roots in the family bakery run by his Mexican mother and Jewish father.

To summarize several of the concepts they have been studying related to plant growth, nutrition, and family relationships, Rosa reads the big book *La gallinita roja* (López 1987), the Spanish version of *The Little Red Hen*. The class lists the steps the hen goes through to grow the wheat and to get the bread to the table. They also discuss how everyone must help in a task if they expect to benefit from it.

Then, in English, Rosa reads *Where Does Breakfast Come From?* (Flint 1998), an informational book showing where the ingredients of a traditional U.S. breakfast, including juice, bread, cereal, eggs, and milk, come from originally. This book has clear photographs and helps the students understand how to read a sequence chart. Following the model provided in *Where Does Breakfast Come From?* the students work in groups. Each group chooses a favorite food, such as pizza, enchiladas, tamales, and even apple pie. They conduct research to find out the ingredients for their dish. Then each group creates a poster listing the ingredients and outlining the steps involved in making their food. They also include information about where each ingredient comes from.

Rosa puts up a large chart showing the food pyramid. She and the students discuss what makes a healthy diet. She asks the students to keep a record of what they eat during the week. At the end of the week, the students use their food journal to evaluate whether or not their diet followed the recommended servings from the food pyramid. Then, in their groups, they analyze the food they had chosen for their poster to see how it compares with the pyramid, and they add this information to the poster. Once students have finished, Rosa has each group make an oral report. They tell what food they chose, the ingredients, the steps involved in making the food, and how healthy this food is. As each group reports, the other groups take notes. The class concludes this activity by ranking the dishes they chose from most to least healthy.

To end this extended unit, Rosa involves her students in a literature study comparing *El hombrecito de pan jengibre* (*The Gingerbread Man*) (Parkes and Smith 1989, 1986) with versions of the story that are culturally relevant for her Mexican students, *La tortilla corredora* (The Runaway Tortilla) (Beuchat and Condemarín 1997) and *The Jalapeño Man* (Leland 2000). The students compare and contrast the three stories. They discuss similarities and differences among the characters, the setting, and the plot sequence. They also vote on their favorite version.

As a final project, the students write their own version of *El hombrecito de pan jengibre*, going through the writing process, drafting, conferring, revising, and editing their stories. Using a word-processing program on the computer, they type their stories, print them, and illustrate each page. As a culminating activity, they go to a kindergarten class and each student reads his or her story to a buddy the teacher has chosen. Both the second-grade students and the kindergartners enjoy this time together, and Rosa and the kindergarten teacher plan to make buddy reading a regular event. Figure 9–1 lists the books Rosa used for her From the Field to the Table unit.

Ada, Alma F. 1990. *Una semilla nada más.* Carmel, CA: Hampton-Brown.

Almada, Patricia. 1997a. *Del padre al hijo.* Crystal Lake, IL: Rigby.

———. 1997b. *From Father to Son.* Crystal Lake, IL: Rigby.

Badt, Karin L. 1994. *Good Morning, Let's Eat!* Chicago: Children's Press.

———. 1995. *Pass the Bread!* Chicago: Children's Press.

Beuchat, Cecilia, and Mabel Condemarín. 1997. *La tortilla corredora.* Boston: Houghton Mifflin.

Bogart, Jo Ellen, illustrator. 1995. *Growing* [Poem]. Bothell, WA: Wright Group.

Boland, Janice. 1998a. *Girasoles.* Katonah, NY: Richard C. Owen.

———. 1998b. *Sunflowers.* Katonah, NY: Richard C. Owen.

Bolton, Faith, and Diane Snowball. 1985. *Growing Radishes and Carrots.* New York: Scholastic.

Buckley, Marvin. 2001. *Corn.* Washington, DC: National Geographic.

———. 2002. *El maíz.* Washington, DC: National Geographic.

Chavarría-Cháirez, Becky. 2000. *Magda's Tortillas/Las tortillas de Magda.* Houston: Arte Publico.

Cumpiano, Ina. 1990. *Pan, pan, gran pan.* Carmel, CA: Hampton-Brown.

Cutting, Brian, and Jillian Cutting. 1995. *Semillas y más semillas.* Trans. G. Andujar. Bothell, WA: Wright Group.

Flint, David. 1998. *Where Does Breakfast Come From?* Crystal Lake, IL: Rigby.

González-Jensen, Margarita. 1994. *Tortillas.* New York: Scholastic.

———. 1997a. *El maravilloso maíz de México.* Crystal Lake, IL: Rigby.

———. 1997b. *Mexico's Marvelous Corn.* Crystal Lake, IL: Rigby.

Hayes, Joe. 2005. *A Spoon for Every Bite/Una cuchara para cada bocado.* El Paso, TX: Cinco Puntos.

Ignacio, Fred. 2000. *Crops.* Carmel, CA: Hampton-Brown.

Jenkins, Rhonda. 1998. *Growing a Plant: A Journal.* Crystal Lake, IL: Rigby.

Jordan, Helene J. 1996. *Cómo crece una semilla.* Trans. M. A. Fiol. New York: HarperCollins.

Kratky, Lada. 1995. *¿Qué sale de las semillas?* Carmel, CA: Hampton-Brown.

———. 1997. *Seeds.* Carmel, CA: Hampton-Brown.

Krauss, Ruth. 1945. *The Carrot Seed.* New York: Scholastic.

(continues)

FIGURE 9–1. Rosa's "From the Field to the Table" Bibliography

Thematic Teaching to Develop Biliteracy

———. 1978. *La semilla de zanahoria.* Trans. A. Palacios. New York: Scholastic.

Leland, Debbie. 2000. *The Jalapeño Man.* College Station, TX: Wildflower Run.

Levy, Janice. 1999. *Abuelito Eats with His Fingers.* Austin, TX: Eakin.

Lomatewama, Ramson, and Graciela Reyes. 1997a. *Cantos al maíz: Un poeta Hopi escribe sobre el maíz.* Crystal Lake, IL: Rigby.

———. 1997b. *Songs to the Corn: A Hopi Poet Writes About Corn.* Crystal Lake, IL: Rigby.

López, Elva R. T. 1987. *La gallinita roja.* New York: Scholastic.

Lucca, Mario. 2001. *Plants Grow from Seeds.* Washington, DC: National Geographic.

———. 2003. *De las semillas nacen las plantas.* Washington, DC: National Geographic.

Marzollo, Jean. 1996. *I'm a Seed.* Carmel, CA: Hampton-Brown.

McMillan, Bruce. 1988. *Growing Colors.* New York: William Morrow.

Merrill, Claire. 1973. *A Seed Is a Promise.* New York: Scholastic.

Mora, Pat. 2001a. *The Bakery Lady/La señora de la panadería.* Houston, TX: Piñata.

Morris, Ann. 1989. *Bread, Bread, Bread.* New York: Mulberry.

Morrison, Rob. 1998. *How Does It Grow?* Crystal Lake, IL: Rigby.

Parkes, Brenda, and Judith Smith. 1986. *The Gingerbread Man.* Crystal Lake, IL: Rigby.

———. 1989. *El hombrecito del pan jengibre.* Crystal Lake, IL: Rigby.

Paulsen, Gary. 1995a. *La tortillería.* Trans. G. d. A. Andújar. Orlando, FL: Harcourt Brace.

———. 1995b. *The Tortilla Factory.* New York: Harcourt Brace.

Scholastic. 1993. "Los panes del mundo." In *Scholastic News.* New York: Scholastic.

Shulman, Lisa. 2004. *Plants We Use.* Barrington, IL: Rigby.

Solano Flores, Guillermo. 1988. *Pon una semilla a germinar.* México, DF: Editorial Trillas.

Walker, Colin. 1992a. *Plants and Seeds.* Bothell, WA: Wright Group.

———. 1992b. *Seeds Grow.* Bothell, WA: Wright Group.

———. 1993a. *Alimento que obtenemos de las plantas.* Cleveland, OH: Simon and Schuster.

———. 1993b. *Las diferentes cosas que vienen de las plantas.* Cleveland, OH: Simon and Schuster.

———. 1995a. *Las semillas crecen.* Trans. G. Andujar. Bothell, WA: Wright Group.

———. 1995b. *Plantas y semillas.* Trans. G. Andujar. Bothell, WA: Wright Group.

Wing, Natasha. 1996. *Jalapeño Bagels.* New York: Atheneum.

FIGURE 9–1. Rosa's "From the Field to the Table" Bibliography (*continued*)

Analysis of Rosa's Theme Study

Rosa helped develop her students' literacy skills in both their languages through extensive reading and writing all organized around a theme that connected to their lives. It is clear that Rosa takes a sociopsycholinguistic view of reading. She always kept the focus on comprehension as she read to students and as they read on their own. Rosa and the students read a wide variety of texts, both fiction and expository, as they investigated their questions. Although she didn't test them on their reading, Rosa had them respond in a variety of ways, through graphic representations, reports, and stories.

Students also wrote every day in response to the academic content they were learning. They wrote their own stories, and Rosa took them through the steps of process writing for this. Students did much of the reading and writing in groups. In their groups, students more proficient in the language of instruction could support their classmates who were still learning the language.

Rosa followed the gradual release of responsibility model. She scaffolded instruction by reading aloud to students and also doing shared reading with big books. The students were further supported by the fact that the texts they read were all on the theme.

Finally, because she organized all the subject area studies around the same theme, her instruction provided a natural preview, view, and review. Since her bilingual students were all Spanish speakers, Rosa introduced new concepts with readings and activities in Spanish before studying them further in English. She also reviewed key concepts and vocabulary in Spanish to be sure that students had a good grasp of the central ideas. Since the concepts were taken from the different content area standards, Rosa was confident that her students were well prepared for the standardized tests they would soon be facing. Rosa is an excellent example of a principled teacher who has a clear view of literacy development and chooses methods and techniques that help all her students develop biliteracy.

 ## Developing Biliteracy by Drawing on Culture

Silvio is a fourth-grade bilingual teacher in a rural school. Some of his students began school as native English speakers, but many came to school speaking only Spanish. The school where he teaches has provided a maintenance bilingual program through the fifth grade because so many of the students are transient, and many come to school in the intermediate grades speaking very little English. Most of the students' families are associated in some way with agriculture, as either laborers in the fields or supervisors. Silvio understands his students and their families well because he was a migrant child. When he was young, a teacher encouraged him, and that encouragement helped him struggle to get through college and become a teacher so that he, in turn, could inspire children.

One of his key concerns as a teacher is that some of his colleagues at the school do not seem to expect much of the students who come to school speaking Spanish. The curriculum that most of these students get in both English and Spanish is simplified, fragmented, and unrelated to their interests or to the reality of their daily lives. Silvio's students have different backgrounds. Some have been in this school or nearby schools since kindergarten. Most of them speak Spanish and some English but have little interest in reading and writing in either language. Several other students are new to his classroom from Mexico or El Salvador and speak only Spanish. He also has two students from Oaxaca, Mexico, whose first language is Mixteco. These students speak a little Spanish, but very little English.

One of Silvio's first decisions is to get his students reading and writing in both Spanish and English, beginning with texts that are not too long to be overwhelming for his students, many of whom are still struggling readers in any language. Since a local poetry festival is coming up, he chooses to start a unit on poetry. He collects a series of poetry resources in Spanish to begin with. He reads some different poems to his students asking them to *"pensar en qué se parecen y en qué se diferencian los poemas"* (think about how the poems are the same and different). He reads some rather sophisticated poetry from Fernando del Paso (1990) and Pablo Neruda (1987), some very short poems from alphabet poetry books (Broeck 1983; Sempere 1987), and some traditional playful poetry by Alma Flor Ada (1992b).

After reading each poem, Silvio asks his students what their impressions are and lists their ideas on chart paper. By the time Silvio has finished reading ten poems, the chart has many different thoughts and questions about the poetry, including *"tiene rima"* (it rhymes), *"me hace sentir confundido"* (it makes me feel confused), *"me gusta porque es alegre"* (I like it because it is happy), *"algunos poemas no tienen rima"* (some poems don't rhyme), *"¿una canción puede ser un poema también?"* (can a song be a poem too?), *"algunos poemas son difíciles para entender"* (some poems are difficult to understand), *"¿por qué escribe poesía un poeta?"* (why does a poet write poetry?), *"algunos poemas tienen palabras extrañas"* (some poems have unusual words).

Silvio and the students look at the chart and talk about their observations and questions. Silvio brings up the poetry festival. This leads to a discussion of how they might prepare for it. Together they decide how they should study poetry together as a class. First, they should read lots of poems in Spanish. Then each student will memorize some poems and practice them in small groups to present to the class and maybe present at the festival.

In addition to reading the poetry of published authors, the students wonder if they can write some poetry of their own during their writing time each day. They decide that after they have read lots of poetry, they will be ready to think about writing their own. In addition, they talk about writing bilingual poems in both Spanish and English and also writing poetry only in English.

Silvio's students begin the year with poetry and revisit poetry throughout the year. In order to get insights into why people write poems and to learn more about poetry as a literary form, the students read *Cantos al maíz* (Lomatewama and Reyes 1997a) and the English version, *Songs to the Corn* (Lomatewama and Reyes 1997b). The poet tells why he writes each poem. He also explains about different kinds of poems. As the year progresses, Silvio draws on resources such as *Días y días de poesía* (Days and Days of Poetry) (Ada 1991) for seasonal poetry ideas. He also reads different poetry books from the Mexican series *Reloj de versos* (Rhyming Clocks) including *Mínima animalia* (The Smallest Animal Kingdom) (Bartolomé 1991), *El himno de las ranas* (The Hymn of the Frogs) (Cross 1992), *Despertar* (Wake Up) (Forcada 1992), and *La luna* (The Moon) (Sabines 1990).

In addition, he reads several poems from another series, *Cantos y cuentos* (Songs and Stories), including *Trotelete* (Frank 1998) and *Un jardin secreto* (A Secret Garden) (Ramírez Castañeda 1998). For English and bilingual poetry, Silvio draws on resources such as *A Chorus of Cultures: Developing Literacy Through Multicultural Poetry* (Ada, Harris, et al. 1993) as well as on local poets and his school library media specialist. Poetry is an excellent way for Silvio's students to develop literacy in both Spanish and English.

The Importance of Agriculture

Silvio sees the excitement of his students as they work with both familiar rhymes and new poetry, but he wants to extend their reading and writing into content areas too. Some of his students are not yet proficient readers and writers in Spanish or in English. Others read and write quite well. Silvio needs to provide literacy experiences that will interest and involve students with very different academic backgrounds and different language proficiency levels. He realizes that an excellent way for his students to develop academic competence and become truly biliterate is by teaching content through a theme that draws on students' backgrounds and experiences.

The small community where he lives and teaches depends heavily on agriculture. All the students in his class understand the importance of the land and of growing crops, including those whose parents are foremen or land owners. He wants all of his students to realize the importance of the work that many of their parents are involved in. Silvio decides to have his students explore the question *¿Por qué es importante la agricultura?* (Why is agriculture important?). He knows that his students' background experiences will help them as they read both literature and content texts on this topic.

Because the students began the year with poetry, it seems natural to Silvio to move into the agriculture theme through poetry. He begins the unit with several folk poems, riddles, and proverbs. Silvio reads some aloud and then gives books to groups and has students choose some favorites to read to the whole class (Ada 1991, 1992a, 1992b, 1992c; Dubin 1984; Peña 1989; Morales and Fernández 1994; Ramírez 1984; Walsh 1994). A favorite of the children with Mexican roots is the bilingual poetry book *My Mexico/México mío* (Johnston 1996). The ideas in these short, accessible texts capture the students' interest.

Then Silvio reads a stanza from the poem *"Son del pueblo trabajador"* (Sound of the Working People) (Ada 1991, 41):

Cuando sale el sol	When the sun rises
las tierras de mi tierra	the earth of my land
cultivo yo,	I cultivate
cuando sale el sol,	when the sun rises
que soy el campesino	I am the fieldworker
trabajador,	laborer
cuando sale el sol.	when the sun rises.

Silvio asks the students to jot down the thoughts or memories this poem brings to mind. They share their ideas in pairs and then make a class list.

Silvio passes out a copy of the stanza for students to take home and read to their parents. He encourages the students to discuss the poem with their family, to find out what ideas it raises for them. He suggests that they write down their parents' impressions and come prepared to share their results in class the next day. Silvio uses this information to create a second list. Then the class compares the two sets of responses to the poem and discusses some of the reasons for similarities and differences. In some cases, the parents have a stronger response because their work experience is more immediate, while the children's impressions have come secondhand as they hear their parents talk about their days in the fields. In other cases, the responses are similar because the children have worked alongside their parents.

From poetry Silvio turns the students to riddles, beginning with the following one for corn (Gallego, Hinojosa-Smith, et al. 1993, 29):

Allá en el llano	There in the plain
está uno sin sombrero.	is one without a hat.
Tiene barbas, tiene dientes	He has a beard, he has teeth
y no es un caballero.	and he is not a horseman.

After reading and guessing several different riddles, the students write their own riddles in pairs and read them aloud for the class to guess. This activity also spills over into English language arts time: The students often use the same topics in English that they first wrote and talked about in their native language.

To further extend the agriculture theme, Silvio reads two stories, *El chivo en la huerta* (*The Goat in the Chili Patch*) (Kratky 1989a, 1992) and "*La marrana dormida*" (The Sleeping Pig) (Seale and Tafolla 1993). Both of these stories are about animals that are in a field of crops where they should not be. The stories describe the attempts of other animals to get them out. In the end, an insect is the hero in each story. These similarities offer Silvio the opportunity to encourage his students to compare and contrast the stories.

Silvio used the above two stories in which onomatopeic words were used to help the main characters rid the crops of different pests. He also brought in poetry and other stories that cleverly used animal sounds and supported his theme including *Sonidos y ritmos* (Sounds and Rhythms) (Dubin 1984), *Pepín y el abuelo* (Pepín and His Grandfather) (Perera 1993), "*Alborada*" (Dawn) (Houghton Mifflin 1993), *El coquí* (Puerto Rican tree frog) (Ada 1992a), and "*Concierto*" (The Concert) (Ada 1992b). These stories offer the students further play with the sounds of language as well as additional opportunities for reading and writing.

Next, Silvio reads the big book *Granjas* (Farms) (Madrigal 1992) to the class. The students are fascinated by the description of *la granja de hortalizas* (the vegetable farm), *la granja lechera* (the dairy), *la granja triguera* (the wheat farm), and *la granja de naranjas* (the orange farm). Silvio asks, "*¿A qué les recuerda lo que leí?*" (What does this remind you of?). The students excitedly share their own and their parents' experiences on the different types of farms, and one proudly tells how his own father often tells him what the book said, "*La agricultura es la actividad más importante del mundo*" (Agriculture is the most important activity in the world) (6).

After this discussion, Silvio explains that the class is going to do different inquiry projects on the topic of *la agricultura y su importancia* (agriculture and its importance), and he asks the students, *"¿Qué más quieren saber ustedes sobre la agricultura?"* (What else would you like to know about agriculture?). The students write questions in groups and then share their questions as Silvio writes them on a large piece of butcher paper. Some students want to know about what kinds of things make the plants on a farm grow better. Some want to know why pineapples and mangos from their countries will not grow in this area. Others want to know why farm laborers earn so little money, and how much it costs to run a farm. Two students want to know more about irrigation, and still others want to know what is necessary to raise farm animals properly. The class decides to form groups to investigate these topics. Each group will write a report to share with the class, and the reports will be combined to create a class book on agriculture.

To get the information that they need, the students decide to use different resources. They plan to interview people in their families and the community, to call or write the local farm bureau for speakers and information, and to look at resource books they have in their classroom including reference books such as *La vida de las plantas* (The Life of Plants) (Costa-Pau 1993), *Plantas* (Plants) and *Animales* (Animals) (Sealey 1979b, 1979a), *Experimenta con las plantas* (*Make It Work! Plants*) (Watts and Parsons 1993, 1992), *Los secretos de las plantas* (*Eyewitness Encyclopedia* Vol. 14: *Plants*) (Burnie 1991, 1989), *Quiero conocer la vida de las plantas* (*Amazing World of Plants*) (Marcus 1987b, 1984b), and *Quiero conocer la vida de los animales* (*Amazing World of Animals*) (Marcus 1987a, 1984a). In addition, they plan to carry out research on the Internet.

Two of Silvio's students who came to his class directly from Mexico had very little previous schooling. The limited texts of the poetry, the riddles, and the limited-text books about plants and animals are accessible to them, especially when the class reads them together or when they have opportunities to read with a buddy. However, Silvio also wants these students to do other reading on their own, so he provides them with books about farms and agriculture that have more limited text to use as they explore their questions. These include books such as *El rancho* (The Ranch) (Almada 1994), *Chiles* (*Peppers*) (Kratky 1995a, 2001), *El campo* (The Country) (Rius and Parramón 1987), *Mi primera visita a la granja* (My First Visit to the Farm) (Parramón and Sales 1990), *Las plantas* (Plants) (Walker 1995a), and *De la semilla a la fruta* (From the Seed to the Fruit) (Zenzes 1987).

Silvio also involves his students in a literature study. He begins with a folktale that teaches the science concept of *cultivos alternados* (rotating crops). First, Silvio reads *Ton-tón el gigantón* (*Hugo Hogget*) (Cumpiano 1992b, 1992a), an Ecuadorian tale about a giant who is tricked by a peasant woman when he demands all the produce of her land. First, she gives him the choice of taking what grows above the ground or below the ground. When he chooses what grows above, she plants potatoes. The next season when he chooses what grows below, she raises beans. Finally, when he wants half the field, she grows wheat and puts in stakes to make it impossible for him to harvest his half of the field. One of the conclusions of the story is that the growing of different crops in the field each year made the harvest better.

After reading and discussing this story with his class, Silvio invites his students to read another version of the story, *El gigantón cabelludo* (The Hairy Giant) (Gondard 1993) and then compare and contrast the two versions. After reading and discussing the two stories, the class also reads and discusses a short content book called *Cultivos alternados* (Rotating Crops) (Gallego, Hinojosa-Smith, et al. 1993). This book gives them additional information about crop rotation.

Another folktale that the students read is *La gallinita, el gallo y el frijol* (The Hen, the Rooster, and the Bean) (Kratky 1989b, 1993). In this cumulative tale, the hen tries to get water to help the rooster get rid of the bean that is caught in his throat. When she asks the river for water, the river asks for a flower. She goes, then, to the flower, who demands thread to tie her vines. When the hen asks the girl for the thread, the girl requests a comb. This series of demands continues until the hen finally gets the needed water to dislodge the bean from the rooster's throat. The students relate this story to another traditional cumulative story, *El gallo que fue a la boda de su tío* (The Rooster Who Went to His Uncle's Wedding) (Ada 1997a, 1998), as well as to the traditional song "I Know an Old Lady Who Swallowed a Fly," which they had learned in English language arts, and the story "The House That Jack Built," which also has a similar cumulative pattern. They decide to look at those stories again and try to find other cumulative stories like them.

Next, Silvio brings out two books in Spanish about children of migrant families who move with the crops: *El camino de Amelia* (Amelia's Road) (Altman 1993a, 1993b) and *Tomates, California* (Seale and Ramírez 1993). He also shows them the bilingual books *Calling the Doves/El canto de las palomas* (Herrera 1995) and *Radio Man/Don Radio* (Dorros 1993). The students discuss the children in these stories. This leads to the topic of rights for farm workers and the hero of the farm workers, César Chávez. Silvio points out several books in the classroom library about the labor leader: *César Chávez: Líder laboral* (César Chávez, Labor Leader) (Morris 1994), *Harvesting Hope: The Story of César Chávez* (Krull 2003), *César Chávez: The Struggle for Justice/César Chávez: La lucha por justicia* (Griswold del Castillo 2002), and *César Chávez: The Farm Workers' Friend* (Fleming 2004). He assigns each book to a group of students and asks them to read the book and then list key events in César Chávez's life. When all the groups have finished, Silvio puts a time line up on the bulletin board. He asks each group for one event. As the groups volunteer their answers, the class decides where the event should go on the time line. Silvio continues to elicit responses until all the groups have reported the events they found.

During English language arts the next day, Silvio asks a group of students to copy a poem in English, "César Chávez, Farm Worker Organizer," onto large chart paper. The poem comes from *Latino Rainbow: Poems About Latino Americans* (Cumpián 1994, 29). The children then discuss how lines like "Tractors have barns, animals have stalls, but the migrant worker has nowhere to lay his head" (29) are related to stories like *El camino de Amelia* and *Tomates, California*. The class then looks at *Earth Angels* (Buirski 1994), a powerful book of photographs and short quotes from field workers about the difficulty of their lives, including the problems of child labor and pesticides. After some discussion, Silvio shows the students three other books that deal with farm workers and their children that he thinks might be interesting reading: *A Migrant Family* (Brimner 1992), *Lights on the River* (Thomas 1994), and *Voices from the Fields* (Atkin 1993).

The weeks that follow in Silvio's room are full of activity. Students read, share, and write about what they are learning. They decide that what they have learned about plants, animals, and agriculture, in general, is important to share with others in their school, and they plan a day when other classes will come into their room so that they can read the stories and reports they have written and explain what they have learned.

The students also want to share with their parents. They want their parents to know what they have learned, but they also want to show their parents their appreciation for the hard work their parents do. After much discussion, the students decide to make a big book titled *La importancia de la agricultura* (The Importance of Agriculture). Every group will contribute two pages to the book. One page will record what they learned in their inquiry and the other will include poems telling how they feel about being part of *la agricultura*. The students will read their pages of the book to their parents during the upcoming Christmas celebration, which will feature refreshments and a piñata. Figure 9–2 lists the books Silvio used for this unit.

Silvio has accomplished his goal. He met state language arts standards by having students read various genres, improve their fluency by reading songs, chants, and poems aloud, and write for a variety of purposes. For social studies standards, he and his students looked at the contributions that various groups have made to the country and the area. In science they learned about how crops grow and about crop rotation. They also began to understand how important agriculture is to the overall economy.

Ada, Alma F. 1991. *Días y días de poesía*. Carmel, CA: Hampton-Brown.

———. 1992a. *Caballito blanco y otras poesías favoritas*. Carmel, CA: Hampton-Brown.

———. 1992b. *Cinco pollitos y otras poesías favoritas*. Carmel, CA: Hampton-Brown.

———. 1992c. *El cuento del gato y otras poesías favoritas*. Carmel, CA: Hampton-Brown.

———. 1997. *El gallo que fue a la boda de su tío*. Boston: Houghton Mifflin.

———. 1998. *The Rooster Who Went to His Uncle's Wedding*. New York: Putnam Juvenile.

Ada, Alma F., Violet J. Harris, and Lee Bennett Hopkins. 1993. *A Chorus of Cultures: Developing Literacy Through Multicultural Poetry*. Carmel, CA: Hampton-Brown.

Almada, Patricia. 1994. *El rancho*. Crystal Lake, IL: Rigby.

Altman, Linda J. 1993a. *Amelia's Road*. New York: Lee and Low.

———. 1993b. *El camino de Amelia*. Trans. D. Santacruz. New York: Lee and Low.

Atkin, Susan B. 1993. *Voices from the Fields: Children of Migrant Farmworkers Tell Their Stories*. Boston: Little, Brown.

Barrera, Rosalinda, and Alan Crawford. 1987. *Vamos*. Boston: Houghton Mifflin.

Barrera, Rosalinda, Alan Crawford, Joan Mims, and Aurelia Davila de Silva, eds. 1993. "Alborada." In *Yo soy yo*. Boston: Houghton Mifflin.

Bartolomé, Efraín. 1991. *Mínima animalia*. México, DF: CIDCLI.

Brimner, Larry D. 1992. *A Migrant Family*. Minneapolis: Lerner.

Broeck, Fabricio V. 1983. *ABC animales*. México, DF: Editorial Patria.

Buirski, Nancy. 1994. *Earth Angels*. San Francisco: Pomegranate Artbooks.

Burnie, David. 1989. *Eyewitness Encyclopedia*, Vol. 14: *Plants*. London: Kindersley.

———. 1991. *Los secretos de las plantas*. Madrid, Spain: Santillana.

Costa-Pau, R. 1993. *La vida de las plantas*. Bogotá, Colombia: Editorial Norma.

Cross, Elsa. 1992. *El himno de las ranas*. México, DF: CIDCLI.

Cumpían, Carlos. 1994. *Latino Rainbow: Poems About Latino Americans*. Chicago: Children's Press.

Cumpiano, Ina. 1992a. *Hugo Hogget: A Story Based on an Ecuadorian Legend*. Carmel, CA: Hampton-Brown.

———. 1992b. *Ton-tón el gigantón*. Carmel, CA: Hampton-Brown.

del Paso, Fernando. 1990. *De la A a la Z por un poeta*. México, DF: Grupo Editorial Diana.

(continues)

FIGURE 9–2. Silvio's Poetry and Agriculture Bibliography

Dorros, Arthur. 1993. *Radio Man/Don Radio*. New York: HarperCollins.

Dubin, Susanna D. 1984. *Sonidos y ritmos*. Boston: Houghton Mifflin.

Fleming, Mara. 2004. *César Chávez: The Farm Workers' Friend*. Barrington, IL: Rigby.

Forcada, Alberto. 1992. *Despertar*. México, DF: CIDCLI.

Frank, José. 1998. *Trotelete*. México, DF: Consejo Nacional de la Cultura y las Artes.

Gallego, Margaret, Rolando Hinojosa-Smith, Clarita Kohen, Hilda Medrano, Juan Solis, and Eleanor Thonis. 1993. *Cultivos alternados*. Orlando, FL: Harcourt Brace Jovanovich.

Gondard, Pierre. 1993. *El gigantón cabelludo*. Orlando, FL: Harcourt Brace Jovanovich.

Griswold del Castillo, Richard D. 2002. *César Chávez: The Struggle for Justice/César Chávez: La lucha por justicia*. Houston, TX: Piñata.

Herrera, Juan F. 1995. *Calling the Doves: El canto de las palomas*. Emeryville, CA: Children's Book.

Johnston, Tony. 1996. *My Mexico—México mío*. New York: G. P. Putnam's Sons.

Kratky, Lada J. 1989a. *El chivo en la huerta*. Carmel, CA: Hampton-Brown.

———. 1989b. *La gallinita, el gallo y el frijol*. Carmel, CA: Hampton-Brown.

———. 1992. *The Goat in the Chili Patch*. Carmel, CA: Hampton-Brown.

———. 1993. *The Hen, the Rooster, and the Bean*. Carmel, CA: Hampton-Brown.

———. 1995. *Chiles*. Carmel, CA: Hampton-Brown.

———. 2001. *Peppers*. Carmel, CA: Hampton-Brown.

Krull, Kathleen. 2003. *Harvesting Hope: The Story of César Chávez*. New York: Harcourt.

Lomatewama, Ramson, and Graciela Reyes. 1997a. *Cantos al maíz: Un poeta Hopi escribe sobre el maíz*. Crystal Lake, IL: Rigby.

———. 1997b. *Songs to the Corn: A Hopi Poet Writes About Corn*. Crystal Lake, IL: Rigby.

Madrigal, Sylvia. 1992. *Granjas*. Carmel, CA: Hampton-Brown.

Marcus, Elizabeth. 1984a. *Amazing World of Animals*. Mahwah, NJ: Troll.

———. 1984b. *Amazing World of Plants*. Mahwah, NJ: Troll.

———. 1987a. *Quiero conocer la vida de los animales*. México, DF: SITESA.

———. 1987b. *Quiero conocer la vida de las plantas*. México, DF: Sistemas Técnicos de Edición.

Morales, Gloria, and Catalina Fernández. 1994. *El torito*. México: CONAFE.

Morris, Clara S. d. 1994. *César Chávez: Líder laboral*. Cleveland, OH: Modern Curriculum.

Neruda, Pablo. 1987. *El libro de las preguntas*. Santiago de Chile: Editorial Andrés Bello.

FIGURE 9–2. Silvio's Poetry and Agriculture Bibliography (*continued*)

Parramón, Josef M., and G. Sales. 1990. *Mi primera visita a la granja*. Woodbury, NY: Barron's.

Peña, Luis d. l. 1989. *Cosecha de versos y refranes*. México, DF: CONAFE.

Perera, Hilda. 1993. *Pepín y el abuelo*. Boston: Houghton Mifflin.

Ramírez, Elisa. 1984. *Adivinazas indígenas*. México, DF: Editorial Patria.

———. 1998. *Un jardín secreto*. México, DF: Consejo Nacional para la Cultura y las Artes.

Rius, María, and Josef M. Parramón. 1987. *El campo*. Woodbury, NY: Barron's.

Sabines, Jaime. 1990. *La luna*. México, DF: CIDCLI.

Seale, Jan, and Carmen Tafolla. 1993. "La marrana dormida." In *Yo soy yo*, ed. Rosalinda Barrera, Alan Crawford, Joan Mims, and Aurelia Davila de Silva. Boston: Houghton Mifflin.

Seale, Jan E., and Alfonso Ramírez. 1993. *Tomates, California*. Boston: Houghton Mifflin.

Sealey, Leonard. 1979a. *Animales*. Barcelona, Spain: Editorial Juventud.

———. 1979b. *Plantas*. Barcelona, Spain: Editorial Juventud.

Thomas, Jane R. 1994. *Lights on the River*. New York: Hyperion.

Walker, Colin. 1995. *Las plantas*. Cleveland, OH: Modern Curriculum Press.

Walsh, María E. 1994. *Matutú marambá*. Buenos Aires: Compañia Editora Espasa Calpe Argentina.

Watts, Claire, and Alexandra Parsons. 1992. *Make It Work! Plants*. London: Two-Can Publishing, Ltd.

———. 1993. *Experimenta con las plantas*. Trans. B. Rodríguez and C. Ginzo. Madrid, Spain: Ediciones SM.

Zenzes, Gertrudias. 1987. *De la semilla a la fruta*. México, DF: Fernández Editores.

FIGURE 9–2. Silvio's Poetry and Agriculture Bibliography (*continued*)

Silvio also accomplished some other things that may be even more important. Through a curriculum that was relevant to the lives of his students, he helped them appreciate what they and their families contribute to society. His students are becoming biliterate by reading both quality literature and informational texts in Spanish and in English, by discussing what they read, and by engaging in meaningful writing. The writing allows students to show what they have learned and how they have been touched by this empowering curriculum.

Conclusion

Our purpose in writing this book was to describe the reading and writing processes in Spanish and in English and to share with teachers ideas about how to best help native Spanish speakers develop biliteracy. We planned to write a short second edition that would cover the basics and serve as a quick reference. However, the book expanded as we attempted to include ideas from the rich research base on bilingual education and reading and writing in two languages. We also wanted to share a sample of the wealth of Spanish literature for young readers and writers. Our book grew because the topic was so important and there was so much to be said.

We do not pretend that we have said all that needs to be said. We have tried, however, to share some of the key ideas that we think all Spanish-English bilingual teachers should know. It is important to consider what the effective features of a quality bilingual or dual language reading and writing program might be. To decide what constitutes effective features, it is critical to understand the reading process. When one understands how readers construct meaning, it is possible to make informed choices about an appropriate reading program. The same kind of informed decision making is important for bilingual teachers in the area of writing. Only when teachers understand how writing develops in Spanish and in English can they support their students as they move from invented spelling to conventional writing.

We develop literacy so that we can understand our world and share that understanding. In our final chapter we have given examples of how two teachers developed quality biliteracy programs by drawing on a wealth of literature and by organizing themes around topics of interest to their students. Teachers working in Spanish-English bilingual and dual language classrooms must not simply teach their students to read and write: they must teach them to think and act to build a better world. Biliterate people are going to be our future leaders, and only if we help our bilingual students understand how to make the world a better place can we say that our teaching has really been successful.

Applications

1. Consider the development of a thematic unit at a specific grade level. Choose a topic or a big question. Look at the content standards for your state for that grade level and identify which standards might be covered within your thematic unit. List the standards.

2. Find some literature and content books in Spanish and in English at your grade level that fit the topic for your thematic unit and meet some of the standards. Bring those books to class to share how you would use them.

3. Work out a plan of activities including materials that you might use over several days during a thematic unit. Incorporate preview, view, and review by having the activities and materials introduced in one language and reinforced in the other. There should be a kind of continual weaving of content back and forth between languages. Bring this plan and the materials to class to share.

References

Literature Cited

Ada, Alma Flor. 1989a. *Los seis deseos de la jirafa.* Carmel, CA: Hampton-Brown.

———. 1989b. *Me gustaría tener . . .* Northvale, NJ: Santillana.

———. 1990. *Una semilla nada más.* Carmel, CA: Hampton-Brown.

———. 1991. *Días y días de poesía.* Carmel, CA: Hampton-Brown.

———. 1992a. *Caballito blanco y otras poesías favoritas.* Carmel, CA: Hampton-Brown.

———. 1992b. *Cinco pollitos y otras poesías favoritas.* Carmel, CA: Hampton-Brown.

———. 1992c. *El cuento del gato y otras poesías favoritas.* Carmel, CA: Hampton-Brown.

———. 1992d. *The Giraffe's Sad Tale.* Carmel, CA: Hampton-Brown.

———. 1997a. *El gallo que fue a la boda de su tío.* Boston: Houghton Mifflin.

———. 1997b. *Gathering the Sun.* New York: Lothrop, Lee and Shepard.

———. 1998. *The Rooster Who Went to His Uncle's Wedding.* New York: Putnam Juvenile.

Ada, Alma Flor, Violet J. Harris, and **Lee Bennett Hopkins.** 1993. *A Chorus of Cultures: Developing Literacy Through Multicultural Poetry.* Carmel, CA: Hampton-Brown.

"Alborada." 1993. In *Yo soy yo,* ed. Rosalinda Barrera, Alan Crawford, Joan Mims, and Aurelia Davila de Silva. Boston: Houghton Mifflin.

Allen, Marjorie, and **Shelly Rotner.** 1991. *Cambios.* Carmel, CA: Hampton-Brown.

Almada, Patricia. 1994. *El rancho.* Crystal Lake, IL: Rigby.

———. 1997a. *Del padre al hijo.* Crystal Lake, IL: Rigby.

———. 1997b. *From Father to Son.* Crystal Lake, IL: Rigby.

Alonso, Fernando. 1989. *La vista de la primavera.* Northvale, NJ: Santillana.

Alshalabi, Firyal M. 1995. *Ahmed's Alphabet Book.* Kuwait: Rubeian.

Altman, Linda Jacobs. 1993a. *Amelia's Road.* New York: Lee and Low.

———. 1993b. *El camino de Amelia*. New York: Lee and Low.

Alvarez, Carmen Espinosa Elenes de. 1979. *Mi libro mágico*. México, DF: Enrique Sainz Editores.

Ambert, Alba. 1997a. *Por qué soplan los vientos salvajes*. Crystal Lake, IL: Rigby.

———. 1997b. *Why the Wild Winds Blow*. Crystal Lake, IL: Rigby.

Aparicio, Eduardo. 1997a. *¡Huracán a la vista!* Crystal Lake, IL: Rigby.

———. 1997b. *Hurricane on Its Way!* Crystal Lake, IL: Rigby.

Atkin, S. Beth. 1993. *Voices from the Fields: Children of Migrant Farmworkers Tell Their Stories*. Boston: Little, Brown.

Atkinson, Katie. 1998. *Hide to Survive*. Crystal Lake, IL: Rigby.

Badt, Karin Luis. 1994. *Good Morning, Let's Eat!* Chicago: Children's Press.

———. 1995. *Pass the Bread!* Chicago: Children's Press.

Barberis. 1974. *¿De quién es este rabo?* Valladolid, Spain: Miñon.

Barrera, Rosalinda, and **Alan Crawford.** 1987. *Vamos*. Boston: Houghton Mifflin.

Barrett, Norman. 1988. *Monkeys and Simians*. New York: Franklin Watts.

———. 1989. *Crocodiles and Caimans*. New York: Franklin Watts.

———. 1991a. *Cocodrilos y caimanes*. New York: Franklin Watts.

———. 1991b. *Monos y simios*. New York: Franklin Watts.

Bartolomé, Efraín. 1991. *Mínima animalia*. México, DF: CIDCLI.

Beal, Kathleen. 2004. *My Rooster Speaks Korean*. Barrington, IL: Rigby.

Beck, Jennifer. 1994. *Patas*. Crystal Lake, IL: Rigby.

Berger, Melvin, and **Gilbert Berger.** 1999. *Do Tarantulas Have Teeth?* New York: Scholastic.

Beuchat, Cecilia, and **Mabel Condemarín.** 1997. *La tortilla corredora*. Boston: Houghton Mifflin.

Bogart, Jo Ellen. 1995. *Growing*. Bothell, WA: Wright Group.

Boland, Janice. 1998a. *Girasoles*. Katonah, NY: Richard C. Owen.

———. 1998b. *Sunflowers*. Katonah, NY: Richard C. Owen.

Bolton, Faith, and **Diane Snowball.** 1985. *Growing Radishes and Carrots*. New York: Scholastic.

Bos, Burny, and **Hans De Beer.** 1989. *Oli, el pequeño elefante*. Barcelona, Spain: Editorial Lumen.

Brimner, Larry D. 1992. *A Migrant Family*. Minneapolis: Lerner.

Broeck, Fabricio Vanden. 1983. *ABC animales*. México, DF: Editorial Patria.

Browne, Anthony. 1983. *Gorilla*. London: Julia MacRae Books.

———. 1991. *Gorila*. México, DF: Fondo de Cultura Económica.

———. 1992. *Zoo*. London: Julia MacRae Books.

———. 1993. *Zoológico*. Méxcio, DF: Fondo de Cultura Económica.

Brusca, María Cristina, and **Tona Wilson.** 1995. *Tres amigos: Un cuento para contar*. Boston: Houghton Mifflin.

———. 1997. *Three Friends*. Boston: Houghton Mifflin.

Buckley, Marvin. 2001. *Corn*. Washington, DC: National Geographic.

———. 2002. *El maíz*. Washington, DC: National Geographic.

Buirski, Nancy. 1994. *Earth Angels*. San Francisco: Pomegranate Artbooks.

Burnie, David. 1989. *Eyewitness Encyclopedia*, Vol. 14: *Plants*. London: Kindersley.

———. 1991. *Los secretos de las plantas*. Madrid, Spain: Santillana.

Cabrera, Miguel. n.d. *Chiquilín*. Caracas, Venezuela: Conceptos.

Calmenson, Stephanie. 1993. *It Begins with an A*. New York: Scholastic.

Canetti, Yanitzia. 1997. *ABC ¡Ya me lo sé!* Boston: Houghton Mifflin.

Canizares, Susan. 1998. *Sun*. New York: Scholastic.

Cassen Mayers, Florence. 1990. *The Wild West*. New York: Harry N. Abrams.

Chanko, Pamela, and **Daniel Moreton.** 1998. *Weather*. New York: Scholastic.

Chapela Mendoza, Luz María. 2000. *Libro integrado*. México, DF: Secretaría de la Educación Pública.

Chavarría-Cháirez, Becky. 2000. *Magda's Tortillas/Las tortillas de Magda*. Houston: Arte Publico.

Cherry, Lynne. 1990. *The Great Kapok Tree*. New York: Harcourt Brace.

———. 1996. *La ceiba majestuosa: Un cuento del bosque lluviosa*. Boston: Houghton Mifflin.

Chin-Lee, Cynthia, and **Terri de la Peña.** 1999. *A es para decir América*. New York: Orchard.

Clark, Patricia N. 2000. *Goodbye, Goose*. Katonah, NY: Richard C. Owen.

Clevidence, Karen. 2004. *A Disaster Is Coming*. Barrington, IL: Rigby.

Comerlati, Mara. 1983. *Conoce nuestros mamíferos*. Caracas, Venezuela: Ediciones Ekaré Banco del Libro.

Costa-Pau, Rosa. 1993. *La vida de las plantas*. Bogotá, Colombia: Editorial Norma.

Costain, Meridith. 1966. *Clouds*. New York: Scholastic.

Cowcher, Helen. 1992. *El bosque tropical*. New York: Scholastic.

Cowley, Joy. 1983. *The Farm Concert*. Bothell, WA: Wright Group.

———. 1987. *Los animales de Don Vicencio*. Auckland, New Zealand: Shortland.

Crimi, Carolyn. 1995. *Outside, Inside*. New York: Scholastic.

Cross, Elsa. 1992. *El himno de las ranas*. México, DF: CIDCLI.

Crum, Mary B. 2004. *The Power of the Wind*. Barrington, IL: Rigby.

Cumpían, Carlos. 1994. *Latino Rainbow: Poems About Latino Americans*. Chicago: Children's Press.

Cumpiano, Ina. 1990. *Pan, pan, gran pan*. Carmel, CA: Hampton-Brown.

———. 1992a. *Hugo Hogget: A Story Based on an Ecuadorian Legend*. Carmel, CA: Hampton-Brown.

———. 1992b. *Ton-tón el gigantón*. Carmel, CA: Hampton-Brown.

Cusick, Pat. 1997. *How's the Weather?* Crystal Lake, IL: Rigby.

Cutting, Brian, and **Jillian Cutting.** 1995. *Semillas y más semillas*. Bothell, WA: Wright Group.

Dawson, Hamish. 1997. *Making a Weather Chart*. Crystal Lake, IL: Rigby.

Dawson, Sarah. 2001. *Animals of the Land and Sea*. Washington, DC: National Geographic.

———. 2002. *Animales de mar y tierra*. Washington, DC: National Geographic.

del Paso, Fernando. 1990. *De la A a la Z por un poeta*. México, DF: Grupo Editorial Diana.

Detwiler, Darius, and **Marina Rizo-Patron.** 1997. *Mi libro del ABC*. Boston: Houghton Mifflin.

Díaz, Katrina. 1997a. *Storm Trackers*. Crystal Lake, IL: Rigby.

———. 1997b. *Tras las tormentas*. Crystal Lake, IL: Rigby.

Dorros, Arthur. 1993. *Radio Man/Don Radio*. New York: HarperCollins.

Drew, David. 1989. *The Book of Animal Records*. Crystal Lake, IL: Rigby.

———. 1990. *Animal Clues*. Crystal Lake, IL: Rigby.

———. 1993. *Pistas de animales*. Crystal Lake, IL: Rigby.

———. 2000a. *Amazing Animals*. Crystal Lake, IL: Rigby.

———. 2000b. *Food Alphabet*. Big book ed. Crystal Lake, IL: Rigby.

Drucker, Malka, and **Rita Pocock.** 1992. *A Jewish Holiday ABC*. New York: Trumpet.

Dubin, Susana Dultzín. 1984. *Sonidos y ritmos*. Boston: Houghton Mifflin.

Ediciones Litexsa Venezolana, ed. 1987. *Aprender a contar*. Caracas, Venezuela: Cromotip.

Ehlert, Lois. 1989. *Eating the Alphabet*. New York: Scholastic.

———. 1990. *Color Zoo*. New York: Trumpet Club.

Ellis, Veronica F. 1997. *La isla de la nube lluviosa*. Boston: Houghton Mifflin.

Fernandes, Eugenie. 1996. *ABC and You*. Boston: Houghton Mifflin.

Fernández, Laura. 1993. "Pío, pío." In *Yo soy yo*, ed. Rosalinda Barrera, Alan Crawford, Joan S. Mims, and Aurelia D. de Silva. Boston: Houghton Mifflin.

Fleming, Denise. 1992. *Count*. New York: Henry Holt.

Fleming, Mara. 2004. *César Chávez: The Farm Workers' Friend*. Barrington, IL: Rigby.

Flint, David. 1998. *Where Does Breakfast Come From?* Crystal Lake, IL: Rigby.

Flores, Guillermo Solano. 1986. *El viento*. México, DF: Editorial Trillas.

———. 1997. *El viento*. Big book ed. Boston: Houghton Mifflin.

Forcada, Alberto. 1992. *Despertar*. México, DF: CIDCLI.

Fowler, Allan. 1991. *Podría ser un mamífero*. Chicago: Children's Press.

Frank, José. 1998. *Trotelete*. México, DF: Consejo Nacional de la Cultura y las Artes.

Gallego, Margaret, Rolando Hinojosa-Smith, Clarita Kohen, Hilda Medrano, Juan Solis, and **Eleanor Thonis.** 1993. *Cultivos alternados*. Orlando, FL: Harcourt Brace Jovanovich.

Gondard, Pierre. 1993. *El gigantón cabelludo*. Orlando, FL: Harcourt Brace Jovanovich.

González-Jensen, Margarita. 1994. *Tortillas*. New York, Scholastic.

———. 1997a. *El maravilloso maíz de México*. Crystal Lake, IL: Rigby.

———. 1997b. *Mexico's Marvelous Corn*. Crystal Lake, IL: Rigby.

Goodall, Jane. 1989. *The Chimpanzee Family Book*. Salzburgo: Neugebaurer.

———. 1991. *La familia del chimpancé*. México, DF: SITESA.

Granados, Antonio. 1989. *Zoológico de palabras*. Hermosillo, Mexico: Editorial Uni-Son.

Grande Tabor, Nancy M. 1992. *Albertina anda arriba*. New York: Scholastic.

Granowsky, Alvin. 1986a. *Los animales del mundo*. Lexington, MA: Schoolhouse Press.

———. 1986b. *¿Por qué nos preocupa?* Lexington, MA: Schoolhouse Press.

Green, Josie. 2005. *Droughts*. Washington, DC: National Geographic.

Greenway, Shirley. 1997. *Two's Company*. Watertown, MA: Charlesbridge.

Griswold del Castillo, Richard de. 2002. *César Chávez: The Struggle for Justice/César Chávez: La lucha por justicia*. Houston, TX: Piñata.

Guarino, Deborah. 1989. *Is Your Mama a Llama?* New York: Scholastic.

———. 1993. *¿Tu mamá es una llama?* New York: Scholastic.

Hayes, Joe. 2005. *A Spoon for Every Bite/Una cuchara para cada bocado.* El Paso, TX: Cinco Puntos.

Herrera, Juan Felipe. 1995. *Calling the Doves/El canto de las palomas.* Emeryville, CA: Children's Book.

Herzog, Brad. 2003. *What's the Weather Outside?* Barrington, IL: Rigby.

Hofer, Angelika, and **Günter Ziesler.** 1988. *The Lion Family Book.* Salzburgo: Neugebaurer.

———. 1992. *La familia del león.* México, DF: SITESA.

Hopping, Lorraine J. 2000. *Today's Weather Is . . . : A Book of Experiments.* New York: Mondo.

Horenstein, Henry. 1999. *A Is for? A Photographer's Alphabet of Animals.* New York: Scholastic.

Houghton Mifflin. 1997. *Mi libro de rimas y canciones.* Boston: Houghton Mifflin.

Hughes, Monica. 1998. *Seasons.* Crystal Lake, IL: Rigby.

Ignacio, Fred. 2000. *Crops.* Carmel, CA: Hampton-Brown.

Ingpen, Robert, and **Margaret Dunkle.** 1987. *Conservation.* Melbourne, Australia: Hill of Content.

———. 1991. *Conservación.* México, DF: Editorial Origen S.A.

Jenkins, Rhonda. 1998. *Growing a Plant: A Journal.* Crystal Lake, IL: Rigby.

Johnston, Tony. 1996. *My Mexico—México mío.* New York: G. P. Putnam's Sons.

Jordan, Denise. 2004. *What Are the Seasons Like?* Barrington, IL: Rigby.

Jordan, Helene J. 1996. *¿Cómo crece una semilla?* New York: HarperCollins.

Kasza, Keiko. 1996. *A Mother for Choco.* Boston: Houghton Mifflin.

———. 1997. *Choco encuentra una mamá.* Boston: Houghton Mifflin.

Kelly, Harold. 2002. *El sol.* New York: Rosen.

Komori, Atsushi. 1996. *Animal Mothers.* Boston: Houghton Mifflin.

———. 1997. *Las mamás de los animales.* Boston: Houghton Mifflin.

Kratky, Lada. 1989a. *El chivo en la huerta.* Carmel, CA: Hampton-Brown.

———. 1989b. *La gallinita, el gallo y el frijol.* Carmel, CA: Hampton-Brown.

———. 1991a. *Animals and Their Young.* Carmel, CA: Hampton-Brown.

———. 1991b. *Los animales y sus crías.* Carmel, CA: Hampton-Brown.

———. 1992. *The Goat in the Chile Patch.* Carmel, CA: Hampton-Brown.

———. 1993. *The Hen, the Rooster, and the Bean.* Carmel, CA: Hampton-Brown.

———. 1995a. *Chiles.* Carmel, CA: Hampton-Brown.

———. 1995b. *Orejas.* Carmel, CA: Hampton-Brown

———. 1995c. *¿Qué sale de las semillas?* Carmel, CA: Hampton-Brown.

———. 1995d. *Veo, veo colas.* Carmel, CA: Hampton-Brown.

———. 1997a. *Ears.* Carmel, CA: Hampton-Brown.

———. 1997b. *I See Tails.* Carmel, CA: Hampton-Brown.

———. 1997c. *Seeds.* Carmel, CA: Hampton-Brown.

———. 2001. *Peppers.* Carmel, CA: Hampton-Brown.

Krauss, Ruth. 1945. *The Carrot Seed.* New York: Scholastic.

———. 1978. *La semilla de zanahoria.* New York: Scholastic.

Krull, Kathleen. 2003. *Harvesting Hope: The Story of César Chávez.* New York: Harcourt.

Kuchalla, Susan. 1982. *Baby Animals.* Mahwah, NJ: Troll.

———. 1987. *¿Cómo son los animales bebés?* México, DF: SITESA.

"Las hormigas marchan." 1993. In *Yo soy yo*, ed. Rosalinda Barrera, Alan Crawford, Joan Mims, and Aurelia Davila de Silva. Boston: Houghton Mifflin.

Lauber, Patricia. 1996. *Hurricanes.* New York: Scholastic.

Leland, Debbie. 2000. *The Jalapeño Man.* College Station, TX: Wildflower Run.

Levy, Janice. 1999. *Abuelito Eats with His Fingers.* Austin, TX: Eakin.

Lomatewama, Ramson, and **Graciela Reyes.** 1997a. *Cantos al maíz: Un poeta Hopi escribe sobre el maíz.* Crystal Lake, IL: Rigby.

———. 1997b. *Songs to the Corn: A Hopi Poet Writes About Corn.* Crystal Lake, IL: Rigby.

Longo, Alejandra. 2004. *Aserrín, aserrán.* New York: Scholastic.

López, Elva R., trans. 1987. *La gallinita roja.* New York: Scholastic.

Lucca, Mario. 2001. *Plants Grow from Seeds.* Washington, DC: National Geographic.

———. 2003. *De las semillas nacen las plantas.* Washington, DC: National Geographic.

Madrigal, Sylvia. 1992. *Granjas.* Carmel, CA: Hampton-Brown.

Mañé, Carmen de Posadas. 1997. *El señor Viento Norte.* Boston: Houghton Mifflin.

Marcus, Elizabeth. 1984a. *Amazing World of Animals.* Mahwah, NJ: Troll.

———. 1984b. *Amazing World of Plants.* Mahwah, NJ: Troll.

———. 1987a. *Quiero conocer la vida de los animales.* México, DF: SITESA.

———. 1987b. *Quiero conocer la vida de las plantas.* México, DF: Sistemas Técnicos de Edición.

Martel, Cruz. 1997. *Días de yagua.* Boston: Hougton Mifflin.

Marzollo, Jean. 1996. *I'm a Seed.* Carmel, CA: Hampton-Brown.

Maurer, Donna. 1996. *Annie, Bea, and Chi Chi Dolores.* Boston: Houghton Mifflin.

McMillan, Bruce. 1988. *Growing Colors.* New York: William Morrow.

McPhail, David. 1989. *Animals A to Z.* New York: Scholastic.

Menchaca, Robert, and **Estella Menchaca.** 1997. *Fue David.* Boston: Houghton Mifflin.

Merrill, Claire. 1973. *A Seed Is a Promise.* New York: Scholastic.

Monreal, Violeta. 1995. *Carlota, reina de las letras, o El rapto de la ñ.* Madrid, Spain: Grupo Anaya.

Mora, Pat. 1994. *Listen to the Desert/Oye al desierto.* New York: Clarion.

———. 2001. *The Bakery Lady/La señora de la panadería.* Houston, TX: Piñata.

Morales, Gloria, and **Catalina Fernández.** 1994. *El torito.* México: CONAFE.

Morris, Ann. 1989. *Bread, Bread, Bread.* New York: Mulberry.

Morris, Clara Sánchez de. 1994. *César Chávez: Líder laboral.* Cleveland, OH: Modern Curriculm.

Morrison, Rob. 1998. *How Does It Grow?* Crystal Lake, IL: Rigby.

Most, Bernard. 1978. *If the Dinosaurs Came Back.* New York: Harcourt Brace.

———.1997. *Si los dinosaurios regresaran.* Boston: Houghton Mifflin.

Neruda, Pablo. 1987. *El libro de las preguntas.* Santiago de Chile: Editorial Andrés Bello.

Nguyen, Rosemary, and **Hieu Nguyen.** 2004. *In the Rain.* Barrington, IL: Rigby.

Pacheco, Lourdes. 2000. *El viento y el sol.* Barrington, IL: Rigby.

Pallotta, Jerry. 1986a. *The Icky Bug Alphabet Book.* New York: Scholastic.

———. 1986b. *The Ocean Alphabet Book.* New York: Trumpet.

———. 1993. *The Extinct Alphabet Book.* New York: Scholastic.

———. 1996. *The Freshwater Alphabet Book*. New York: Trumpet.

Paqueforet, Marcus. 1993a. *A comer, mi bebé*. México, DF: Hachette Latinoamérica/SEP.

———. 1993b. *A dormir, mi bebé*. México, DF: Hachette Latinoamérica/SEP.

———. 1993c. *A pasear, mi bebé*. México, DF: Hachette Latinoamérica/SEP.

———. 1993d. *Un cariñito, mi bebé*. México, DF: Hachette Latinoamérica/SEP.

Parker, John. 1997. *Wind and Sun*. Crystal Lake, IL: Rigby.

Parkes, Brenda. 1986. *Who's in the Shed?* Crystal Lake, IL: Rigby.

———. 1990. *¿Quién está en la choza?* Crystal Lake, IL: Rigby.

Parkes, Brenda, and **Judith Smith.** 1986. *The Gingerbread Man*. Crystal Lake, IL: Rigby.

———. 1989. *El hombrecito del pan jengibre*. Crystal Lake, IL: Rigby.

Parramón, Josep M., and **G. Sales.** 1990. *Mi primera visita a la granja*. Woodbury, NY: Barron's.

Paulsen, Gary. 1995a. *La tortillería*. Orlando, FL: Harcourt Brace.

———. 1995b. *The Tortilla Factory*. New York: Harcourt Brace.

Peña, Luis de la. 1989. *Cosecha de versos y refranes*. México, DF: CONAFE.

Perea Estrada, Altamira. 1996. *Un abecedario muy sabroso*. New York: Scholastic.

Perera, Hilda. 1993. *Pepín y el abuelo*. Boston: Houghton Mifflin.

Pratt, Kristin Joy. 1993. *Un paseo por el bosque lluvioso/A Walk in the Rainforest*. Nevada City, CA: Dawn.

Quinn, Pat, and **Bill Gaynor.** 1999. *El poder del viento*. Huntington Beach, CA: Learning Media.

Ramírez Castañeda, Elisa. 1984. *Adivinazas indígenas*. México, DF: Editorial Patria.

———. 1998. *Un jardín secreto*. México, DF: Consejo Nacional para la Cultura y las Artes.

Ritchie, Rita. 1999. *Mountain Gorillas in Danger*. Boston: Houghton Mifflin.

Rius, María, and **Josep María Parramón.** 1987. *El campo*. Woodbury, NY: Barron's.

Sabin, Francene. 1985. *Whales and Dolphins*. Mahwah, NJ: Troll.

Sabines, Jaime. 1990. *La luna*. México, DF: CIDCLI.

Samoyault, Tiphaine. 1998. *Alphabetical Order: How the Alphabet Began*. New York: Viking.

Sanchez, Isidro. 1989. *El elefante*. Barcelona, Spain: Multilibro.

Sandved, Kjell B. 1996. *The Butterfly Alphabet*. New York: Scholastic.

Scholastic. 1993. "Los panes del mundo." *Scholastic News*. New York: Scholastic.

Seale, Jan Epton, and **Alfonso Ramírez.** 1993. *Tomates, California*. Boston: Houghton Mifflin.

Seale, Jan, and **Carmen Tafolla.** 1993. "La marrana dormida." In *Yo soy yo*, ed. Rosalinda Barrera, Alan Crawford, Joan Mims, and Aurelia Davila de Silva. Boston: Houghton Mifflin.

Sealey, Leonard. 1979a. *Animales*. Barcelona, Spain: Editorial Juventud.

———. 1979b. *Plantas*. Barcelona, Spain: Editorial Juventud.

Sempere, Vicky. 1987. *ABC*. Caracas, Venezuela: Ediciones Ekaré-Banco del Libro.

Shannon, George. 1996. *Tomorrow's Alphabet*. Hong Kong: South China Printing.

Sharp, Kathie. 1998. *Rain, Snow, and Hail*. Crystal Lake, IL: Rigby.

———. 2006. *Weather Words*. Austin, TX: Harcourt Achieve.

Shulman, Lisa. 2004a. *Plants We Use*. Barrington, IL: Rigby.

———. 2004b. *The Wonderful Water Cycle*. Barrrington, IL: Rigby.

Singer, Arthur. 1973. *Wild Animals: From Alligator to Zebra*. New York: Random House.

Smith, Cathy. 2001. *Animals with Armor*. Washington, DC: National Geographic.

———. 2002. *Animales con armadura*. Washington, DC: National Geographic.

Solano Flores, Guillermo. 1988. *Pon una semilla a germinar*. México, DF: Editorial Trillas.

Stolz, Mary. 1997. *Una tormenta nocturna*. Boston: Houghton Mifflin.

Sullivan Carroll, Kathleen. 1996. *One Red Rooster*. Boston: Houghton Mifflin.

Thomas, Jane Resh. 1994. *Lights on the River*. New York: Hyperion Books for Children.

Tsang, Nina. 2004. *The Weather*. Barrington, IL: Rigby.

Urbina, Joaquín. n.d. *La culebra verde*. Caracas, Venezuela: Gráficas Armitano.

Wachter, Joanne. 2004. *Around the Sun*. Barrington, IL: Rigby.

Waite, Judy. 2000. *Fox, Beware!* Barrington, IL: Rigby.

———. 2004. *Look Out the Window*. Barrington, IL: Rigby.

Walker, Colin. 1992a. *Plants and Seeds.* Bothell, WA: Wright Group.

———. 1992b. *Seeds Grow*. Bothell, WA: Wright Group.

———. 1993a. *Alimento que obtenemos de las plantas*. Cleveland, OH: Simon and Schuster.

———. 1993b. *Las diferentes cosas que vienen de las plantas*. Cleveland, OH: Simon and Schuster.

———. 1995a. *Las plantas*. Cleveland, OH: Modern Curriculum.

———. 1995b. *Las semillas crecen*. Bothell, WA: Wright Group.

———. 1995c. *Plantas y semillas*. Bothell, WA: Wright Group.

Walsh, María Elena. 1994. *Matutú marambá*. Buenos Aires, Argentina: Compañia Editora Espasa Calpe Argentina.

Watts, Claire, and **Alexandra Parsons.** 1992. *Make It Work! Plants*. London: Two-Can Publishing, Ltd.

———. 1993. *Experimenta con las plantas*. Madrid, Spain: Ediciones SM.

Wellington, Monica. 1997. *Night House Bright House*. New York: Dutton.

West, Loretta. 2006. *Maya's Storm*. Austin, TX: Harcourt Achieve.

Wexo, John Bonnett. 1981. "Los animales en extinción." *Zoobooks*. San Diego, CA.

Wilbur, Richard. 1997. *The Disappearing Alphabet Book*. New York: Scholastic.

Willow, Diane, and **Laura Jacques.** 1993. *Dentro de la selva tropical*. Watertown, MA: Charlesbridge.

Wing, Natasha. 1996. *Jalapeño Bagels*. New York: Atheneum.

Woolley, Marilyn. 2003. *Cuando llueve*. Washington, DC: National Geographic.

Wong, George. 2001. *Animals and Plants Live Here*. Washington, DC: National Geographic.

———. 2002. *Animales y plantas viven aquí*. Washington, DC: National Geographic.

Wright, Alexandra. 1992. *Will We Miss Them?* Watertown, MA: Charlesbridge.

———. 1993. *¿Les echaremos de menos?* Watertown, MA: Charlesbridge.

Zak, Monica. 1989. *Salvan mi selva*. México, DF: Sistemas Técnicos de Edición.

Zawisza, Tita. 1982. *Conoce a nuestros insectos.* Caracas, Venezuela: Ediciones Ekaré-Banco del Libro.

Zenzes, Gertrudias. 1987. *De la semilla a la fruta.* México, DF: Fernández Editores.

Professional Works Cited

Adams, Marilyn. 1990. *Beginning to Read: Thinking and Learning About Print.* Cambridge: MIT Press.

———. 1994. "Modeling the Connection Between Word Recognition and Reading." In *Theoretical Models and Processes of Reading,* ed. R. Ruddell, M. Ruddell, and H. Singer, 838–63. Newark, DE: International Reading Association.

Akhavan, Nancy L. 2004. *How to Align Literacy Instruction, Assessment, and Standards and Achieve Results You Never Dreamed Possible.* Portsmouth, NH: Heinemann.

Allen, Janet. 2002. *On the Same Page: Shared Reading Beyond the Primary Grades.* Portland, ME: Stenhouse.

Allen, Roach Van. 1976. *Language Experiences in Communication.* Boston: Houghton Mifflin.

Anderson, Richard, Elfrida Hiebert, et al. 1985. *Becoming a Nation of Readers: The Report of the Commission on Reading.* Champaign, IL: Center for the Study of Reading.

Anthony, Edward. 1965. "Approach, Method, and Technique." In *Teaching English as a Second Language: A Book of Readings,* ed. H. Allen and R. Campbell, 4–8. New York: McGraw-Hill.

Armbruster, Bonnie, and **Jean Osborn.** 2001. *Put Reading First: The Research Building Blocks for Teaching Children to Read.* Washington, DC: U.S. Department of Education.

Atwell, Nancie. 1987. *In the Middle: Writing, Reading, and Learning with Adolescents.* Portsmouth, NH: Boynton/Cook.

———. 1998. *In the Middle: New Understandings About Writing, Reading, and Learning.* Portsmouth, NH: Heinemann.

Barbosa Heldt, Antonio. 1971. *Como han aprendido a leer y a escribir los mexicanos.* México, DF: Editorial Pax-Mexico.

Barrera, Rosalinda. 1981. "Reading in Spanish: Insights from Children's Miscues." In *Learning to Read in Different Languages,* ed. S. Hudelson. Washington, DC: Center for Applied Linguistics.

Bellenger, Lionel. 1979. *Los métodos de lectura.* Barcelona, Spain: Oikos-Tau.

Berdiansky, Betty, B. Cronnell, et al. 1969. *Spelling-Sound Relations and Primary Form-Class Descriptions for Speech Comprehension Vocabularies of 6–9 Year Olds.* Inglewood, CA: Southwest Regional Laboratory for Educational Research and Development.

Braslavsky, Berta. 1962. *La querella de los métodos in la enseñanza de la lectura.* Buenos Aires, Argentina: Kapelusz.

———. 1992. *La escuela puede.* Buenos Aires, Argentina: Aique.

———. 2004. *¿Primeras letras o primeras lecturas?* Buenos Aires, Argentina: Fondo de la Cultura Económica.

Bruno de Castelli, Elba, and **Rebecca Beke.** 2004. "La escritura: Desarrollo de un processo." *Lectura y vida* XXV (3): 6–15.

Buchanan, Ethel. 1989. *Spelling for Whole Language Classrooms.* Winnipeg, MB: Whole Language Consultants.

Burton, Shelia, and **Faye Ong.** 2000. *Science Content Standards of California Public Schools.* Sacramento: California State Department of Education.

California Department of Education. 1999. *English-Language Arts Content Standards for California Public Schools Kindergarten Through Grade Twelve.* Sacramento: California Department of Education.

Calkins, Lucy. 1986. *The Art of Teaching Writing.* Portsmouth, NH: Heinemann.

———. 1991. *Living Between the Lines.* Portsmouth, NH: Heinemann.

———. 2003. *The Nuts and Bolts of Teaching Writing.* Portsmouth, NH: Heinemann.

Cañado, María Luisa Pérez. 2005. "English and Spanish Spelling: Are They Really Different?" *The Reading Teacher* 58 (6): 522–30.

Castedo, Mirta, and **Cinthia Waingort.** 2003. "Escribir, revisar y reescribir cuentos repetitivos: Segunda parte." *Lectura y vida* XXIV (2): 36–48.

Chall, Jean. 1967. *Learning to Read: The Great Debate.* New York: McGraw Hill.

Chomsky, Carol. 1970. "Reading, Writing, and Phonology." *Harvard Education Review* 40 (2): 287–309.

Clymer, Theodore. 1963. "The Utility of Phonic Generalizations in the Primary Grades." *The Reading Teacher* 16 (January): 252–58.

Coles, Gerald. 2000. *Misreading Reading: The Bad Science That Hurts Children.* Portsmouth, NH: Heinemann.

Collier, Virginia. 1989. "How Long? A Synthesis of Research on Academic Achievement in a Second Language." *TESOL Quarterly* 23 (3): 509–32.

———. 1995. "Acquiring a Second Language for School." *Directions in Language and Education* 1 (4).

Collier, Virginia, and **Wayne Thomas.** 2004. "The Astounding Effectiveness of Dual Language Education for All." *NABE Journal of Research and Practice* 2 (1): 1–19.

Crawford, James. 2004. *Educating English Learners.* Los Angeles: Bilingual Education Services.

Crowell, Caryl G. 1995. "Documenting the Strengths of Bilingual Readers." *Primary Voices K-6* 3 (4): 32–37.

Cummins, Jim. 1981. "The Role of Primary Language Development in Promoting Educational Success for Language Minority Students." In *Schooling and Language Minority Students: A Theoretical Framework,* 3–49. Los Angeles: Evaluation, Dissemination and Assessment Center, California State University, Los Angeles.

———. 1994. "The Acquisition of English as a Second Language." In *Kids Come in All Languages: Reading Instruction for ESL Students,* ed. K. Spangenberg-Urbschat and R. Pritchard, 36–62. Newark, DE: International Reading Association.

———. 2000. *Language, Power and Pedagogy: Bilingual Children in the Crossfire.* Tonawanda, NY: Multilingual Matters.

daCruz-Payne, Carleen, and **Mary Browning-Schulman.** 1998. *Getting the Most Out of Morning Message and Other Shared Writing.* New York: Scholastic.

Denton, Carolyn, Jan Hasbrouck, et al. 2000. "What Do We Know About Phonological Awareness in Spanish?" *Reading Psychology* 21: 235–52.

Dewey, John. 1929. *My Pedagogic Creed.* Washington, DC: The Progressive Education Association.

Dubois, María Eugenia. 1984. "Algunos interrogantes sobre comprensión de la lectura." *Lectura y Vida* 4: 14–19.

———. 1995. "Lectura, escritura y formación docente." *Lectura y vida* 16 (2): 5–12.

Duer, Ariel. 2004. "Los maestros recién recibidos no saben cómo enseñar a leer." Reportaje a la pedagoga Berta Braslavsky. *Clarin.* Buenos Aires, Argentina: Clarín.

Edelsky, Carole. 1986. *Writing in a Bilingual Program: Había una vez.* Norwood, NJ: Ablex.

———. 1989. "Bilingual Children's Writing: Fact and Fiction." In *Richness in Writing: Empowering ESL Students,* ed. D. Johnson and D. Roen, 165–76. New York: Longman.

Edelsky, Carole, Karen Smith, and **Christian Faltsis.** In press. *Content-Area Inquiry in Multilingual Classrooms.* Portsmouth, NH: Heinemann.

Elley, Warwick. 1998. *Raising Literacy Levels in Third World Countries: A Method That Works.* Culver City, CA: Language Education Associates.

Fader, Daniel. 1976. *The New Hooked on Books.* New York: Berkeley.

Ferreiro, Emilia. 1994. "Diversidad y proceso de alfabetización: De la celebración a la toma de conciencia." *Lectura y vida* 15 (3): 5–14.

Ferreiro, Emilia, Clotilde Pontecorvo, et al. 1996. *Caperucita Roja aprende a escribir: Estudios psicolingüísticos comparativos en tres lenguas.* Barcelona, Spain: Gedisa Editoria.

Ferreiro, Emilia, and **Ana Teberosky.** 1979. *Los sistemas de escritura en el desarrollo del niño.* México, DF: Signi Ventiuno Editores.

———. 1982. *Literacy Before Schooling.* Portsmouth, NH: Heinemann.

Fitzgerald, Jill. 2000. "How Will Bilingual/ESL Programs in Literacy Change in the Next Millennium?" *Reading Research Quarterly* 35 (4): 520–23.

Fletcher, Ralph. 1992. *What a Writer Needs.* Portsmouth, NH: Heinemann.

Flurkey, Alan. 1997. "Reading as Flow: A Linguistic Alternative to Fluency." In *Education.* Tucson: University of Arizona.

Foorman, Barbara R., Jack M. Fletcher, et al. 1998. "The Role of Instruction in Learning to Read: Preventing Reading Failure in At-Risk Children." *Journal of Educational Psychology* 90: 37–55.

Freeman, David, and **Yvonne Freeman.** 1997. *Invitaciones.* Boston: Houghton Mifflin.

———. 2004. *Essential Linguistics: What You Need to Know to Teach Reading, ESL, Spelling, Phonics, and Grammar.* Portsmouth, NH: Heinemann.

———. 2005. "Literacy Essentials for Dual Language Programs." *Language Magazine* 4 (5): 24–28.

Freeman, Yvonne. 1987. The Contemporary Spanish Basal in the United States. Unpublished doctoral dissertation. Tucson: University of Arizona.

———. 1988. "The Contemporary Spanish Basal Reader in the United States: How Does It Reflect Current Understanding of the Reading Process?" *NABE Journal* 13 (1): 59–74.

———. 1993. "Celebremos la literatura: Is It Possible with a Spanish Reading Program?" *Report Card on Basal Readers: Part II,* ed. P. Shannon and K. S. Goodman, 115–28. New York: Richard C. Owen.

Freeman, Yvonne, and **Maricela Bonett-Serra.** 2000. "El diseño de un programa efectivo para el desarrollo de la escritura." *Legenda* 3 (4–5): 45–50.

Freeman, Yvonne S., David E. Freeman, and **Sandra Mercuri.** 2005. *Dual Language Essentials for Teachers and Administrators.* Portsmouth, NH: Heinemann.

Freeman, Yvonne S., Yetta M. Goodman, et al. 1995. "Revalorización del estudiante bilingüe mediante un programa de lectura basado en literatura auténtica." *Lectura y vida* 16 (1): 13–24.

Freeman, Yvonne S., and **Lynn Whitesell.** 1985. "What Preschoolers Already Know About Print." *Educational Horizons* 64 (1): 22–25.

Freire, Paulo, and **Donaldo Macedo.** 1987. *Literacy: Reading the Word and the World.* South Hadley, MA: Bergin and Garvey.

Garan, Elaine. 2002. *Resisting Reading Mandates.* Portsmouth, NH: Heinemann.

Gelb, I. 1978. *Historia de la escritua.* Madrid, Spain: Alianza Editorial.

Gibbons, Pauline. 2002. *Scaffolding Language: Scaffolding Learning.* Portsmouth, NH: Heinemann.

Goldenberg, Claude, and **Ronald Gallimore.** 1991. "Local Knowledge, Research Knowledge, and Educational Change: A Case Study of Early Spanish Reading Improvement." *Educational Researcher* 20 (8): 2–14.

Goodman, Kenneth. 1965. "Cues and Miscues in Reading: A Linguistic Study." *Elementary English* 42 (6): 635–42.

———. 1967. "Reading: A Psycholinguistic Guessing Game." *Journal of the Reading Specialist* (May): 126–35.

———. 1984. "Unity in Reading." In *Becoming Readers in a Complex Society: Eighty-Third Yearbook of the National Society for the Study of Education,* ed. A. Purves and O. Niles, 79–114. Chicago: University of Chicago Press.

———. 1986. *What's Whole in Whole Language.* Portsmouth, NH: Heinemann.

———. 1989. *Lenguaje integral.* Mérida, Venezuela: Editorial Venezolano C.A.

———. 1993. *Phonics Phacts.* Portsmouth, NH: Heinemann.

———. 1995. *El lenguaje integral.* Buenos Aires, Argentina: Aique.

———. 1996. *On Reading.* Portsmouth, NH: Heinemann.

Goodman, Yetta M., and **Bess Altwerger.** 1981. *Print Awareness in Preschool Children.* Occasional Paper, No. 4. Tucson: University of Arizona.

Goodman, Yetta M., and **Kenneth S. Goodman.** 1990. "Vygotsky in a Whole Language Perspective." In *Vygotsky and Education: Instructional Implications and Applications of Sociohistorical Psychology,* ed. L. Moll, 223–50. Cambridge, MA: Cambridge University Press.

Graves, Donald. 1983. *Writing: Teachers and Children at Work.* Portsmouth, NH: Heinemann.

———. 1994. *A Fresh Look at Writing.* Portsmouth, NH: Heinemann.

Greene, Jay. 1998. *A Meta-analysis of the Effectiveness of Bilingual Education.* Claremont, CA: Tomas Rivera Policy Institute.

Halliday, Michael A. K. 1975. *Learning How to Mean.* London: Edward Arnold.

Hansen, Jane. 1987. *When Writers Read.* Portsmouth, NH: Heinemann.

Harste, Jerome. 1992. *Reflection Connection.* Niagara Falls, NY: Whole Language Umbrella.

Harwayne, Shelley. 2000. *Lifetime Guarantees: Toward Ambitious Teaching*. Portsmouth, NH: Heinemann.

Hendrix, Charles. 1952. *Cómo enseñar a leer por el método global*. Buenos Aires, Argentina: Editorial Kapelusz.

Holdaway, Don. 1979. *The Foundations of Literacy*. New York: Scholastic.

Hornberger, Nancy, ed. 2003. *Continua of Biliteracy: An Ecological Framework for Educational Policy, Resarch, and Practice in Multilingual Settings*. Clevedon, UK: Multilingual Matters.

Hoyt, Linda. 1999. *Revisit, Reflect, Retell: Strategies for Improving Reading Comprehension*. Portsmouth, NH: Heinemann.

———. 2000. *Snapshots: Literacy Minilessons Up Close*. Portsmouth, NH: Heinemann.

———. 2002. *Make It Real: Strategies for Success with Informational Texts*. Portsmouth, NH: Heinemann.

———. 2005. *Spotlight on Comprehension: Building a Literacy of Thoughtfulness*. Portsmouth, NH: Heinemann.

Hudelson, Sarah. 1981. "An Investigation of the Oral Reading Behaviors of Native Spanish Speakers Reading in Spanish." In *Learning to Read in Different Languages*, S. Hudelson. Washington, DC: Center for Applied Linguistics.

———. 1986. "ESL Children's Writing: What We've Learned, What We're Learning." In *Children and ESL: Integrating Perspectives*, ed. P. Rigg and D. S. Enright, 23–54. Washington, DC: Teachers of English to Speakers of Other Languages.

———. 1989. *Write On: Children Writing in ESL*. Englewood Cliffs, NJ: Prentice Hall Regents.

Hughes, Margaret, and **Dennis Searle.** 1997. *The Violent E and Other Tricky Sounds*. York, ME: Stenhouse.

Hunter, Madeline C. 1994. *Enhancing Teaching*. New York: Macmillan.

Krashen, Stephen. 1996. *Under Attack: The Case Against Bilingual Education*. Culver City, CA: Language Education Associates.

———. 2004. *The Power of Reading: Insights from the Research*. Portsmouth, NH: Heinemann.

Kucer, Stephen, and **Cecilia Silva.** 2006. *Teaching the Dimensions of Literacy*. Mahwah, NJ: Lawrence Erlbaum.

Laminack, Lester, and **Katie Wood.** 1996. *Spelling in Use: Looking Closely at Spelling in Whole Language Classrooms*. Urbana, IL: National Council of Teachers of English.

Lindholm-Leary, Kathryn J. 2001. *Dual Language Education*. Clevedon, UK: Multilingual Matters.

López Guerra, Susana, and **Marcelo Flores Chávez.** 2004. "Colonialismo y modernidad: La enseñanza del español en la Nueva España." *Odiseo Revista de Pedagogía* 2 (3) (noviembre): www.odiseo.com.mx

McCollum, Pam. 1999. "Learning to Value English: Cultural Capital in Two-Way Bilingual Programs." *Bilingual Research Journal* 23 (2 and 3): 113–14.

Moreno, María Stella Serrano. 1982. "La enseñaza-aprendizaje de la lectura." In *Escuela de educación*, 262. Mérida, Venezuela: Universidad de los Andes.

Moustafa, Margaret. 1997. *Beyond Traditional Phonics: Research Discoveries and Reading Instruction*. Portsmouth, NH, Heinemann.

North Central Regional Educational Laboratory (NCREL). 2001. *History of Professional Development in Reading Instruction.* Retrieved 7/23/05 www.NCREL.org /litweb/pd/history.php

Opitz, Michael. 2000. *Rhymes and Reasons: Literature and Language Play for Phonological Awareness.* Portsmouth, NH: Heinemann.

Opitz, Michael, and **Michael Ford.** 2001. *Reaching Readers: Flexible and Innovative Strategies for Guided Reading.* Portsmouth, NH: Heinemann.

Owocki, Gretchen, and **Yetta Goodman.** 2002. *Kidwatching: Documenting Children's Literacy Development.* Portsmouth, NH: Heinemann.

Pacheco, Margarita. 1992. *La metodología de enseñanza de la lecto-escritura: Una experiencia de lectura activa en el aula.* Caracas, Venezuela: Cooperativa Laboratorio Educativo.

Parkes, Brenda. 2000. *Read It Again! Revisiting Shared Reading.* Portland, ME: Stenhouse.

Paulson, Eric, and **Ann Freeman.** 2003. *Insight from the Eyes: The Science of Effective Reading Instruction.* Portsmouth, NH: Heinemann.

Pearson, P. David, and **M. C. Gallagher.** 1983. "The Instruction of Reading Comprehension." *Contemporary Educational Psychology* 8 (3): 317–44.

Pellicer, Félix. 1969. *Didáctica de la lengua Española.* Madrid, Spain: Magisterio Español.

Pilgreen, Janice. 2000. *The SSR Handbook: How to Organize and Manage a Sustained Silent Reading Program.* Portsmouth, NH: Heinemann.

Porlán, Rafael. 1993. *Constructivismo y escuela: Hacía un modelo de enseñanza-aprendizaje basado en la invesitgación.* Sevilla, Spain: Díada Editora S.L.

Ramírez, J. David. 1991. *Final Report: Longitudinal Study of Structured English Immersion Strategy, Early-Exit and Late-Exit Bilingual Education Programs.* Washington, DC: U.S. Department of Education.

Read, Charles. 1971. "Pre-school Children's Knowledge of English Phonology." *Harvard Education Review* 41 (1): 1–34.

Rigg, Pat, and **D. Scott Enright.** 1986. *Children and ESL: Integrating Perspectives.* Washington, DC: Teachers of English to Speakers of Other Languages.

Rodríguez, María Elena. 1995. "Hablar en la escuela: ¿Para qué? ¿Cómo?" *Lectura y vida* 16 (3): 31–40.

Rolstad, Kellie, Kate Mahoney, et al. 2005. "A Meta-analysis of Program Effectiveness Research on English Language Learners." *Educational Policy* 19 (4): 572–94.

Romero, Guadalupe. 1983. *Print Awareness of the Pre-school Bilingual Spanish-English Speaking Child.* Tucson: University of Arizona.

Routman, Regie. 2000. *Conversations: Strategies for Teaching, Learning, and Evaluating.* Portsmouth, NH: Heinemann.

Samway, Katharine Davies, Gail Whang, and **Mary Pippitt.** 1995. *Buddy Reading: Cross Age Tutoring in a Multicultural School.* Portsmouth, NH: Heinemann.

Schickedanz, Judith A., and **Renée M. Casbergue.** 2004. *Writing in Preschool.* Newark, DE: International Reading Association.

Sequeida, Julia, and **Guillermo Seymour.** 1995. "El razonamiento estratégico como factor de desarrollo de la expresión escrita y de la comprensión de lectura." *Lectura y vida* 16 (2): 13–20.

Shannon, Patrick. 1989. *Broken Promises*. Granby, MA: Bergin and Garvey.

———. 1991. *The Struggle to Continue: Progressive Reading Instruction in the United States*. Portsmouth, NH: Heinemann.

Simon, T. 1924. *Pédagogic expérimentale*. Paris: Armand Colin.

Skutnabb-Kangas, T. 1979. *Language in the Process of Cultural Assimilation and Structural Incorporation of Lingusitic Minorities*. Washington, DC: National Clearinghouse for Bilingual Education.

Smith, Frank. 1971. *Understanding Reading*. New York: Holt, Rinehart and Winston.

———. 1973. *Psycholinguistics and Reading*. New York: Holt, Rinehart, and Winston.

Solé i Gallart, Isabel. 1995. "El placer de leer." *Lectura y vida* 16 (3): 25–30.

Stanovich, Keith. 1986. "Matthew Effects in Reading: Some Consequences of Individual Differences in the Acquisition of Literacy." *Reading Research Quarterly* 21: 360–407.

———. 1996. "Word Recognition: Changing Perspectives." In *Handbook of Reading Research: Volume II*, ed. R. Barr, M. Kamil, P. Moosenthal, and P. D. Pearson, 418–52. Mahwah, NJ: Erlbaum.

———. 1998. "Twenty-five Years of Research on the Reading Process: The Grand Synthesis and What It Means for Our Field." *Forty-seventh Yearbook of the National Reading Conference*, ed. T. Shanahan and F. Rodriguez-Brown, 44–58. Chicago: National Reading Conference.

Strauss, Steven. 2005. *The Linguistics, Neurology, and Politics of Phonics: Silent "E" Speaks Out*. Mahwah, NJ: Lawrence Erlbaum.

Strecker, Susan, Nancy Roser, et al. 1998. *Toward Understanding Oral Reading Fluency*. Oak Park, WI: National Reading Conference Yearbook.

Taylor, Denny. 1998. *Beginning to Read and the Spin Doctors of Science: The Political Campaign to Change America's Mind About How Children Learn to Read*. Urbana, IL: National Council of Teachers of English.

Testimony of G. Reid Lyon on Children's Literacy. 1997. Washington, DC: Committee on Education and the Workforce, U.S. House of Representatives.

Texas Education Agency (TEA), Division of Curriculum. 1998a. *Texas Essential Knowledge and Skills, Kindergarten* 75 (49): 1–6. Austin: TEA. www.tea.state.tex.us

———. 1998b. *Texas Essential Knowledge and Skills, Kindergarten* 76 (47): 11–3. Austin: TEA. www.tea.state.tex.us

———. 1998c. *Texas Essential Knowledge and Skills, Grade 1*. Provision 110.3: 1–38. Austin: TEA. www.tea.state.tex.us

Thomas, Wayne P., and **Virginia P. Collier.** 1997. *School Effectiveness for Language Minority Students*. Washington, DC: National Clearninghouse of Bilingual Education.

———. 2002. *A National Study of School Effectiveness for Language Minority Students' Long-Term Academic Achievement*. Center for Research on Education, Diversity, and Excellence. Retrieved 7/20/05: www.crede.org/research/llaa/1.1_final.html.

Thonis, Eleanor. 1976. *Literacy for America's Spanish-Speaking Children*. Newark, DE: International Reading Association.

———. 1983. *The English-Spanish Connection*. Northvale, NJ: Santillana.

Trelease, Jim. 1992. *Hey! Listen to This: Stories to Read Aloud*. New York: Penguin.

———. 2001. *The Read-Aloud Handbook*. New York: Penguin.

Turbill, Jan. 2002. "The Four Ages of Reading Philosophy and Pedagogy: A Framework for Examining Theory and Practice." *Reading Online* (Feb.). Retrieved 7/20/05: www.readingonline.org.

U.S. Congress. House. 1994. *Goals 2000: Educate America Act.* HR 1804. 103d Cong., 2d sess.

Vygotsky, Lev. 1962. *Thought and Language.* Cambridge: MIT Press.

Weiss, Maria J., and **Ranae Hagen.** 1988. "A Key to Literacy: Kindergartners' Awareness of the Functions of Print." *The Reading Teacher* 41 (6): 574–78.

Wilde, Sandra. 1992. *You Kan Red This! Spelling and Punctuation for Whole Language Classrooms, K–6.* Portsmouth, NH: Heinemann.

Willig, Ann. 1985. "A Meta-analysis of Selected Studies on the Effectiveness of Bilingual Education." *Review of Educational Research* 55: 269–317.

Zutell, Jerry, and **Timothy Rasinski.** 1991. "Training Teachers to Attend to Their Students' Oral Reading Fluency." *Theory into Practice* 30: 211–17.

Index

National Institutes for Child Health and Human Development (NICHD), 34
National Reading Panel (NRP), 33

onomatopoeic method, 101
Opitz and Ford, 140
Opitz, Michael, 135
organizing around themes, 209

Pacheco, Margarita, 97
Parkes, Brenda, 137
Paty, 163
Paulson and Freeman, 55
phonemic awareness, 33, 38
phonic stage, 195
phonics, 40
phonics or phonetic method, 102
Pilgreen, Janice, 142
poetry and agriculture bibliography, 229
poetry unit, 222
political influences on bilingual education, 16
predicting, 56
prephonetic stage, 166
principled eclecticism, 120
principled teachers, 124
prism models, 11
process approach to writing, 156
Proposition 227, 4
psycholinguistic guessing game, 55
psychological strategies, 55
Put Reading First, 18, 34, 93

Quincy method, 84

Ramírez study, 7
Read-Aloud Handbook, 133
read-alouds, 132
Read, Charles, 184
reading mandates, 5
Rébsamen, 82
research on word recognition views of reading, 32
reversals, 168
Rhonda, 169
Roberto, 70

Rolstad, Mahoney, and Glass meta-analysis, 8
Rosa, 210

Sam, 188
sampling text, 55
Schickedanz and Casbergue, 161
scientific management, 84
scribble writing, 161
semantic cues, 58
Shannon, Patrick, 81, 84
shared reading, 134
Silabario de San Miguel, 80
Silvio, 221
sociopsycholinguistic view of reading, 26, 54
stages and levels of writing development, 165
stages of writing, 163
Stanovich, Keith, 32
Strauss, Steven, 35
sustained silent reading (SSR), 140
syllabic hypothesis, 188
syllabic method, 104
syntactic cues, 57
syntactic/semantic stage, 205
synthetic methods, 80, 98

techniques, 144
Teresa's unit, 66
Texas Essential Knowledge and Skills standards (TEKS), 27, 67
Thomas and Collier, 11
traditional view of writing, 155
Trelease, Jim, 133
Turbill, Jan, 85

universal process, 61

Vygotsky, Lev, 131

weather bibliography, 52
whole language, 87
Willig meta-analysis, 8
word recognition view of reading, 26, 31

zone of proximal development (ZPD), 131